COLUMBIA COLLEGE LIBRARY
600 S. MICHIGAN AVENUE
CHICAGO, IL 60605

COLUMBIA COLLEGE CHICAGO

3 2711 00138 0751

Elder Abuse
A Public Health Perspective

Randal W. Summers
Allan M. Hoffman
Editors

W9-CZU-701

DISCARD

American Public Health Association
Washington, DC

ENTERED OCT 1 7 2007

American Public Health Association
800 I Street, NW
Washington, DC 20001–3710
www.apha.org

© 2006 by the American Public Health Association

Library of Congress Cataloging-in-Publication Data
Elder abuse : a public health perspective / Randal W. Summers, Allan M. Hoffman, editors.
    p. cm.
    ISBN-13: 978-0-87553-050-5
    ISBN-10: 0-87553-050-8
        1. Older people--Abuse of--United States. 2. Abused elderly--United States. 3. Older
people--Health and hygene--United States. 4. Medical policy--United States. I. Summers, Randal
W., 1946- II. Hoffman, Allan M. (Allan Michael) III. American Public Health Association.

HV6626.3.E436 2006
362.6--dc22   2006048365

All rights reserved. No part of this publication may be reproduced, stored in a retrieval system,
or transmitted in any form or by any means, electronic, mechanical, photocopying, recording,
scanning, or otherwise, except as permitted under Sections 107 and 108 of the 1976 United States
Copyright Act, without either the prior written permission of the Publisher or authorization
through payment of the appropriate per-copy fee to the Copyright Clearance Center [222
Rosewood Drive, Danvers, MA 01923, (978) 750-8400, fax (978) 750-4744, www.copyright. com].
Requests to the Publisher for permission should be addressed to the Permissions Department,
American Public Health Association, 800 I Street, NW, Washington, DC 20001-3710; fax (202)
777-2531.

Georges C. Benjamin, MD, FACP
Executive Director

Publications Board Liaison: Burt Wilcke

Printed and bound in the United States of America
Set In: Palatino and Gill Sans
Interior Design and Typesetting: Terence Mulligan
Cover Design: Irma Rodenhuis
Printing and Binding by United Book Press, Baltimore, Maryland

ISBN-13: 978-0-875530-50-5
ISBN: 0-87553-050-8

1500 07/06

This book is dedicated to our families, with love.

To Randal's family:
Tully, Vivian, Quinn, Aja, Joan, Jamie, Kim, Dawn, Alycia, Anita, and Norman

To Allan's family:
Andrew, Emily, Elijah, Tim, and Annie

We would also like to express our sincere gratitude to all the contributing authors.

Table of Contents

Foreword

Protection from elder abuse is a key concern for AARP members and the public at large. The risk of physical and emotional harm, in the community and in residential care settings, grows as the number of people living into advanced old age increases. This detailed volume addresses a key issue facing older people and, indeed, our entire society.

Widely used estimates of elder abuse prevalence and incidence show that the problem is huge and growing. The National Elder Abuse Incidence Study estimated that abuse, neglect, and self-neglect of adults age 60 and over in domestic settings totaled approximately 551,000, and that about 84 percent of elder abuse incidents go unreported. The 2004 Survey of State Adult Protective Services (APS) found that in 2003, APS agencies received over 565,000 reports of suspected elder and vulnerable adult abuse. This study found almost a 20 percent increase in reports of abuse and neglect and a 15.6 increase in substantiated cases in the four years since the last APS survey was conducted in 2000. These figures are alarming—and should be a wake up call for us all.

Elder abuse is a public health problem as well as a criminal justice issue. It is an epidemic that affects the community as a whole. This volume helps identify some of the key barriers to understanding and addressing elder mistreatment, including widely varying definitions of elder abuse, a dearth of reliable data on its frequency, a lack of consensus about causes and effective preventive measures, a national policy void, and a lack of funds for both research and implementation of interventions. As a leading elder abuse researcher recently stated, "Although elder abuse has had its share of horror stories, exposés, and Congressional hearings, somehow they have failed to capture the attention required for significant research funding, federal policy, or comprehensive programming." (Anetzberger, 2005)

The key question is posed by Randal Summers and Allan Hoffman in this volume's introduction: How can we deal with this problem? Consistent with the public health ethic of "maximum health for all" and "assuring the conditions in which people can be healthy," the appropriate and humane starting point is to improve detection of abuse and provide quality care for victims. The development of standards of care and standardized models of evaluation and intervention and the recognition of "at risk" factors and indicators of abuse by health care professionals is critical to achieving this goal. Further, the volume's attention to the key role of home care nurses and physical therapists in identifying, reporting, and perhaps most importantly, preventing abusive situations through timely intervention and assistance is significant. Older persons living in the community may be at greater risk of abuse than those living in institutional settings where initiatives such as ombudsman programs and staff monitoring and training requirements provide a formal framework for safeguarding residents. Through sharing of information, routine examinations, and interactions with patients, families, and caregivers, home care nurses and physical therapists can perform a similar function in community settings.

Another significant theme in the volume is the importance of understanding cultural factors, particularly as they relate to encouraging the identification of abusive situations involving older minority persons and the likelihood that older minority victims and their families will seek and/or accept assistance and services. Recent research indicates that older minority populations may be over-represented among victims of elder abuse. Given that the proportion of older minorities is expected to increase significantly in the future, it is critical to achieve a greater understanding of the impacts of cultural factors in order to respond effectively to the needs of an increasingly diverse older population. I second the call by Summers and Hoffman to foster collaborative efforts, particularly with the criminal and civil justice systems, and to enhance public awareness of elder abuse.

AARP is also striving to find answers to the question about how we deal with the problem of elder abuse. We are working to advance the field in a number of areas including communications and programmatic initiatives, research, and adoption and implementation of improved federal and state policies. The general public and too many policy makers are unaware that elder abuse is a serious problem. AARP recognizes that we must do more to bring this issue to light. In Maryland, for example, the AARP State Office co-sponsored a series of town hall style meetings with the State Attorney General that focused on preventing elder abuse and neglect. These meetings were cited by the Attorney General as a strong and positive influence in raising the awareness of elder abuse to the citizens of Maryland. Our California State Office worked with the Attorney General in that state to create an awareness manual entitled "A Citizen's Guide to Preventing and Reporting Elder Abuse." This manual includes information on the warning signs of abuse and how to file a report. AARP has also initiated the first national evaluation of guardianship monitoring practices in over fifteen years. This research includes a national survey of experts with frontline experience—judges, court managers, guardians, elder law attorneys, and legal representatives of people with disabilities; site visits; and the development of best practices.

The challenges we face in preventing and stopping the abuse of our most vulnerable citizens are formidable. However, the knowledge, empathy, and commitment to improve the current situation expressed by the authors in this volume are a ray a hope. On behalf of the AARP, I commend the efforts of the American Public Health Association to strengthen the ability of the nation's public health professionals to deal effectively with the problem of elder abuse. This book serves as a guidebook to help us all face up to this urgent challenge.

John C. Rother
Director, Policy and Strategy
AARP

Acknowledgements

We wish to give special thanks to all the dedicated professionals at APHA who made this publication possible:

Nancy Persily and Burton W. Wilcke, Jr., Publications Board; Ellen Meyer, Director of Publications; Terence Mulligan, Book Production Manager; Tara Kelly, Desktop Publishing Manager; and Irma Rodenhuis, Graphic Designer.

INTRODUCTION

Randal Summers and Allan Hoffman

Toward the end of World War II, our young service men and women began coming home. This gave rise to an unprecedented population explosion now referred to as the "baby boom." Here we are, decades later, and this segment of the population is now entering the retirement years. On the whole, life has been "good" for most and there is an expectation that the retirement years will be a peaceful continuation. The surviving parents of "baby-boomers" are now in their 70s and 80s. Many of these elders occupy a place somewhere along a continuum from independence (living in their own home) to dependence (living with family, or in a senior's retirement home or long term care facility). One might conclude that this is the natural "cycle of life." However, there is another side to this "cycle of life"—a side, which reflects all that is ignoble in our society.

It is comprised of interpersonal behavior (intentional or unintentional) that causes pain and suffering (physical or emotional) for people in the "sunset" years of their lives. This Public Health enemy is called elder abuse. The title of this work makes reference to the Public Health perspective. Although the study of elder abuse tends to focus on the victimization of individuals, it truly is a study of the health of our communities.

HOW PREVALENT IS ELDER ABUSE?

It is difficult to accurately portray the extent of this problem because so much of it is "hidden" or unreported. In a study supported by the National Center on Elder Abuse (1998) it was estimated there were between 820,000 and 1,860,000 abused elderly in our country in 1996. Statistical data on reported cases of abuse indicated a 150% increase from 1986 to 1996. Today, there are well over 2 million cases per year suggesting that this is not only a serious problem but it is one of epidemic proportions. What is even more disconcerting is the increasing trend predicted with the "graying of America."

WHAT ARE THE UNDERLYING CAUSES?

Because there are many dynamics associated with elder abuse the underlying causes may vary. For example, the causes may differ for domestic abuse compared to the abuse occurring in nursing homes or other institutions. The causes may vary in domestic settings depending on the type of abuse, the sex of victims, the sex of perpetrators and whether the abuser is the elder's spouse or adult child or a non-family caregiver. A number of chapters in this volume address 'cause' and Chapter 7 identifies the values and ethical principles that are violated in elder abuse.

IS ELDER ABUSE UNIQUE TO PARTICULAR GROUPS IN OUR SOCIETY OR TO THE U.S. AS A COUNTRY?

Although the majority of research studies about elder abuse focus on the white, non-Hispanic population, there is ample evidence to suggest that elder abuse knows no racial or ethnic boundaries. Chapter 5 in this volume addresses elder abuse in minority populations (Latinos, African Americans, Asian, Pacific Islanders and Native Americans). The chapter addresses the cultural implications involved in the definition of elder abuse and the appropriate interventions.

Elder abuse is not confined to the U.S. Chapter 6 explores elder abuse in other countries and maintains that although there are many challenges associated with international investigation, many nations are acknowledging that elder abuse is a significant social problem. The World Health Organization plays an important role by increasing awareness of elder abuse and recommending the public health sector's active involvement.

HOW CAN WE DEAL WITH THIS PROBLEM?

Elder abuse poses a serious public health issue today and is expected to intensify in the future. Like many social problems, it requires a Public Health approach that draws on scientific knowledge which spans a broad range of professional disciplines. It is an approach that focuses on the definition of the problem, the identification of risk factors and the development, implementation, and monitoring of prevention and intervention strategies/programs.

The framework of chapters in this volume supports this Public Health approach. For example, reference is made to the definition and prevalence of elder abuse and in particular the data associated with specific types of abuse. Other chapters identify risk factors and point out that we still have much to learn about the problem (profiling perpetrators, for example).

Chapter 5 explores the cultural dynamics and implications with an increasingly diverse population. Certain chapters focus on prevention and intervention. Chapter 3, for example suggests the use of a specific model with Care Pathway Guidelines for professionals. Chapter 11 highlights Social Services and Health Care interventions in elder abuse. In addition, various resources are listed for individuals seeking help and for professionals who want to know where to find more information.

The purpose of this book is consistent with the fundamental Public Health goal of "maximum health for all" (Schneider, 2000). Our intent is to provide greater insight into the many facets of the problem and provide meaningful support to the professionals who are touched by this tragic epidemic either in their personal lives or in carrying out their Public Health mission of "assuring the conditions in which people can be healthy" (*The Future of Public Health*, 1988).

REFERENCES

Institute of Medicine (US), committee for the Study of the Future of Public Health, *The Future of Public Health* (Washington, DC: National Academy Press, 1988)

National Center on Elder Abuse. (1998). *The National Elder Abuse Incidence Study: Final Report.* Available at

Schneider, Mary-Jane (2000). *Introduction to Public Health,* Gathersburg, Maryland. Aspen.

ELDER ABUSE: DEFINITION AND SCOPE OF THE PROBLEM

Tina Fryling, Randal Summers, and Allan Hoffman

The phrase "elder abuse" is used to describe violence, neglect, and other crimes aimed at elderly persons. Much research has been directed towards the concept of elder abuse; however, no universal definition of the phenomenon exists. Like child abuse, the term "elder abuse" refers to abuse at the hands of a caregiver of an elderly person, including institutional employees. The abuse takes many forms, including physical abuse, mental abuse, financial abuse, and both passive and active neglect. The results of this abuse range from emotional suffering and inhumane living conditions, along with severe suffering and pain and even death.

Despite the government's funding of programs to combat elder abuse and despite increased involvement in this area from the criminal justice system, elder abuse continues to grow, and no easy solutions exist. Various theories attempt to explain why elderly persons are abused at alarming rates and provide some suggestions as to how social service agencies could attempt to combat this growing problem.

There is a general reluctance on the part of society to accept the fact that we are not treating our elderly people as "sweet old grandparents." Americans have a highly idealized notion of family life and find it difficult to accept the fact that abuse exists within the family, especially when it is directed toward elderly people. It is also quite disturbing to acknowledge that the large number of elderly people that reside in nursing facilities and other care-giving institutions are in danger of being abused. Hence, it is easier to ignore elder abuse than to accept it and attempt to develop remedies. However, the tragedy of elder abuse is being recognized more often by our public health, social service, criminal justice and health care systems as an important problem to be studied and solved.

DEFINITION OF ELDER ABUSE

The term "elder abuse" was first coined in the late 1970s during congressional hearings which focused on the mistreatment of elderly persons. ("Elder Abuse" 1992) However, depending on the study being undertaken or the group or agency defining the problem, "elder abuse" may be defined in varying ways. For example, although some literature defines elder abuse as being abuse focused on persons age fifty (50) and older, other studies have defined the term in respect to persons over sixty (60) or even over sixty five (65). After abuse of the elderly became a focus of social policy, the term "elder abuse" was sensationalized and sometimes substituted with the terms "granny bashing," and, in the medical press, "granny battering."

Elderly persons can be victims of abuse either in their own homes, in the homes of a family member, friend or other private caregiver, or in a nursing home or other institutional setting. The term "elder abuse" generally describes all of the following: physical abuse, psychological abuse, material abuse, active neglect, and passive neglect of elderly persons. (Wolf and Pillemer, 1989) More specifically, these categories include sexual abuse, overdosing or withholding an elderly person's necessary medications, and the general humiliation or harassment of an elderly person. Financial abuse is another category of abuse which is unfortunately promulgated both by private and institutional caregivers.

Abuse by Guardians and/or Family Members

Many elderly persons reside with a family member, such as their child or another close relative, and thus may be subjected to abuse by those caregivers. Other elderly persons have been officially declared incompetent by the court and have been appointed a "guardian" to maintain their finances and oversee their care and major life decisions. A guardian may or may not be a relative, and is unfortunately generally held to a fairly low standard in making choices about a person's finances and care. For example, the guardian of a sixty-six year old woman who suffered from schizophrenia was sued for failing to place the woman in an institution, when the woman was in danger of harming herself in a home-care setting. The woman, consistent with previous behavior, left a burning cigarette in her bed, which caused a house fire and her subsequent death. The guardian was limited to using the least restrictive means in caring for the woman, and the woman may not have wanted to be placed in an institution. Thus, a court determined that the guardian did not abuse her ward.

The prevalence of abuse by a family member is difficult to study because the abuse by a family member is often not reported. Abused elderly people may not report the abuse because they fear reprisals from their caregiver or love their abusive children too much to turn them in to authorities. In an investigation, the House Select Committee on Aging found that because of such fear or because they depended on their abusers, only one out of every six elderly people who were abused ever brought the abuse to the attention of authorities. As with other dark figures of crime, we will never know exactly how many cases of elder abuse are never reported.

Many abused persons are also not in a position to report their abuse because as part of the abuse they are not taken to doctors appointments or out of the abuser's home for any reason. Most states have reporting acts that require a health care provider to report suspected elderly abuse, similar to reporting statutes for child abuse. However, these statutes can only be of help if the elderly person is actually permitted by his or her caregiver to actually obtain medical care or speak in private to a provider.

Elderly people may remain in abusive relationships "by choice, because of counter balancing factors or because the alternatives (such as institutionaliza- tion) appear more negative or frightening." In addition, "pride, embarrassment, fear, isolation, lack of access to services, and mental confusion are all obstacles to (elderly persons) acknowledging abuse and seeking professional assistance."

Also, statutes which make elder abuse criminal are often ineffective because they are rarely utilized by an elderly victim. Elderly people are reluc- tant to criminally prosecute a family member, especially when that relative is his or her child. An elderly person can be institutionalized after reporting that he/she is being abused. Elderly people do not want to be uprooted from their homes even if that home is abusive, and most often do not wish to spend the remainder of their lives in an institution. Additionally, the criminal justice sys- tem can cause both physical and emotional strain on a victim, especially when that victim is elderly, and most victims of elder abuse do not want to deal with the stress of testifying in court regarding their abuse.

Some elder abuse actually comes in the form of spousal abuse. Certainly spousal abuse does not take place only among younger couples, and spouses or intimate partners with a history of abuse do not suddenly stop abusing a partner in their later years. Additionally, some spousal abuse begins only after a person is elderly, especially if the elderly victim suffers from some condition such as Alzheimers or Dementia, which could cause their care-giving spouse to engage in violence out of frustration. Thus, some theories which purport to explain domestic violence may also explain some incidents of elder abuse.

Offenders (Perpetrators)

We see some of these theories operationalized when we examine the characteristics of the offenders or perpetrators of elder abuse. In 1990, the majority of offenders were male. However, by 1996 both males and females accounted almost equally for elder abuse incidents. When offenders are reviewed by type of abuse by gender, the area of neglect is the only area that has relatively equal representation.

- Neglect: 52.4% female offenders, 47.6% male offenders
- Emotional/psychological abuse: 39.9% female offenders, 60.1 male offenders
- Financial/material exploitation: 40% female offenders, 60% male offenders
- Physical abuse: 37.5 female offenders, 62.6% male offenders
- Abandonment: 16.6% female offenders, 83.4% male offenders

When the age of offenders is reviewed we find that most offenders are in the younger age group although for most types of abuse those under 40 and those older than 80 offend the most.

- 65 % of offenders are 59 years and younger
- 10% of offenders are between 60 and 69
- 25% of offenders are age 70 and older

It is often thought that abuse occurs at the hands of institutional or non-family care-givers. Contrary to belief, most offenders are the adult children of the victims:

- Adult Children: 47%
- Spouse: 19%
- Grandchild: 9%
- Other relative: 9%
- Sibling: 6%
- In-home service provider: 3 %
- Out-of home service provider: 1%

Abuse in Nursing Homes and Other Institutions

Employees of nursing homes and other caregiving institutions also engage in elder abuse. Although ombudsman programs and other statutory reporting requirements should theoretically reduce the incidence of abuse in nursing homes, all forms of abuse nevertheless take place in such institutions.

A report from the Special Investigations Division, Committee on Government Reform of the United States House of Representatives published on July 31, 2001 focused on the abuse of nursing home residents. That report indicated that thousands of nursing homes, over thirty percent (30%) of those in the United States, were cited for abuse. Some of these violations were so severe that they caused the resident's death. The violations included direct physical abuse, verbal abuse, and the act of allowing one patient to harm another. There were also many incidents of nursing home personnel ignoring complaints of sexual or other serious abuse; in fact, such failure to investigate was the most frequent abuse violation reported. Many nursing homes were also cited for failing to develop and implement policies that would lessen incidents of abuse, even though such policies are generally mandatory. (*Abuse* 2001).

It is possible that the statistics gathered on nursing home abuse might be slightly more accurate than statistics gathered for other forms of elder abuse. Nursing homes are inspected and are subject to government regulations, especially if residents receive funding from Medicare or Medicaid. There also exists a formal complaint process in nursing homes and states must investigate those complaints once they are lodged.

Nursing home violations consist of all forms of physical abuse, including broken bones, bruises, and lacerations. State inspection reports also demonstrate many reported cases of sexual abuse to nursing home residents by other residents or by staff, from incidents of fondling to rape. Nursing home residents also complained of verbal abuse, which many times causes a patient to fail to ask for help or for medical care, a form of forced self-neglect. (*Abuse*, 2001).

TYPES OF ABUSE

Physical Abuse

Physical abuse involves the use of physical force to harm or impair an elderly person. Any sort of physical violence or such actions as burning, the inappropriate use of drugs—such as over-medicating a person or even failing to give a person proper medication, the use of physical restraints, and even force feeding are considered physical abuse. (National Centeron Elder Abuse 1998). As with children, it may be difficult to determine whether physical injuries were a result of abuse or an accident such as a fall.

Physical incidents of elder abuse can also include sexual abuse, which includes any sexual acts for which the elderly person has not given or is incapable of giving consent. Coerced nudity and taking sexually explicit photographs of an elderly person is also considered physical and mental abuse.

Mental Abuse

Any infliction of anguish, pain, or distress in an elderly person is considered mental abuse. Specific examples include "treating an older person like an infant; isolating an elderly person from his/her family, friends, or regular activities; giving an older person the 'silent treatment;' and enforced social isolation." (National Center on Elder Abuse 1998). As discussed previously, when caregivers verbally abuse or threaten a victim, that victim may then be less likely to request care or make their needs known, which then leads to a lack of proper care and medical services for that victim.

Financial Abuse

Elderly persons are often an easy target for financial abuse both in private homes and in institutional settings because they often give their caregiver control over their finances. Any illegal or improper use of an elderly person's funds is considered financial abuse. Incidents of financial abuse include forging an elderly person's signature, forcing them to sign any document, such as a will or contract, that would benefit the person who is forcing the signature, and stealing and/or misappropriating funds from the elderly person. Many elderly persons are either coerced into turning over or decide on their own to turn over their financial freedom to someone else in the form of a power of attorney or guardianship, and very often the elderly person consequently has little control over the funds they have turned over. Even elderly persons without official paperwork requiring them to turn over financial control to a third party feel obligated to give their caregiver control of their finances in return for the care they are receiving. Additionally, an elderly person may not know who to turn to even if he believes those funds are being abused. If the caregiver that is taking financial advantage of them is also the person providing him with transportation and phone services, the elderly person may not have contact with anyone other than the caregiver in order to lodge a complaint.

In the area of financial abuse of the elderly, a question exists regarding whether an adult child is "abusive" of the parent if he or she does not financially support that parent. In *Stone v. Brewster*, a domestic relations court adjudicated a claim that was brought to force a person to financially support his parents. The court stated that a statutory obligation arises only after the court determines the parent's need for support, the child's ability to furnish such support, and the extent to which such support should be furnished. Courts do occasionally find through the interpretation of statutes or by common law that a person is legally obligated to assume a "duty of care" for his/her elderly parent. However, because this "duty of care" refers only to financial care, not to a duty to care for an elderly parent's physical and emotional needs. Many people may respond to their duty of care by placing their elderly parent in a nursing home, thus eliminating the possibility of at home abuse, but subjecting the person to abuse by institutional caregivers. Additionally, as discussed below, a person providing resources for a parent or other elderly relative may become stressed due to the financial strain that is created and physical or mental abuse might occur as a result of that stress.

Neglect

Most elder abuse initially takes the form of physical abuse or neglect; financial abuse, abuse of basic constitutional rights, and psychological abuse follow. Neglect is any refusal or failure to fulfill an elderly person's needs. Many cases of elder abuse involve neglect due to a family member's inability or non-interest in providing proper care to an elderly person who is living in their home. Issues in this area again involve the question of what duties a person actually must perform for an elderly person. Neglect can be inflicted upon an elderly person by family caregivers or even by in-home service providers that have been hired to provide certain types of assistance to an elderly person, whether it be medical care, psychological care, or assistance with general daily needs. "Passive neglect" refers to a failure to care for a person or non-intended neglect that might take place due to a person's lack of knowledge of how to care for an elderly person's needs (Krummel, 1996). Active neglect involves withholding something from a person that they clearly need to survive. (Rathbone-McCuan and Voyles, 1982). Often, the line is blurred between active neglect and outright physical or mental abuse.

Clearly the failure to provide life necessities for an elderly person is a form of neglect. Food, water, clothing, shelter, medication, and personal safety are all life necessities. Many neglect cases revolve around unsanitary living conditions caused by the caregiver ignoring the person. In Texas, an elderly woman was found in a great deal of pain, lying in her own urine and excrement, wtih bedsores on her heel, back, and hip that were so large they had eaten away her flesh to the bone. She had also sustained second degree burns on her inner thighs from lying in her own urine. Upon her entry to the hospital, medical workers even found maggots in her bed sores. The woman had been tucked away in an upstairs bedroom of her son's home and he had done his best to keep other members of the family from visiting her. The woman was in great need of medical care but clearly unable to summon help for herself. (Billingslea v. Texas). This type of neglect may obviously also be considered to rise to the level of physical abuse.

A California Court was able to hold a woman liable for failing to help her father even when she was not his direct caregiver, thereby extending liability to people who are aware of possible abuse and do nothing within their powers to halt it. The Court indicated that a stranger who saw an elderly person in need on the street did not have a duty to help that person; the duty only applied to a relative or someone close to that person. In the California case, the decedent's daughter was required to maintain him to the extent of her ability, and since she knew of the peril he was in while residing with her brothers who could not properly care for him, she was required to exercise a minimal duty of care that would avoid general negligence on her part.

Some elder abuse literature also lists "self-neglect" as one category of neglect. Certainly some older persons engage in behavior that threatens his or her own safety or health, in the form of a failure to eat, take medications, or perform proper hygiene. The issues involved in self-neglect are whether a person who realizes that the elderly person is neglecting him or herself has a duty to report that person. This issue becomes quite difficult, as an adult would have to be considered incompetent before another adult could make decisions for him/her. Many adult children of elderly parents do not want to deal with trying to take away his or her parent's autonomy.

The term "granny dumping" has also been used to refer to the ultimate form of neglect where an elderly person, often suffering from Alzheimers or some other form of dementia is abandoned in some public place by his or her family. The person may not know their own name, much less who left them there, and they then become a ward of the state.

PREVALENCE OF ELDER ABUSE: RATES AND STATISTICS

As more elderly people reside with adult caregivers, a higher possibility exists that those people may ultimately be victims of abuse. Numerous studies have been undertaken in the attempt to determine the amount of elder abuse that takes place in various countries throughout the world. Clearly, like any study of victimization, a number of factors make statistics inaccurate. As previously discussed, there is always a "dark figure" of crime in any area, and this figure exists most likely at a high rate in the area of elder abuse because many elderly persons living with a caregiver do not report the abuse they are facing, either because they are afraid to or because they are isolated and thus unable to come into contact with anyone who they could report it to. However, results of studies which have been done will be summarized herein.

The National Elder Abuse Incidence Study estimated that in 1996, 449,924 persons aged sixty (60) and over experienced abuse and/or neglect in domestic settings. That number was based on information from only 20 counties in 15 states. That study also reported that only twenty one percent (21%) of all cases were actually reported to an agency or substantiated by an agency. (National Center on Elder Abuse 1998). Findings from a random sample estimated that as many as 701,000 to 1,093,560 elderly persons are abused in our nation. This correlates to an estimate of 32 elderly persons per 1000 that are subjected to some form of maltreatment. (Pillemer and Finkelhor, 1988).

Research in Canada estimates that 98,000 to 137,000 elderly persons are abused in Canada. (Podnieks, 1992). This survey estimated that approximately 40 persons per 1,000 elderly individuals in Canada experienced some sort of abuse or maltreatment at the hands of a caregiver or other relative, including partner violence.

Elderly people are exposed to home and institutional caregivers for extended periods of time, allowing abuse to be "repeated," and the term "elder abuse" generally refers to such repeated abuse. One time thefts, assaults, or scams directed at the elderly, while prevalent in society, are theoretically not considered "elder abuse." Obviously the biggest difficulty in determining the prevalence of elder abuse is the fact that, as stated previously, most elderly persons who are being abused are being controlled by their caregiver. Thus, there is no way these persons can report their abuse. Hence, the assumption is that findings in these areas are very low and that the prevalence of abuse of the elderly is much higher than determined in any study that has been undertaken thus far.

In 1980, more than twenty-five million Americans were age sixty-five or older. By 1990, thirty one million Americans, almost thirteen percent of the population of the United States were at least sixty-five years of age. It is estimated that by the year 2030, persons ages sixty and older will number 85 million, while the number of persons ages 85 and over will number 8 million. (Wallace at 239). High estimates indicate that five percent of the total elder population is abused each year. This would mean that 1.5 million elderly people are currently abused each year. As the population of elderly people rises, incidents of elder abuse will also rise. Despite the high incidence of elder abuse in the United States, the problem has only recently gained attention as an area for our legal system to deal with.

Studies performed by the National Center on Elder Abuse demonstrates the rise in elder abuse, or at least a rise in reporting of elder abuse, in the past decade. In 1986, 117,000 cases of elder abuse were reported; by 1990, that rate had risen to 211,000 and in 1996 that number was 293,000. Specifically, the numbers have broken down as follows: physical abuse (15.7 percent), sexual abuse (.04 percent), emotional abuse (7.3 percent), neglect (58.5 percent), financial exploitation (12.3 percent), all other types (5.1 percent) and unknown (.06 percent). (Toshio, T. 1996). Mandatory reporting statutes and more education in the health care and social work settings regarding this problem may have increased reporting; the rising number of elderly people in our society and the number of persons living in institutions or with caregivers could also have contributed to this jump in incidents.

Although mandatory reporting requirements exist in the area of elder abuse, it is far less likely to be reported than is child abuse. Perhaps one reason for this discrepancy is that child abuse is often noticed by school officials or day care center workers. Children often interact with others outside of the home. In contrast, elderly people who are abused are often unable to leave the abuser's home. Thus, there is little chance that a person from outside of the home will even have the opportunity to become aware of cases of elder abuse.

Regarding nursing home violations, the percentage of nursing homes cited for abuse violations has tripled since 1996. (Abuse, 2001). In 2000, sixteen percent (16%) of all nursing homes in the United States were cited for abuse violations during their annual inspections. This was a ten and one tenth percentage (10.1%) increase since 1996. This increase may be a result of more reporting, more incidents, or other political measures, such as a repeal of the Boren Amendment, which guaranteed that nursing homes would receive enough funding to provide adequate care to their residents. (Abuse, 2001). Nursing home reports still are not 100% accurate, especially considering that institutions that do not accept medicare or medicaid money do not have to report to or be inspected by the federal government. In fact, the majority of research done in the area of elder abuse in nursing homes has been done based solely on official reports or complaints lodged with the state. There would clearly be many victims who would not report their victimization, either because of a fear of repercussions by staff or other residents, or because they are unable to tell their experience to anyone due to dementia or an inability to communicate. However, with one out of every three nursing homes being cited for violating federal standards which were promulgated to prevent elder abuse in nursing facilities, it is clear that abuse in nursing homes is a very prevalent problem.

CAUSES/THEORIES OF ELDER ABUSE

Both an elderly person and his/her family must make very important decisions when the elderly person needs care. Literature examining elder abuse sometimes attempts to excuse abusers and find fault with the elderly person in order to blame the victim for the abuse. Sociological studies emphasize the stress that an adult child goes through when taking an elderly parent into the home, and then examine what the elderly person does that could anger his/her caregiver. Emphasizing what the elderly person may do to cause the abuse suggests that battering a parent is acceptable as long as there is a "good reason" for the abuse. This type of attitude is unfortunate and may truly hamper the possibility of remedying the growing problem of elder abuse.

General sociological theories that explain violence in general are often used to explain elder abuse. Nadien (1995) suggests that the following theories are applicable: psychoanalysis, social learning theory, social exchange theory, conflict theory, role-learning theory, situational theory, and functionalism. The family stress theory is also a widely promulgated theory to explain elder abuse. (Steinmetz, 1988). These theories will be expanded upon below.

The Decision to Care for an Elderly Parent

Adult children and other relatives of elderly persons assume a caregiving role for various reasons. First, an adult child may feel that putting an elderly parent in a nursing home would be a waste of the elderly person's assets, which would instead be inherited by the child if not used up during the elderly person's life. In addition, adult children may expect that their elderly parents will act as live-in babysitters and will help with the housework, although failing health and mental abilities may prevent the elderly person from assuming any of these duties. Finally, while adult children are often motivated to care for their elderly parents out of love, they may also feel a sense of responsibility, duty, or guilt. Often, the decision to accept an elderly parent into the home is hasty and the adult child feels as though no other alternative exists. The forces that motivate someone to care for an elderly parent vary and may not be focused towards furthering the parent's best interests.

The Decision to Enter an Abuser's Home

The elderly person also enters the home of his/her adult child for varying reasons, and the decision to do so is often difficult. Most often, the elderly person has no resources and no alternative place to live. Once the elderly person enters the other parties' household, his/her personal autonomy is challenged. An elderly parent who once ruled a home with an iron glove may do the same in a caregiver's home. In addition, the former caregiver now must be cared for. The elderly person may resist the care offered by family members, which can result in abuse by the caregiver, who will force care upon the elderly person. The elderly person may have no mechanism with which to avoid that force except through violence to the caregiver; such violence invites further abuse by the caregiver, who is usually stronger than the elderly person and, consequently, more abusive.

The Difficulties in Caring for an Elderly Person

The elderly person's dependency on the caregiver signifies a role reversal between the two parties. The adult child, who used to depend on a parent for advice and support, is now expected to care for that person. In contrast, the parent who used to be responsible for his son or daughter is now powerless and in a position of dependency. This reversal of roles is overwhelming to the adult child and humiliating to the parent.

This role reversal creates new rights, responsibilities, and obligations for the caregiver. The caregiver experiences stress and anger because of a lack of personal time or a lack of privacy, or by rivalry, especially between mothers and daughters, of how to manage the household and the children. The duties the caregiver is expected to perform are stressful and demanding. Caring for an elderly person with physical or psychological problems is a constant, twenty-four hour per day job, often with no respite for the caregiver. Frustration can often lead to physical violence or an apathetic attitude towards the elderly person, which in turn results in neglect.

Financial difficulties also lead to stress and abuse. Household resources may not stretch far enough to accommodate the needs of the immediate family and the elderly person. Often, college or wedding plans for the caregiver's children must be balanced with household income that is already decreasing due to retirement. This leaves little money with which to care for an elderly person and can cause resentment towards the elderly person; medication and medical equipment needed to provide proper care to the elderly person is costly. Medical costs are often not compensated by government programs and therefore must be fully paid by the family out of the elderly person's already dwindling assets.

The "social exchange theory" promulgates that when a victim depends on a caregiver financially, emotionally, and physically, that dependence can lead to abuse. The result of the dependence is that the caregiver may feel as though he is being "taken advantage of" by the elderly person, which may lead to resentment. Another form of the social exchange theory asserts that the abuser is actually dependent on the victim; some caregivers depend on their victim for financial assistance and/or housing. (Wallace 1998). Such dependence may result in the caregiver trying to control all aspects of the elderly person's life.

Abuse can provide that desired control, as a victim is more likely to obey a caregiver who has control. Conflict theories explain elder abuse in terms of power and resources. The theory states that a caregiver will have money, power, and control, and the elderly person may have none of those resources. Thus, the person with control abuses the person who has none. Some abusers may even obtain physical pleasure from controlling and tormenting a victim. The abuser may have been an abused child, sometimes by the parent he/she is now abusing. Such incidents support the "cycle of violence" theory which suggests that those who are abused tend to abuse others. However, Galbraith (1989) has determined that most cases of elder abuse do not involve a cycle of violence. In any event, the use of social learning theories to explain elder abuse has been the focus of much disagreement among researchers in the area of elder abuse.

In addition to the above case-specific causes of abuse of the elderly, many blame elder abuse on the presence of ageism in our society. Ageism is the "widespread negative attitude about the class" of elderly people. While it may seem that most people think of elderly people as "loving grannies," in fact, many people see elderly people as a burden on our society. Our youth-oriented society often does not accept the problems that come with an aging population. While elder abuse may or may not be caused by ageism, the lack of effective statutes and programs which deal with elder abuse may be a result of this poor attitude toward the elderly. The "functionalism theory" states that if a caregiver believes that an elderly person is stupid or weak, due to ageism, they will be less likely to care appropriately for that person.

The elderly are often easy targets for abuse because they are almost always in a position of financial dependency and psychological dependency on the children with whom they reside. Elderly people look to their children for social companionship after spouses and friends are gone. In addition, elderly people are often dependent on their children to take care of their legal and financial obligations. However, the adult child may resent being the center of the elderly person's universe, and this resentment may lead to retaliation and abuse.

While women are often the primary care providers for the elderly in homes, women are also increasingly members of the work force. The duties of caregiver often fall on women, but the added stresses of job and family make caring for an elderly person a great burden. Women ultimately take on the duties of both the physical and financial support of elderly parents, and such duties are often manifested through abuse. The "family stress theory" asserts that elder abuse is caused by the stress brought on a family when an elderly person is taken into the home. This includes financial stress and the general stress of having more people living within a household. Similarly, psychoanalytic theories blame the psychological makeup of the abuser for the abuse; for example, a caregiver might be depressed or have an anger control problem, which leads to abuse.

Abuse in nursing homes can be caused by different factors than abuse by a general caregiver, although stress can also cause institutional abuse. Although a caregiver in a nursing home is able to escape and perhaps detach himself or herself from the situation more than someone caring for an elderly person in his/her home, work in an institution can be extremely stressful. A shortage of nursing staff, burnout, and inadequate training all contribute to abuse in such settings.

Financial abuse exists as a result of the level of control such institutions may have over a person's finances. Often an elderly person has no family members to supervise his or her finances or advocate for him or her in cases of questionable missing funds. Low wages also contribute to the temptation of institutional employees to steal from the residents. Patients of a nursing home are often out of their rooms for meals, appointments, doctors visits, and other activities, which provides a time period for staff or visitors to steal from that person's room. Additionally, a victim complaining that something was stolen from him or her might be ignored and their complaints might be considered to be due to dementia. In fact, staff may rationalize that a person with dementia will not remember what possessions he or she had anyway. The prevalence of theft from patients is difficult to gauge because many nursing homes do not wish for researchers to pursue this issue and that many times the victim may not be competent to discuss whether he or she was victimized.

Some suggest that one problem in adjudicating elder abuse cases results from the difficulty at times to separate fact from fiction when an elderly person discusses his or her mistreatment. Elderly people can suffer from depressive paranoia, which could cause them to "make up" stories of abuse. While this may make the job of the investigator of elder abuse more difficult, this theory is a result of ageism. To assume that elderly people are less believable than other people is an unfortunate, and often inaccurate, stereotype. If the same theory was asserted for children who claim they are abused or for wives who claim their husbands beat them, we would nevertheless take the steps to examine whether the actual abuse occurred.

Additionally, a family member may simply lack the skills necessary to properly take care of an elderly person. A parent with Alzheimer disease who tends to wander and act out may be difficult for a caregiver who does not understand the disease to deal with. The "role theory" explains elder abuse in this manner; that the role of caregiver is basically thrust upon a person and that by role playing, a caregiver or an elderly person might come to understand what is desired in their role as either caregiver or patient. Understanding the perspective of the other person involved may be helpful in avoiding abuse. Situational theory focuses on the isolation that a person might feel if they are a caregiver. Being isolated and having little emotional support may lead to abuse. The role theory and isolation may be particularly applicable to persons who are giving care to their elderly spouses. An elderly person may have a difficult time understanding why a spouse with dementia or other mental health issues is acting out toward him and may have little support from or little contact with the outside world. Such a scenario can easily lead to frustration, extreme stress, and ultimately abuse.

Although universal agreement on the definition, prevalence and cause of elder abuse is lacking there is ample evidence to suggest we have a major public health concern in our country. Furthermore, given the age demographic (graying of America) there is the likelihood that the problem will continue to escalate. Metaphorically, if this public health problem was seen as a forest fire hazard, the index would read "Danger."

REFERENCES

Billingslea v. Texas, 780 S.W.2d 420, 424 (Tex. 1989).

"Elder Abuse." Infolink 1 (17). (National Victim Center, Washington D.C.) 1992.

Galbraith, M.W. (1989). "A Critical Examination of the Definitional, Methodological and Theoretical Problems of Elder Abuse," in R. Filenson and S.R. Ingman (eds.), *Elder Abuse: Practice and Policy*, Human Sciences Press, New York.

Garfield, Audery S. (1991). Note, Elder Abuse and the State's Adult Protective Services Response: Time for a Change in California. *42 Hastings L.J. 859.*

Greene, Jan (2001). When Not Treating Pain Equals Abuse. *H and HN: Hospitals and Health Networks*, Vol. 75 Issue 10, p 34.

Harris, S. (1996). For Better or for Worse: Spouse Abuse Grown Old. *Journal of Elder Abuse and Neglect*. Vol. 8, No. 1, 1-33.

Krummel, S. (1996). Abuse of the elderly. In D.M. Busby (Ed.), *The Impact of Violence on The Family* (pp. 123-148). Boston: Allyn and Bacon.

Nadien, M.B. (1995). Elder violence (maltreatment) in domestic settings: Some theory and research. In L.L. Adler and F.L. Denmark (Eds.), *Violence and the Prevention of Violence* (pp. 177-190). Westport, CT: Praeger.

National Center on Elder Abuse. (1998). *The National Elder Abuse Incidence Study: Final Report*. Available at

Pillemer, K. and Finkelhor, D. (1988). The Prevalence of Elder Abuse: A Random Sample Survey. *Gerontologist*, Vol. 28, No. 1, 51-57.

Podnieks, E. (1992). National Survey on abuse of the Elderly in Canada. *Journal of Elder Abuse and Neglect*, Vol. 4, No. 1/2,5 - 58.

Rathbone-McCuan, E. and Voyles, B. (1982). Case detection of abused elderly parents. *American Journal of Psychiatry, 139*(2), 189-192.

Steinmetz, S.K. (1988). *Duty Bound: Elder Abuse and Family Care.* Newbury Park, California: Sage Publications.

Stone v. Brewster, 218 A.2d 41 (D.C. 1966).

Sullivan v. Craine (Ohio App. 10 Dist.)

Toshio, T. (1996). Elder Abuse in Domestic Settings. *Elder Abuse Information Series #1.* Washington, D.C. National Center for Elder Abuse.

Wolf, R. and Pillemer, K. (1989). *Helping Elderly Victims.* New York, Columbia University Press.

———— (1992). 138 Cong. Rec. H8969-01 (Older American Act Amendments of 1992) (Thursday September 22).

———— (2001). Abuse of Residents Is a Major Problem in U.S. Nursing Homes, Special Report prepared for Rep. Henry A. Waxman, U.S. House of Representatives.

3

CARE PATHWAY MODEL AND GUIDELINES FOR HEALTH CARE PROFESSIONALS

Tom Miller

Health care professionals recognize the importance of standards of care and standardized models of evaluation and intervention in cases of elder abuse. This chapter focuses on risk factors, the trauma accommodation experienced by elderly who are abused, physical and behavioral indicators of elder abuse, a model algorithm of care for victims of elder abuse, a care pathway for health care professionals to follow in cases of elder abuse and a case study exemplifying the intervention strategies health care providers should consider in such an event. Algorithms and care pathways are being utilized to assure consistency in the evaluation and interventions offered where the spectrum symptoms of domestic violence are identified in the course of counseling. A review of the literature on the use of treatment guidelines is offered, as are treatment and legal considerations and community resources available to the public health and health care professional.

Victims of elder abuse are seeking the assistance of health care professionals with an understanding and sensitivity to their needs and with the expectation that a standardized model of care and treatment will be provided. While each individual brings a unique and highly individualized case to the health care provider, the need for standardized models of care becomes essential to assure consistent standards of care for each person.

Health care providers have begun to utilize clinical algorithms and pathways of care in order to standardize the clinical care provided to individuals who are diagnosed and treated for domestic violence issues. Developments in the health care system have driven important changes that have provided shifts in traditional paradigms of service to more clinically relevant and standardized approaches to assessment and treatment. This chapter describes a model that includes algorithms and care pathways that have been developed and implemented in order to coordinate a standard approach to treatment for victims of domestic violence. The use of such treatment guidelines has gained considerable attention in the managed care arena among health care professionals (Griffith, 1999).

ASSESSING ELDER ABUSE

The presence of depression in traumatized victims of abuse has been well-documented (Conte, Berlinger, Schwerman, 1987; Russell, 1983; Veltkamp and Miller, 1994). The protracted depression is reported as a most common symptom along with aggravated depressive symptoms, hyperarousal, intrusive thoughts, insomnia, psychosomatic symptomatology, and dissociation commonly associated with the post traumatized period. The paralysis of apathy and helplessness, the intense internalized anger, the debased self-image, and ruminations of guilt, all are recognized within the cluster of depressive symptomatology frequently recognized in victims of prolonged abuse.

Long-term traumatized individuals who have been abused (Horowitz and Soloman, 1978; Frayberg, 1980) show anxiety, agitation and hypervigilance which is most recognized not only in their insomnia and startle reactions, but also in tension headaches, abdominal pain, gastrointestinal disturbances, and other forms of somatization. Victims of prolonged trauma are as well users of the art of altered consciousness as a means of coping and controlling the situation and the perpetrator. Through dissociative experiences, including suppression and denial, they are able to cope through the immediacy of the trauma but often suffer at later times from disturbances of memory and concentration because of their conditioned experience to the dissociative form of coping. Adult survivors of child sexual abuse and adult victims of domestic violence use these dissociative capacities in their adaptation and accommodation to stressful life experiences.

Victims of elder abuse (Miller and Veltkamp, 1996) may well experience a more complex picture of psychopathology. They are, in fact, victims of a disorder of extreme stress which must capture the manifestations of repeated and prolonged abuse and its resultant impact on personality development that is not usually seen in situations of more acute stressful nature. Counselors have come to the realization that the significance of prolonged and repeated traumatization as seen through domestic violence and physical and sexual abuse warrant careful consideration in providing a counseling intervention.

RISK FACTORS IN ELDER ABUSE

Health care professionals recognition of "at risk" factors is crucial. The "at-risk" factors in domestic violence focus on two elements: (1) a multigenerational pattern of abuse, and (2) a family constellation of "at-risk" factors as reflected in the "victim-victimization" spectrum. Multigenerational patterns of abuse on to subsequent generations, perpetuating a "cycle of violence" (Walker, 1998). Persons most prone to violent behavior experience financial problems, frequent moves, substance abuse, and isolation from peer groups and family support systems, which often include ingredients that leads to family violence. Efforts to recognize "high-risk" individuals and to provide early intervention in the form of prevention and education may be of considerable benefit in reducing spouse and child abuse in all segments of the pop-

Table 1: Victim-Victimizer Spectrum

Survivor	Victimizer
Isolation from others	History or pattern of abuse
Feeling of helplessness	Learned violent behavior
Vunerable	Unstable
Secrecy	Low self-esteem
Indecision	Impulsive
Poor self-confidence	Impaired judgment
Low self-esteem	Narcissistic
Fear, anxiety, depression	Alcohol and/or substance abuser
Impaired ability to judge trustworthiness in others	Control and power seeking
Accomodates to the victimization	Perpetuates continued forms of victimization

ulation. Table 1 identified as the victim-victimizer spectrum summarizes risk factors for both the victim and the perpetrator.

In addition to the factors identified in the "victim-victimizer" spectrum, the family constellation of at-risk factors in abusing families may include the following characteristics:

- An elder partner may be extremely passive, dependent, and/or reluctant to assert oneself in the face of an abusive situation.
- Poor marital relationship, a lack of constructive communication or poor interpersonal relationship.
- The perpetrator turns outside the family or toward the victim to relieve and displace emotional tension and stress.
- The elderly person may feel emotionally deprived and turn to the perpetrator for support and emotional nurturance, and in the process becomes abused.
- The issue of control is a big factor in elder abuse situations
- Perpetrators use control to force victims to comply with their wishes.
- Generational boundaries are often unclear between the perpetrator and elder abuse victim.
- There is a lack of social contacts outside the family.

- Caretakers have inadequate coping skills, particularly under stress.
- Family problems become family secrets, therefore not allowing change or intervention to occur within the cycle of violence.
- Substance abuse is sometimes a factor in cases involving domestic violence.

There are specific behavioral indicators of abuse frequently seen in spouses and children who have been abused. Any one of these behaviors may be the victim's way of communicating to the physician or health care professional that something is wrong, that he or she is being abused. A mistake frequently made by health care professionals is that these behaviors are viewed as "the problem," rather than the symptom of a far greater family problem, namely domestic violence. The most prominent physical and behavioral indicators are summarized in Table 2 and address both the child and the spouse. These indicators become important to the counselor in screening for domestic violence in the care pathway.

ACCOMMODATION OF TRAUMA AND ABUSE IN THE ELDERLY

The trauma of physical and/or psychological abuse for the victim is often a difficult experience to understand and accommodate. The Trauma Accommodation Syndrome (Miller and Veltkamp, 1998) is based on DSM IV criteria (American Psychiatric Association, 1994) and outlines how the victim processes trauma such as abuse. There is usually extreme difficulty in discussing any aspect of the victimization. The victim confronted with such abuse often passes through a series of stages in dealing with this trauma. The initial stage is one of *victimization*, which is recognized as the stressor and is usually realized as an acute physical and/or psychological traumatization. The person's response is usually one of feeling overwhelmed and intimidated, and the locus of control for the victim is more of an external nature. It is not uncommon for the victim to think recurringly of the stressful experience and to focus on the intimidating act, as well as the physical pain associated with the abuse. Figure 1 summarizes the stages or phases the victim often experiences along with clinical indicators present during each stage.

This *acute stage* of trauma involving feelings of helplessness and fear is followed by a stage involving more cognitive disorganization and confusion. This stage is marked by a vagueness in understanding both the concept of abuse and the expectations associated with the demands of the perpetrator. The third stage may involve denial and a conscious inhibition wherein an effort is made on the part of the victim to actively inhibit thoughts and feelings related to the abuse. This can involve revisiting the cognitive disorganization phase and the earlier memories, with flashbacks to the acute physical and psychological trauma. This stage can also realize avoidance involving unconscious denial, wherein the victim is not aware of his effort to avoid the psychological trauma associated with the abuse. The victim, therefore, unconsciously denies or minimizes the abuse and/or any efforts to respond to the

Table 2: Physical and Behavioral Indicators of Elder Abuse

Physical Indicators
Malnourishment and dehydration
Unexplained bruises and welts
Unexplained burns, especially on soles, palms, back or buttocks
Immersion burns, pressure sores or ulcers
Rope burns on arms, legs, neck or torso
Unexplained fractures to skull, nose, or facial structure; in various stages of
    healing; multiple or spiral fractures
Unexplained lacerations or abrasions to mouth, lips, gums, eyes, or external
    genitalia

Behavioral Indicators
Emotional constriction and blunted affect

Fear of adult contacts
Extreme withdrawal or aggressiveness

Extreme rejection or dependence
on caretakers

Apprehension, fearfulness
Afraid to go home
Depression and isolation
Phobias, anxiety
Sleep disturbance
Withdrawn, inhibited behavior
Obsessive-compulsive behavior

Material/Financial Indicators
Lack of knowledge of financial
assets
Unusual banking activity
Living conditions vary from value
of estate
Documents for signature drawn
without elders knowledge and
approval
Lost or missing personal assets
Isolation from family and friends
Variation in signatures on legal
papers and checks

Abuse of a Sexual Nature
Difficulty in walking or sitting
Torn, stained, or bloody underclothing
Bruises or bleeding in external genitalia, vaginal, or anal areas
Venereal disease or sexually transmitted disease
Sleep disturbances
Withdrawn or regressed behavior
Secondary enuresis or encopresis
Poor interpersonal skills
Self-report of abuse
Anorexia or loss of appetite
Extreme self-blame for the abuse
Extreme expressed fears

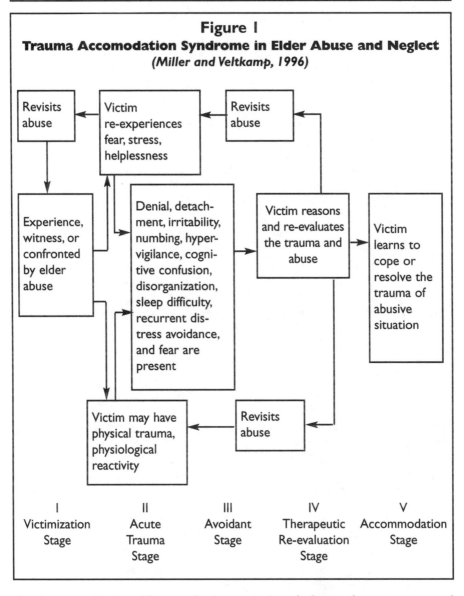

Figure I
Trauma Accomodation Syndrome in Elder Abuse and Neglect
(Miller and Veltkamp, 1996)

abusing experiencing. This results in stagnation, feelings of entrapment, and often results in the victim accommodating the pain of the abuse.

This *avoidant stage* may be followed by a stage of *therapeutic re-evaluation*, where a "significant other" usually supports the reasoning through and the re-evaluation of this psychological and physical trauma associated with the abuse. In this stage, the victim may begin to disclose specific content relevant to the abuse. The phase of therapeutic re-evaluation and reasoning is significant in that it indicates that conscious support has been realized by the victim in passing from the avoidant phase to the issues, activities, and trauma of the abusing experience(s).

The final stage is one of accommodation, which involves coping and/or resolution, wherein the victim has been able to deal with the issues of the abuse and comes to a better understanding of the significance of the abuse and the perpetrator. The victim is viewed at this stage as: (1) being more open to talking about the incident, (2) being able to express thoughts and feelings more readily, and (3) being committed to both assessment and therapy where the victim may discharge some of the aggressive feelings toward the perpetrator. It is clearly at this stage that the victim has realized an alliance with the counselor, significant others and/or other professionals in: (1) exploring the original abusive experience, (2) dealing with both the physical and psychological stressors involved, (3) attending to the repressed material and the process of either conscious inhibition or unconscious denial utilized during the avoidant stage, (4) focusing on self-understanding, psychological and emotional support of others in comprehending the rationale for the abusing experiences, and (5) exploring appropriate psychosocial lifestyles to determine the degree of therapeutic intervention yet required.

Risk factors once identified can best be monitored by the use of a practice guideline which have been guided by clinical research studies (Miller and Veltkamp, 1998). These studies and clinical evidence have identified the effects of victimization in cases of elder abuse. Cicchette and Olsen (1987) in the Harvard Maltreatment Project, realized that adult victims were often over controlled in their management of feelings and impulses during the victimization process and therefore significantly at risk for developing psychopathology (Walker, 1998). Among the most relevant characteristics of at-risk individuals are children who: (1) have a history of family violence, abuse, or neglect; (2) have recognized family disorganization; (3) experience a lack of acceptance and a lack of interest on the part of the family of the victim; and (4) have poor quality of communication with others in and beyond the family (Veltkamp and Miller, 1990).

There is considerable evidence in the health care literature (Griffith, 1998, Sackett, 1997, Eddy, 1996) that the use of algorithms and care pathways based on clinical research will help in standardizing care and providing the necessary ingredients for effective diagnostic and counseling interventions. The goal is to make the client management guideline the accepted professional behavior and a reward in itself (Griffith, 1999). To the extent that this is successful, five components that occur: (1) the clinical guideline is widely used and becomes habitual, (2) multidisciplinary professionals can use it to anticipate care events, (3) counselors can use it as a shorthand or outline to guide their decisions and their communications to others. The individual plan becomes the exception to the guideline, (4) the logistics for delivering the guideline components are convenient and reliable. Intermediate methods or strategies in the guideline must be readily available and delivered uniformly in terms of quality and timeliness, and (5) the guideline defines the measures of performance and incorporates information collection that can be used for its evaluation and improvement. The individualized plans counselors may use also contribute information for guideline revision.

Figure 2
Model Algorithm for Elder Abuse Intervention

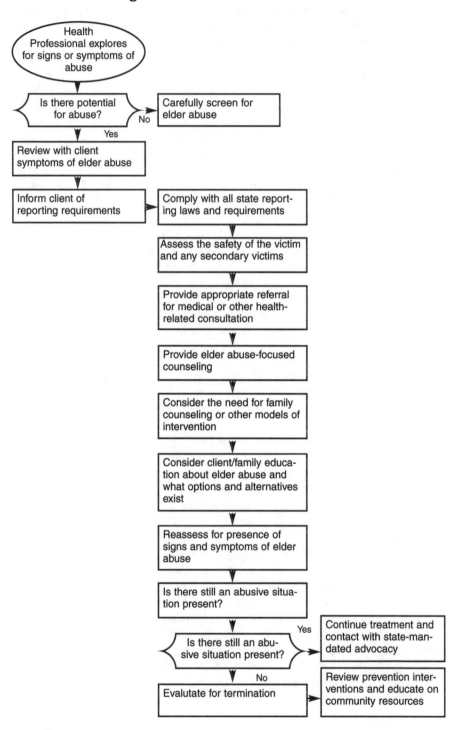

A MODEL ALGORITHM OF CARE FOR VICTIMS OF ELDER ABUSE

Clinical algorithms and care pathways delineate specific timelines in which intervention should occur. They further address the decision-making process, the clinical services offered and the potential interactions among multi-disciplinary health care professionals and providers for specific needs of patients referred. Clinical information systems capable of supporting the functional requirements of comprehensive critical pathway also provide direction to the development and implementation of algorithms appropriate for change (Miller and Veltkamp, 1996). The clinical algorithm for an abusive situation or for family violence is summarized in Figure 2. Sometimes the client will present with symptoms or complaints not of the abuse but of some other related symptomatology. The clinical algorithm moves through the history and systems review, the identification of symptoms and the diagnostic criteria for acute and/or chronic trauma. It also considers symptoms, specific treatment and supportive care, and how the counselors can reassess and monitor an abusive situation over time.

The care pathway delineates the specific timelines in which assessment and treatment or interventions must occur. Note with specificity the importance of the legal and ethical responsibilities within the abuse spectrum. Specific emphasis here is on reporting child and adult abuse to the appropriate local state Department of Social Services unit. In addition, specific information related to office management for clients who present with problems associated with domestic violence are summarized in Figure 3, the care pathway or guideline for domestic violence. These become the critical ingredients to be considered in a care pathway that would provide standardized care and treatment for the victim of domestic violence and abuse.

CLINICAL INTERVENTIONS AND LEGAL CONSIDERATIONS

Counseling of an abused person and/or the perpetrator is a complex process, which may involve a multidisciplinary team. Collaboration, cooperation, mutual respect, and understanding of each other's roles are essential to the success of the therapeutic process. The reporting law recognizes the need for open communication in the area of abuse and recognizes no privileged relationships beyond the attorney-client relationship. Siblings must also be addressed in abuse cases. In physical and sexual abuse cases, the siblings have often been exposed to the same family themes as the victim; and in many cases, the siblings may also have been abused. They may also feel guilty that they had not attempted to intervene and stop the abusive pattern. The following are important areas for counselors to address:

1) Abide by all reporting laws and facilitate appropriate medical care immediately.
2) Maintain the therapeutic relationship with the victim. The elder victim's contact with the perpetrator should be monitored. Reducing the

Figure 3
Integrated Sample Care Pathway for Client
with Indicators of Elder Abuse

Activity	Visit 1	Visits 2-5	Visit 6	Visit 8
Assessment	Abuse Screening		PRN Assessment	Depression Screening
Intervention	Abide by reporting requirements for abuse in your jurisdiction	Abuse focused Mental Health Education & Counseling Brief Therapy		Consider for Individual Counseling; Family Counseling
Consults/ Assessment Considered	Internist Psychologist Psychiatrist Mental Health Counselor OB/GYN	Follow-up with consultant	Integrate counseling and recommenda- tions	
Client/Family Education				Encourage client and family edu- cation, review "cycle of vio- lence" theory, and encourage victim-initiated interventions and control

degree of environmental change is crucial for children. Maintaining the victim's relationship with peers, the community contacts, neighbors and church, are important to reduce risk of further problems.

3) Reduce risk for further abuse/neglect by providing suspected or reported information to authorities as identified in state reporting laws.

4) Refer to clinician specializing in elder abuse to monitor clinical indicators and assess if the victim is showing signs and symptoms of abuse.

5) If victim cannot be protected in their home or living site, they should be removed from the home environment through legal advocacy referral often through the county attorney's office.

COMMUNITY RESOURCES

Miller and Veltkamp (1998) have summarized the spectrum of community resources available to the counselor and other health care professionals. These include the following:

1) Safe shelters and 24-hour crisis line: Be aware of services that provide a place where victims and perpetrators may call anytime, day or night, to receive counseling, information, referrals, and screening for abusive situations.

2) Counseling and casework services: These services are designed to facilitate the victim's exploration of alternatives to being abused and provide eventual return to the community and a non-explicated or abusive relationship.

3) Legal advocacy programs: Programs such as these provide a legal advocate to act as a liaison between the victim of domestic violence, whether residing at a shelter or not, and the court system counselor's should work closely with legal advocacy system.

4) Hospital advocacy program: This service provides a hospital advocate who will meet the victim at the hospital to provide information, support, medical treatment and referrals to other medical and health related professional services.

5) Perpetrator's Intervention Programs: This service provides perpetrators the opportunity to seek alternatives to violence and break down the isolation they may feel and provide alternatives to physically, psychologically, and sexually abusive behaviors they have likely developed as a part of their behavior pattern.

6) Community education: Counselors should participate in community education and service programs on issues of domestic violence to improve public awareness of the scope of abuse and family violence in the community.

The Case of Asking Abuse Related Questions

Ron is a 67-year-old white married male veteran who suffered a brain stem stroke seven years ago. He was currently in a semi-private room in a skilled nursing facility. He is a quadriplegic with limited ability to communicate although his mental status shows he is oriented to time, place, person and self.

He receives physical therapy, speech therapy and occupational therapy along with routine medical and skilled nursing care. Ron has been showing signs of depression and agitation but has been unable to communicate with health care personnel other than through eye contact blinking and limited efforts toward nodding his head.

During a monthly staffing, he was asked a number of routine medical and clinically diagnostic questions with limited response. In a post staffing individual contact with the patient, he was asked the question "are you satisfied with your care?" He responded with what seemed to be negative eye movements from left to right. Among the questions that followed, he was asked if he was being abused in anyway. He indicated a positive response with his eyes. Subsequently, it was discerned that he was being fondled regularly at night by his roommate. The nursing home immediately moved the patient to a private room, notified adult protective services by phone and initiated an internal and external investigation. The perpetrator was isolated until the investigation could be completed.

The results of both the internal and external investigation revealed a pattern of sexual abuse on the part of the perpetrator. The victim's depressive features subsided once he had been provided a safe environment and staff responded to his abuse. Preventative steps taken included:

WEB-BASED RESOURCES

The Administration on Aging (AoA)

The Administration on Aging (AoA) is the only federal agency dedicated to policy development, planning, and the delivery of supportive home and community-based services to our nation's diverse population of older persons and their caregivers. They provide critical information and assistance and programs that protect the rights of vulnerable, at-risk older persons through the national aging network. State elder abuse prevention activities include:

- Professional training, workshops for adult protective services personnel and other professional groups, statewide conferences open to all service providers with an interest in elder abuse, and development of training manuals, videos, and other materials.
- Coordination among state services systems and among service providers, creation of elder abuse hotlines for reporting, formation of statewide coalitions and task forces, and creation of local multi-disciplinary teams, coalitions and task forces;
- Technical assistance, development of policy manuals and protocols that outline the proper or preferred procedures for assessment and reporting.
- Public education, development of elder abuse prevention education campaigns for the public, including media public service announcements, posters, flyers, and videos.

- AoA funds the national Center on Elder Abuse as a resource for public and private agencies, professionals, service providers, and individuals interested in abuse prevention.

> Administration on Aging
> U.S. Department of Health and Human Services
> Washington, DC 20201
> Email: aoainfo@aoa.gov
> Website: http://www.aoa.gov

- Legislatures in all 50 states have passed some form of elder abuse prevention laws. Laws and definitions of terms vary considerably from one state to another, but all states have set up reporting systems. Generally, adult protective services (APS) agencies receive and investigate reports of suspected elder abuse.

National Center on Elder Abuse (NCEA) – www.edlerabusecenter.org
Elder Abuse Prevention – www.oaktrees.ore/elder/
The National Elder Abuse Incidence Study –
    www.aoa.gov/abuse/report/default.htm
Elder Abuse Preventon – Administration on Aging Fact Sheet –
    www.aoa.gov/factsheets/abuse/html
NCPEA Home Page – www.preventelderabuse.org/
MEDLINEplus: Elder Abuse –
    www.nlm.nih.gove/medlineplus/edlerabuse.html
Elder Abuse and Neglect: In Search of Solutions –
    www.apa.org/pi/aging/eldabuse.html
Elder Abuse Law – www.elderabuselaw.com/
Actions on Elder Abuse – freespece.virgin.net/man.web/aea/
Elder Abuse in the United Kingdom – www.elderabuse.org.uk/

CONCLUSION

In the case of elder abuse, health care professionals must be sensitive to a standardized model and respond to the needs of individuals who have been victimized through elder abuse. A model algorithm for abuse is summarized herein as is a standardized care pathway that is beneficial to the new paradigms of health care delivery. Health care professionals must understand the transforming paradigms effecting health care service provision through managed care and that practice guidelines are a critical ingredient in today's health care environment.

Several therapeutic approaches may be beneficial with elder abuse situations (Westcot and Dries, 1990) but much depends on the competencies and abilities of the victim of elder abuse. All are dependent on therapists taking the time to get to know the unique aspects of the victim-perpetrator situations. Assessment of the unique as well as universal aspects of elder abuse always precedes therapeutic interventions. To effectively treat victims of elder abuse, therapists must help them work together as a team systematically. (Gladding, 1998).

Solution-focused therapy may be particularly helpful to elder abuse victims because it helps them focus on certain aspects of their lives by finding exceptions to difficult situations and doing something different (deShazeer, 1991; O'Hanlon and Weiner-Davis, 1989). The emphasis on making small changes is ideally suited to elder abuse victims in which there is much unrest and the ability to participate in therapeutic work is limited because of demands and fatigue. However, if victims perceive when they are in harmony with each other, they can then focus their energy and efforts on cultivating these exceptional times and in the process make significant and healthy changes.

Bowen family therapy is employed because of its emphasis on resolving the past and examining historical family patterns (Bowen, 1978). Through the construction of a genogram, perpetrators may come to notice and deal with the absent person or persons that have influenced them positively or negatively previously. For example, a solo parent may realize he is still trying to live up to the words of his mother who admonished him to "stay married at all costs" and "always put your children's needs before your own." In the process of constructing a genogram, such "ghosts" from the past lose their power to interfere with the family's present interactions because they are recognized as historical figures over which one has control (Goldenberg and Goldenberg, 1994).

Experiential family therapy, especially as advocated by Virginia Satir (1967), may be useful for elder abuse victims in helping their family members enact metaphorically—through sculpting and choreography—troublesome and unresolved situations. The feelings that arise in connection with these symbolic experiences often experience affective relief from circumstances they can no longer influence or control.

Regardless of what theoretical approach is employed with elder abuse victims, health care professionals should keep in mind the intervention must be tailor made to the needs of the victim and the circumstances of the abuse. This will require special attention to the physical, psychological, emotional, and dynamic complexity of the abusive situation.

Health care professionals should determine the applicability of these evolving concepts to their organizations and evaluate the impact on the quality and continuity of health care delivery with respect to all clinical disorders including the impact of elder abuse on health and adjustment of clients. The algorithm and care pathway only provide a framework. Health care providers should systematically operationalize and implement health care delivery to victims of elder abuse. Success of prevention programs, as well as intervention strategies, will depend on competencies of health care providers in making fundamental use of standardized models of assessment and intervention in cases of elder abuse.

Acknowledgements
The authors wish to acknowledge the assistance of Lane J. Veltkamp M.S.W., Brenda Frommer, Dale Dubina, Tag Heister, Deborah Kessler, Breston Britner, Ph.D., Beth Alexander, Ph.D,.Carrie Ogtz, Celena Keel, Shannon Nelson, Tina Lane, Amber Alexander, and Robert Kraus, M.D for their contributions to the completion of this chapter.

REFERENCES

American Psychiatric Association. (1994). *Diagnostic and Statistical Manual - IV- Revised.* Washington, D.C.

Cicchetti, D., and Olsen, K. (1987), The developmental psychopathology of child maltreatment. In: *Handbooks of Developmental Psychopathology,* ed. M. Lewis and S. Miller. New York: Plenum.

Conte, J.R., Berlinger, L., and Schwerman, J. R. (1987). The Impact of Sexual Abuse on Children. Final Technical Report: National Institute of Mental Health, Project No. MH 37133.

Eddy, D.M. (1996). "Guidelines—How Should They Be Designed?" *Clinical Decision Making: From Theory to Practice.* Sudbury, MA: Jones and Bartlett, 34-40.

Frayberg, J.T. (1980). Difficulties in separation-individuation as experienced by offspring of Holocaust survivors. *Amercian Journal of Orthopsychiatry,* 50 (8): 87-95.

Griffith, J.R. (1998). *Designing 21st Century Healthcare: Leadership in Hospitals and Healthcare Organizations,* Chicago: Health Administration Press, 247-65.

Gladding, S. T. (1998). *Family Therapy.* New Jersey: Prentice Hall Publishers.

Griffith, J.R. (1999). *The Well Managed Health Care Organization.* Chicago, Ill: Health Adminstration Press.

Horowitz, M. J., and Solomon, G. F. (1978). Delayed Stress Response in Vietnam Veterans. In C.R. Figley (Ed.), *Stress Disorders Among Vietnam Veterans.* New York: Brunner/ Mazel.

Miller, T. W., and Fiebelman, N. D. (1989). Truamatic Stress Disorder: Diagnostic and Clinical Issues in Psychiatry. In T. W. Miller (ed.), *Stressful Life Events.* New York: International Universities Press, Inc.

Miller, T. W. and Veltkamp, L. J. (1996) Theories, Assessment and Treatment of Domestic Violence. *Directions in Clinical and Counseling Psychology.* New York: Hatherleigh Company, Limited.

Miller, T. W., and Veltkamp, L. J. (1998). *Clinical Handbook of Adult Abuse and Exploitation.* Madison Ct.: International Universities Press, Incorporated.

National Center for Child Abuse and Neglect (1996). *Study Findings: National Study of the Incidence and Severity of Child Abuse and Neglect.* Washington, D. C.: U. S. Government Printing Office.

Russell, D. (1983). The Incidence and Prevalence of Intrafamilial and Extrafamilial Sexual Abuse of Female Children. *Child Abuse and Neglect,* 7, 56-63.

Sackett, D.L. (1997). *Evidence-Based Medicine: How to Practice and Teach EBM.* New York: Churchill Livingstone Publishers.

Veltkamp, L. J. and Miller, T. W. (1990). Clinical Strategies and Recognizing Spouse Abuse. *Psychiatric Quarterly,* 61 (3): 181-189.

Veltkamp, L. J. and Miller, T. W. (1994) *Clinical Handbook of Child Abuse and Neglect.* Madison CT: International Universities Press, Inc.

Walker, L. B. (1998) Domestic Violence. In: Miller, T. W. and Veltkamp, L. J. *Clinical Handbook of Adult Abuse and Exploration.* Madison CT: International Unversities Press Incorporated.

4

CAREGIVER STRESS AND NURSE/HEALTH THERAPIST IDENTIFICATION OF ABUSE IN THE HOME

Denise Bender

In the late 1980s, responding to the national interest in elder abuse, Congress used the Omnibus Budget Reconciliation Act to enact major reforms for the nursing home industry (OBRA, 1987). Institutional standards required in order to qualify for Medicare and Medicaid funds were amended to improve the training and competency of caregivers working with the institutionalized elderly (42 USC §§ 1395i-3, 1987; 42 USC § 1396r, 1987). As a result, health care providers working in hospitals and nursing homes became sensitized to watch for abuse, particularly among institutionalized patients.

Institutional initiatives such as ombudsman programs, increased staff scrutiny, and training programs to educate those who came into contact with the elderly residents did help to safeguard those living in long-term care settings. While these Federal actions brought about important reforms in the management of the problem of elder abuse, the changes had little impact on the safety of community dwelling elders. There is a lack of knowledge and awareness in the general public about how to identify and appropriately respond to abuse, especially when the questionable behavior occurs in a home environment (Wieland, 2000). As already observed with the issues of child abuse and domestic violence, social attitudes shape ideas about what type and severity of behavior is required before an action is considered abusive (Reay and Browne, 2001). Many adult children would deny that expressing verbal frustration about the failure of a parent to function at a level of overly high expectations could be considered mental abuse. Others would view their failure to monitor the safety of an older adult as a momentary lapse in judgment, rather than as neglect (Nadworny, 1994). Health providers, keenly aware of the piecemeal nature of many elder care arrangements, might rationalize that a caregiver willing to provide even a marginal quality of care was better than nothing at all. Episodes of elder abuse could be excused or overlooked, because busy home care providers did not know which questions to ask or felt unprepared to label observed behaviors as abuse (Marshall, Benton, and Brazier, 2000).

A study by Lachs (1998) reinforces the urgent need for some type of monitoring of elders living in the community. His research found that the risk of death was more than three times higher for those elders with a history of abuse (1998). National statistics from Adult Protective Services (APS) reported that 49% of the reports of abuse that it receives concerning community-dwelling elders could be substantiated (Teaster, 2000). Although another 39% of the reports were eventually dismissed as unsubstantiated, the APS data clarified that this dismissal does not mean that abuse did not occur. The dismissal may have been granted because the burden of proof demanded by the state was not met (NEAIS, 1998). Demographics on the frequency of elder abuse uniformly agree that the reported rate of incidence of abuse reflects only a small portion of the actual occurrence of abuse (Pillemer and Finkelhor, 1988). These statistics identified an under-protected group of elders that encompasses all races, genders, and economic groups. The dignity of living and aging safely in one's own home was denied to them and they often lived at the mercy of their caregivers.

It is difficult to monitor what goes on in the privacy of a private home or apartment. Many aging, but independently living adults do not routinely interact with persons other than family. It is not atypical for an elder to have outlived friends or to have moved away from long-term support systems in order to live closer to a child. The onset of a noticeable decline in physical mobility or development of an illness is often the first time that community dwelling elder must begin on-going contact with outside persons. Unfortunately, brief contact with medical persons is sometimes inadequate to allow identification of an abusive situation.

The doctor usually has the first contact with an older adult who has problems managing changes in medical or functional status. This point-of-entry role identifies the physician as the first professional who has an opportunity to screen for the possibility of elder abuse. Ideally, any suspicious changes would be noticed immediately based on the long-standing relationship of trust and familiarity that existed between the physician and the patient (Jogerst, Dawson, Hartz, Ely, and Schweitzer, 2000). Since the onset of managed care, research shows that the doctor-patient relationship has changed significantly. In a survey on the impact of managed care on physicians' practice, results indicated physicians feel they have less time for their patients because of an increased emphasis on productivity (Feldman, Novack, and Gracely 1998). The shortened length of visits leaves physicians with little opportunity to closely observe and question the patient for physical and emotional health issues related to abuse, especially if the patient is not forthcoming about the problem (Hoban, 2000).

Many older persons with significant changes in health status require multi-disciplinary home care services. A physician's referral to a home care agency involves several other professional disciplines with the patient. This includes home health agency nurses and physical therapists who fulfill an important role in detection of elder abuse. In addition to the examination of discipline specific health related issues, each of these professionals assesses the general well being of the patient and family environment. This improves the likelihood that abuse will be detected and addressed. (Swagerty, Takahashi, and Evans, 1999).

The home care nurse usually acts as the home care services coordinator for a particular patient. The nurse monitors the care provided by therapists, aides, and others to ensure that all of the patient's needs are met. Providers such as physical therapists and nurses often have frequent enough interactions to develop on-going relationships of trust with the patient. During that time, the physician may only be involved peripherally in the care, and actually see the patient only a few times. Through shared documentation, routine medical examination procedures, and peer conversations about interactions with the patient, family, and/or caregivers, these team members have many opportunities to share suspicions and work together to identify and intervene in abusive or potentially abusive situations (Holland, Kasraian, and Leonardelli, 1987; Wieland, 2000).

This on-going proximity to the older patient highlights the importance of therapists and nurses recognizing and accepting a primary role in the identification of abuse. All 50 states and the District of Columbia have passed laws that established adult protective services and defined some level of professional responsibility for reporting suspected abuse. Currently, the criteria for determining which professionals are required to report abuse include physical therapists and nurses (http://www.elderabusecenter.org). The American Physical Therapy Association and the American Nursing Association both require members to practice according to a strict code of ethics (APTA, 1999; http://www.nursingworld.org/ethics/code). These codes charge members of both professions with the duty to protect the safety and dignity of all patients. Elder abuse puts both the dignity and the safety of older patients at risk, and tolerance of abusive behaviors would violate these codes.

Home care professionals may overlook the signs and symptoms of elder abuse in a home care patient because of preconceived beliefs about who typically comprises the segment of the population (Wolfe, 1998). As in all other forms of family violence, elder abuse statistics show that the problem occurs in all social and cultural demographics (Nadworny, 1994). There is no area in the United States that can be identified as having an abnormal prevalence of elder abuse, although APS reporting percentages are higher in the western states (NEAIS, 1998). The expected victim of elder abuse is a single Caucasian female over the age of seventy-five who is financially dependent and either physically or mentally impaired (Bradley, 1996; NEAIS, 1996). Within this category, certain sub-populations who are more at risk than others. Many abused older persons are depressed or confused (Wolfe, 1998). Approximately 75% of abuse victims are no longer independent in the performance of self-care activities (NEAIS, 1998). The presence of one or any combination of these impairments significantly increases the physical and psychological demands of care giving (Wolf, 1997).

There is no formula to distinguish between the caregiver who will be able to cope with these responsibilities and the one who will retaliate with abuse. Elder abuse is classified as a form of intimate abuse (Wolfe, 1998) and although not always the case, the abusers often occupy a relationship of trust with the older adult (Marshall, Benton, and Brazier, 2000). According to a national report from APS; the abuser frequently fits within an identifiable profile. Typically, the abuser is a Caucasian male between the ages of 40 and 59 (NEAIS, 1998) who has a familial tie to the abusee (Teaster, 2000). The primary relationship between abuser and victim is that of an adult child with the spouse or life partner identified as the second most prevalent category (Wolfe, 1998; NEAIS, 1996). Caregiver involvement with alcohol or drug abuse is commonly found among abusers (Hyde-Robertson, Pirnie, and Freeze, 1994; Swagerty, Takahashi, and Evans, 1999).

There are various theories offered to explain the reasons that abuse occurs. Some abuse is attributed more to caregiver stress than to a malicious desire to hurt an older person (Marshall, Benton, and Brazier, 2000; Sengstock and Barrett, 1993). Caregivers with a limited understanding of the burden they have accepted, or with physical, financial, or emotional stresses directly related to the care giving role may feel justified in engaging in abusive behaviors toward the family member (Nadworny, 1994).

A home health care provider is in an ideal position to monitor family dynamics and to continually assess both situational stress, and the quantity of stressors occurring within a short period of time at each visit (Hyde-Robertson, 1994; Sengstock and Barrett, 1993). Johnson (1991) identifies several key primary and secondary caregiver stress factors that place a patient at greater risk for abuse. The primary factors include isolation, perceived burden, dependency (financial and physical), and stress (Fusco, 1991; Holland, Kasraian, and Leonardelli, 1987). Of secondary impact, but more remediable from the nurse and therapists' viewpoint, are issues of amount of knowledge and understanding about the process of aging, and lack of exposure to resources to remediate this lack of awareness. Caregivers with little knowledge concerning which behaviors are typical in aging persons may develop unreasonable expectations and feel increased levels of frustration with their tasks. Unfamiliarity with the services available for respite, emotional support, medical information, and financial assistance within the caregiver's community can contribute to a feeling of helplessness and isolation (Hoban, 2000).

The mere existence of any or all of these factors in a care giving relationship is not a definite harbinger of abuse. The individual caregiver's ability to adjust to, and cope with, any or all of these factors on an on-going basis provides the best indicator of the likelihood that abuse will occur. A nurse or physical therapist who includes the home care patient's environment as an essential component of their overall health assessment may be able to identify and address coping problems exhibited by caregivers before the abuse begins.

Despite great strides in awareness of the existence of elder abuse, the actual and suspected incidence of abuse, as documented by the NEAIS report and the National Center on Elder Abuse strongly suggest that many potential opportunities to identify abuse are missed (NEAIS, 1998). Even the comprehensive nature of the nursing and physical therapy assessments may result in observation of abuse-related symptoms but fail to properly identify or intervene when abuse has occurred. The fault for this can be attributed to two reasons. Until recently, elder abuse was not viewed as an important and frequently encountered medical issue. As a result, didactic information on elder abuse was either not included or addressed in an abbreviated manner in many professional curriculums (Hazzard,1995; Woodtli and Breslin, 2002). Students were not taught to routinely screen for abuse related findings or instructed as to appropriate questioning techniques designed to elicit this information (Woodtli and Breslin, 2002). Unless serious injury or a significant number of unexplained physical injuries were present, busy home care practitioners often accepted the explanations provided by either the caregiver or the older adult. The abused patients, often embarrassed by the events or in fear of retaliation by the abuser, can add to the confusion by downplaying injuries or attributing the suspicious findings to other, more benign causes (Bradley, 2000; Harrell, Toronjo, McLaughlin, Pavlik, Hyman, and Dyer, 2002).

The second reason for failure to identify the problem relates to the expectation of the health provider to encounter normal and expected age-related changes. The physical and cognitive signs and symptoms of elder abuse are not always unexpected or clearly attributable to a specific cause. Seemingly suspicious signs and symptoms such as hair loss, bruising, weight loss, dehydration, falls, and mental confusion are also signs and symptoms of medical changes related to aging (Bradley, 1996; Wolf, 1997). This makes it difficult for a home health provider to identify abuse with certainty. Elder abuse is more likely to be detected if the initial and subsequent evaluations of a patient's health status by a physical therapist or nurse consider the possibility that physical abuse may have occurred since the last visit. A heightened sense of awareness during all patient interactions increases the likelihood that a provider can detect a pattern of atypical findings. This type of pattern indicates that further investigation is needed.

Detection of elder abuse begins when the multi-disciplinary home health team members first encounter the patient (Swagerty, Takahashi, and Evans, 1999). A patient interview traditionally begins the evaluation process, allowing the nurse and therapist to gather related medical information while assessing the cognition, psychological status, and home environment. Ideally, the presence of the caregiver is minimized during the interview to allow the provider a chance to develop a rapport with the patient (Swagerty, Takahashi, and Evans, 1999). The refusal of a caregiver to leave a competent patient alone with the practitioner during the interview is the first potential sign that the care giving relationship may not be appropriate. This behavior can be the result of a desire to help the provider obtain complete and accurate information, or it can suggest an attempt to direct and perhaps limit the interview (Hoban, 2000). Although the provider should make every effort to interview the adult patient in privacy, if the patient consents to the other person's presence, the provider must allow it.

There are also times when the cognitive or physical status of the patient limits the ability to accurately respond to questions. When it is necessary to interview the caregiver for information, the therapist or nurse should perform the interview in the presence of the patient (APTA, 2000). This interview yields not only medical information, but allows the provider to assess the caregiver's knowledge of aging, environmental stressors, attitude toward the patient and expectations concerning the amount of care needed by this patient (Hoban, 2000). If possible, the patient can later be asked to confirm or modify the responses provided by the caregiver.

The presence of the caregiver should not add a third person to the patient-provider relationship. Caregiver involvement in the interview might be necessary to provide information, but the allegiance of the therapist or nurse is to the patient alone. Behaviors including interruption of the patient, contradiction of the information provided by the patient, or attempts to either bond or control the interview process should raise questions in the provider's mind concerning the caregiver. These actions may suggest the existence of an abusive relationship. The therapist or nurse, while mindful of the need to avoid antagonizing the caregiver, must explore this possibility further if any of these behaviors are noted.

Through use of direct and indirect questioning, the provider can structure an interview to create opportunities for the patient to confide (Swagerty, Takahashi, and Evans, 1999). Direct questioning, which consists of asking whether abuse has occurred or if anyone in the home has hurt the patient or similar questions, is one option. Its benefits include a decreased likelihood of misunderstanding the intent of the question and a chance to directly observe the patient's response. In the early stages of establishing rapport, the patient may not trust the provider enough to honestly answer the question. The phrasing of questions could inadvertently suggest to the patient that there is a particular response the provider wishes to receive. Other patients, particularly in situations where no abuse is occurring, may feel offended or uncomfortable. The provider must make every effort to keep the questions and the tone of the interview non-judgmental and comfortable (Marshall, Benton, and Brazier, 2000).

Indirect questioning, which consists of asking more open-ended questions about issues related to abuse, is another option. Questioning patients about feelings of fear elicited by anyone involved in their life can provide opportunities for unstructured conversation that yield information a provider may not typically solicit. A potential problem with an indirect approach is the vague nature of the questions. A patient may misinterpret the question and respond inaccurately. Alternatively, a patient may respond to the question by providing an equally indirect response, thus providing information that could be wrongly interpreted by the provider.

Whether direct or indirect questioning is attempted, a nurse or therapist should adopt a standardized series of questions to ensure that the screening is adequate to detect all forms of elder abuse. There are many questionnaires in use today. Most include a mixture of direct and indirect style questions and build in a deliberate repetitiveness to the series of questions to allow examination of answers for consistency. The Elder Assessment Instrument (EAI) screening tool is one example of a comprehensive questionnaire that can be quickly completed by any provider during a home visit to identify potential issues of neglect and abuse (Fulmer, 2003). Originally intended for use in a busy emergency room, it is equally suitable to incorporate into the initial home care evaluation performed by either the nurse or the physical therapist. (2003)

The physical examination portion of the evaluation is usually performed after the interview. In addition to the routine assessments of medical status, functional mobility, and self-care ability, there are particular behaviors, responses, and physical findings that might suggest elder abuse is a problem. Although the term "elder abuse" can encompass an entire gamut of behaviors that cause injury to an older adult, the National Elder Abuse study identified seven main categories of abuse (NEAIS, 1998). The four categories described below are the types of abuse most likely to be encountered and identified by therapist or nurse during home visits.

NEGLECT

Neglect is the considered the most common type of elder abuse (Bradley, 1996; Fisher and Dyer, 2003) and accounts for 48.7% of the occurrences (NEAIS, 1998). Demographic figures indicate that women make up a disproportionate percentage of this category (NEAIS, 1998). The two distinct types of neglect include caregiver neglect and self-neglect (APTA, 2000). In neglect, as compared to physical abuse, the therapist or nurse is not always able to find physical signs and symptoms to justify suspicions. It may be only a perceived inadequacy of care that makes a provider look more closely at a care giving situation.

Caregiver neglect includes the failure to provide the physical and emotional supports necessary to either prevent harm to the patient or to ensure that the patient is able to function at the highest possible level (AMA, 1994, p. 10). Possible explanations include, but are not limited to, caregiver ignorance concerning appropriate care, inadequate level of assistance, financial constraints, or unwillingness of the older adult to accept care giving assistance (Marshall, Benton, Brazier, 2000). Self-neglect may be determined when a patient engages in behavior that places health or safety at risk, whether the decision stems from conscious choices or an inability to perform self-care. According to a nationwide study (NEAIS, 1998), the APS receives more reports of self-neglect than of caregiver neglect. Home health providers should closely monitor independently living patients with a medical diagnosis of depression for signs of self-neglect. Using these operational definitions, nurses and therapists may identify the presence of neglect even in situations where the older patient or the caregiver tries to provide an adequate level of care (APTA, 2000; AMA, 1994; Marshall, Benton, and Brazier, 2000).

Neglect, whether self-initiated or due to inadequate assistance from a caregiver, might easily be missed due to its subtle presentation. It can appear deliberate, as seen in a refusal to provide the essential level of care required to maintain health and safety or inadvertent, as shown by inadequate knowledge or a lack of concern for safeguarding the safety or health of a patient.

Caregivers may override questions concerning the appropriateness of care by attributing the signs of neglect to depression, uncooperativeness, or general cognitive deterioration. Although no single sign is indicative of neglect (APTA, 2000; AMA, 1994; Bradley, 1996), home care providers should watch for evidence of:

Inappropriate Decision-Making on Behalf of the Elder

Examples may include the provision of clothing that is inadequate for the weather, minimal attention or concern about potential falls risks in the home, or failure to comply with the recommended medication or treatment programs. The nurse or therapist should question the caregiver if any of these are observed, and monitor the situation to identify any observable pattern of unsafe choices on behalf of the patient.

Living Environment

The caregiver of a dependent patient may have difficulty keeping the home environment as clean as the health provider may desire, especially if there are pets or a number of people living in the home. There are also cultural and societal factors that affect how someone chooses to live. It is important to avoid making a judgment of neglect merely because someone chooses to live in a manner that is different than what is typically encountered. Therapists and nurses should look for evidence that significant and potentially dangerous living conditions exist. These may include infestations of insects or rodents, food and dirty dishes left on counters for extended periods of time, lack of heat, or deterioration of the housing structure (APTA, 2000; AMA, 1994).

General Deterioration of Health and Well Being

The home care therapist or nurse should suspect neglect when the physical appearance of the patient seems unsatisfactory. While isolated episodes of soiled clothing or bedding, urine or fecal stains on clothing, body odor, or untrimmed hair and fingernails can be found in any patient, repeatedly noting some combination of these elements should arouse suspicion. Failure to provide or maintain dentures, glasses, hearing aids, and other assistive equipment necessary for the patient's daily function without adequate reason also suggests neglect (Hoban, 2000). The home care team needs to first determine that the caregiver and patient understand the importance of routinely using these devices before making any determination that a caregiver is deliberately withholding them.

EMOTIONAL ABUSE

Emotional abuse accounts for approximately 35.4% of the reported cases (Bradley, 1996). The term "emotional abuse" includes conduct that causes psychological anguish in older adults (AMA, 1994 p. 10). This distress may be caused by either verbal or non-verbal behaviors (Hoban, 2000; Hogstel and Curry, 1999; Marshall, Benton, and Brazier, 2000) exhibited by the caregiver. These behaviors may include:

Inappropriate Interactions Between Caregiver and Older Person

The nurse or therapist may overhear or have a patient report receiving threats of present or future harm insults, derogatory comments, or general disrespect from a caregiver. For those statements not directly observed, the health provider needs to evaluate the frequency of the statements and any special circumstances surrounding the events before taking any action. Providers also need to be alert to evidence of isolation of the older person, whether from community activities or within the house itself. Locks placed on the outside of bedroom doors may suggest that a caregiver is locking the patient into the room. Un-emptied commodes, evidence of previous meals, and unauthorized restraint use may indicate that the patient remains in one room for most of the day. Conversations with the caregiver can help the provider decide if these action were taken to ensure the client's safety, to minimize the caregiver burden, or in an attempt to isolate or punish the older adult.

FINANCIAL ABUSE

Despite its prevalence (Bradley, 1996; Hogstell and Curry, 1999), financial abuse is difficult for the nurse or therapist to identify. A certain amount of financial co-dependency between the older adult and the caregiver can exist without any incidence of abuse. An older adult may no longer have the ability or interest to manage financial issues and may choose to vest this authority in a caregiver. Abuse occurs when another person deliberately violates a position of trust (either actual or implied) and misuses or misappropriates an older adult's financial resources for personal gain (APTA, 2000; AMA, 1994), and was found to occur in 30.2% of the reported incidents (Bradley, 1996; NEAIS, 1998).

The issue of financial abuse is difficult for the home care therapist or nurse to recognize because they usually have few discussions with the patient or family about financial issues. Financial stability is a constant worry for many older adults. Attitudes toward money vary according to culture, socialization, and custom, and what may seem abusive behavior by an adult child could reflect a personal money management choice by the parent. Some older adults fear outliving their resources and insist upon engaging in unnecessary cost-saving activities in attempts to stave off poverty. Despite these variations, financial behaviors that might trigger suspicions in the health care providers that impropriety has occurred include:

Changes in Living Circumstances

When physical or cognitive health deteriorates, an adult caregiver may move into the home of the older adult to provide supervision and assistance.

This arrangement sometimes results in a shared responsibility for shopping, bill payments, and other money-related issues. This can be a mutually beneficial relationship. A health provider should become suspicious if valuable or expensive items disappear from the home without the patient being able to explain the absence. Overheard arguments between the older person and the caregiver concerning the need to borrow money should also alert the provider to the need to monitor for potential abuse in this area. Events that might suggest greater scrutiny should be paid to the potential for this type of abuse include:

A Significant Change in The Older Adult's Standard of Living

The food or clothing supplied for the patient should be monitored to detect any marked decrease in quality or quantity. This should be compared to the standard of living enjoyed by the caregiver.

Reports of Unexpected Changes in an Elder's Ability to Meet the Costs of Health Care

Medications, disposable supplies, and equipment are the most costly elements in a home patient's plan of care. Many older adults living on a fixed income do have problems covering unexpected or prolonged expenses. Health providers should remain alert for comments that suggest an older person now needs to ask the caregiver for permission to incur an expense, or was told that he/she could no longer afford to purchase a necessary item. Home care services may be abruptly discontinued, citing cost as the reason, even though the care is still obviously needed and the costs have not significantly changed. An older patient may confide that caregivers are demanding access to checks or to bank accounts or insisting that modifications to wills are made. Although not specifically health related, financial abuse affects the overall well being of the patient. Its detection falls within the scope of practice of a home health practitioner. (APTA, 1999; *http://www.nursingworld.org/ethics/code*).

PHYSICAL ABUSE

Physical abuse is identified in 25.6% of the reported incidents (Bradley, 1996; NEAIS, 1996). It is defined as actions that result in physical injury or potential injury to the elder and includes all acts of violence that result in pain, injury, impairment, or disease (AMA, 1994). Commonly identified acts of physical abuse include slapping, pushing, shaking, inappropriately restraining, pinching, and beating (APTA, 2000). Despite its lower rate of occurrence when compared to neglect or financial abuse, this is the type of abuse that a nurse or physical therapist may identify more readily, since it tends to elicit more recognizable signs and symptoms. Commonly observed findings may include:

Patches of Baldness with Bruising or Bloody Appearance in The Scalp

While thinning hair is commonly found with aging, someone who remains supine in bed or restrained in a high-backed chair or recliner for prolonged periods of time may show increased hair loss along the back of the skull. The home care aide might report an unwillingness of the patient to have the hair washed or combed, or an observation of blood on the bed linens.

Varied Colors of Bruising Layered in the Same Location

Bruising easily occurs in the geriatric population due to the fragile nature of aging skin. A variety of colors of bruising may indicate the presence of injuries in a variety of healing stages (Harrell, Toronjo, McLaughlin, Pavlik, Hyman, and Dyer, 2002; Wolf, 1998). This suggests repeated trauma to the area. The nurse or therapist should remain alert to environmental hazards that could account for this finding, and should discuss these observations with the patient and caregiver before concluding that abuse may have occurred.

Bruising in Atypical Locations or with a Shape that Suggests Contact with a Cord, Tape, Hand, or Other Object

Bruises due to accidental trauma are often irregularly shaped and in areas (e.g. tibial crests, shoulders, forehead or lateral hips) that frequently bump against objects in the home environment. Bruising along the breasts, abdomen, thighs, or buttocks are less commonly incurred in everyday activities and discovery of these should be questioned (AMA, 1994; APTA, 2000;). Findings of burns, handprints on upper arms or face, loosened teeth, broken dentures or glasses, or any unexplained swelling without an associated episode of trauma should also elicit suspicions of abuse (Harrell, Toronjo, McLaughlin, Pavlik, Hyman, and Dyer, 2002).

Decubiti Present in an Ambulatory Patient

Older persons with limited mobility are at a higher risk for development of pressure ulcers, even with the best of care (Brandeis, Berlowitz, and Katz, 2001). Prolonged sitting can lead to pathological tissue pressures within hours. The pressure problem is exacerbated for a person with incontinence of bowel or bladder since the prolonged pressure will affect tissues that are already at risk due to moisture. Homebound patients who are restrained to a chair for prolonged periods by belt, straps, or by elevation of the footrest are at a greater risk to develop pressure sores (2001). Health professionals should question the onset of redness, tenderness, or skin breakdown in the areas of the coccyx, sacrum, or ischeal tuberosities, especially when noted in a patient who is not bedridden (Hoban, 2000). Observation of the wrists, ankles, and torso of the patient may reveal chafed and reddened areas that suggest unauthorized restraint use has occurred.

Inappropriate Handling of Patient by Caregiver

Caregivers, especially informal family caregivers, may have little training or experience in how to safely transfer or ambulate with older persons. Family assistance offered during mobility activities often appears clumsy, rushed, or inappropriate, even when provided with the best of intentions. Despite this, therapists and nurses should not observe instances of rough handling, pushing, pinching, or prodding when the caregiver interacts with the older person. Careful attention to the attitude and the interaction between the caregiver and the elder person during movement activities allows the provider to distinguish between inexperience and malicious intention (Harrell, Toronjo, McLaughlin, Pavlik, Hyman, and Dyer, 2002).

SEXUAL ABUSE

Older adults of sound cognition are still sexual beings capable of engaging in consensual sexual activities. Abuse occurs when the adult does not consent or is incapable of consent to behaviors ranging from exposure to rape. At a frequency of 0.3% (Bradley, 1996), the low percentage of reports of sexual abuse seems to suggest that it is not much of a problem for the older population. Just as is suspected for elder abuse in general, there is a strong likelihood that older persons, particularly women, may not report sexual abuse. There are a variety of reasons to explain this. Women who grew up in a time when sexual issues were not routinely discussed might lack the words or the comfort level to discuss what has happened. When the sexual abuser is a spouse or partner, the abused person may not know that the behavior could qualify as abuse (Basile, 2002). The physical therapist may want to consider the possibility of sexual abuse if unexplained changes in a patient's mobility or sitting comfort are observed. The nurse and the aide may identify bruises along breasts, thighs, and abdomen when assisting with the intimate tasks of toileting and bathing. Other observations that might arouse suspicion in providers include:

Evidence of Sexual Activity

The presence of blood or semen on the sheets or undergarments of the older adult who is sexually inactive suggests abuse.

Report of Sexual Abuse by a Patient

An older person may make a direct statement or indirect questioning by the therapist or nurse about suspicious findings may elicit the report that sexual abuse has occurred (Pritchard, 1992).

INTERVENTION

The main responsibility of a home health provider is to identify that an abusive situation actually exists. Accurate identification demands a high level of evaluative skills and clinical judgment from the provider, as well as an awareness of those subpopulations most likely to at risk for abuse (Sengstock and Barrett, 1993). Most home care agencies have policies that direct a therapist or nurse to discuss suspicious findings with the health care team and supervisor to confirm that abuse exists. Each provider should carefully document the behaviors, statements, and physical findings that indicated the presence of abuse. If granted permission by the patient, the inclusion of photographs of bruises, burns, or ligature marks provide additional visual support for the statements (AMA, 1994; APTA, 1999;).

The next step, taking action to intervene, is a more involved task. There is considerable variation in both the reporting requirements, the investigatory authority of each state's elder abuse statute, and in the severity of the civil and criminal penalties associated with the elder abuse (http://www.abanet.org/aging/). All states have a "good Samaritan" protections offering immunity from criminal or civil liability if a health provider, acting in good faith, reports a suspicion of elder abuse (AMA, 1994; APTA, 2000). Despite this protection, home health practitioners might feel unprepared or unwilling to make the decision that abuse exists and intervention is needed (Marshall, Benton, and Brazier, 2000). Reasons range from a fear of legal reprisals (AMA, 1004), concern over possible misidentification of abuse (Hazzard, 1995), and lack of familiarity with reporting standards and procedures (Marshall, Benton, and Brazier, 2000). Information on identification, intervention, and management of elder abuse should be woven through the didactic and the clinical components of all health providers' curriculum (Hazzard, 1995). Expanding the number of opportunities for interdisciplinary interaction with case studies and problem-based learning experiences help students to understand their roles and responsibilities in the detection of elder abuse. These experiences also familiarize each discipline with the scope of examination and assessment done by the other providers likely to interact with the home care patient.

Professional development from continuing education courses is an important part of improving the understanding and comfort of practicing home health providers with the reporting requirements for elder abuse (Jogerst, Dawson, Hartz, Ely, and Sweitzer, 2000). In addition to discussing the requirements and procedures for a particular state, the educational module must also explain the limitations of the APS ability to intervene. Professional ethics demand that the home health providers document all findings and contact the APS about suspected abuse regardless of the patient's willingness to seek help (APTA, 1999; http://www.nursingworld.org/ethics/code). When notified of an abusive situation, APS will investigate and make recommendations. At this point, the momentum of the intervention may halt. A competent older adult, unlike an abused child, may choose to refuse intervention (Harrell, Toronjo, McLaughlin, Pavlik, Hyman, and Dyer, 2002; Swagerty, Takahashi, and Evans, 1999). Even if no intervention is presently accepted, the information generated by the home health provider is still important. APS and the home care agency will have a file of previous reports to use if more episodes occur in the future.

Another important responsibility of home care nurses and physical therapists requires them to go beyond the step of simply identifying and reporting episodes of elder abuse. The best interests of the patient are not served if a health provider feels no responsibility to take action until abuse has occurred. Patient-centered management of a home care patient requires an initial evaluation of the caregiver-patient dynamics as part of the overall assessment of medical factors (Reay and Browne, 2001). The role in home care filled by physical therapists and nurses allows close contact with any aides, family members, and other persons who come into regular contact with the older adult. Willingness to engage these persons in conversations about the impact of the care giving responsibilities on their lives allows providers to proactively identify potentially abusive situations and offer assistance (Hyde-Robertson, 1994).

Decreasing the caregiver burden through enhancing awareness of community resources is an essential duty of the health care team (Holland, Kasraian, and Leonardelli, 1987). Appropriate community resources include medical education seminars, support groups, and respite activities. Depending on state and local resources, these community-based interventions are designed to meet the family caregiver's need for access to current medical information and emotional support through interaction with persons facing similar stresses. The nurse or therapist needs to tailor these recommendations to fit the circumstances of the caregiver. According to Alexy (2000), many caregivers who are referred and would like to participate in these community activities face barriers to their participation in traditional support group. The constant on-call nature of care giving responsibilities can make it impossible for those who most need support to regularly attend any scheduled group meeting. The therapist or nurse involved in the case has the level of knowledge of the range of available community resources to assist the caregiver in finding one that fits. Suggestions for respite care, recommendations for more appropriate assistive equipment, and frank conversations about the caregiver's perception of burden should be part of every initial patient contact.

Elder abuse is not an easy problem to manage. It typically comes to the attention of the medical profession only after physical or emotional damage has already occurred. More education and resources are required to prepare health providers and community agencies to develop a more comprehensive approach to support older adults in the community. Home health therapists and nurses, because of their familiarity with the aging population, can provide valuable insight concerning the physical, social, financial, and supportive needs of community dwelling older adults.

REFERENCES

American Medical Association. (1994). *Diagnostic and Treatment Guidelines on Elder Abuse and Neglect*. Chicago; AMA.

American Physical Therapy Association. (2000). *Guidelines for Recognizing and Providing Care for Victims of Elder Abuse*. Alexandria; APTA.

Alexy, E. M. (2000). Computers and Caregiving: Reaching out and Redesigning

Interventions for Homebound Older Adults and Caregivers. *Holistic Nurs Prac,* 14(4), 60–66.

Basile, K.C. (2002). Attitudes Toward Wife Rape: Effects of Social Background and Victim Status. *Violence Victim,* 17(3),341-354.

Baker, A. A. (1977). "Granny Battering." *Modern Geriatrics,* 5, (8), 20-24.

Bradley, M. (1996). Caring for Older People: Elder Abuse. *BMJ,* 313(7056), 548-550.

Brandeis, G.H., Berlowitz, D.R., and Katz, P. (2001). Are Pressure Ulcers Preventable? A Survey of Experts. *Adv in Skin and Wound Care,* 14(5), 245-248.

Feldman, D. S., Novack, D. H., and Gracely, E.(1998). Effects of Managed Care on Physician-Patient Relationships, Quality of Care, and the Ethical Practice of Medicine: A Physician Survey. *Arch Int Med,* 158(15), 1626-1632.

Fisher, J.W., and Dyer, C.B. (2003). The Hidden Health Menace of Elder Abuse. Physicians Can Help Patients Surmount Intimate Partner Violence. *Postgrad Med.,* 113 (4). Retrieved August 20, 2003 from http://www.postgradmed.com/issues/2003/04_03/apr03.htm .

Fulmer, T. (2003). Elder Abuse and Neglect Assessment. *J Gerontol Nurs,* 29(6), 4-5.

Harrell, R., Toronjo, C.H., McLaughlin, J., Pavlik, V.N., Hyman, D.J., and Dyer, C.B. (2002).

How Geriatricians Identify Elder Abuse and Neglect. *Am J Med Sci,* 323(1), 34-38.

Hazzard, W.R. (1995). Elder abuse: Definitions and Implications for Medical Education. *Acad Med,* 70(11), 979-981.

Hoban, S. (2000). Elder Abuse and Neglect: It Takes Many Forms—If You're Not Looking, You May Miss It. *Am J Nurs,* 100(11), 49-50.

Hogstel, M.O., and Curry, L.C. (1999). Elder Abuse Revisited. *J Gerontol Nurs,* 25(7),10-18.

Holland, L.R., Kasraian, K.R., and Leonardelli, C.A. (1987). Elder Abuse: An Analysis of The Current Problem and Potential Role of the Rehabilitation Professional. *Phys and Occupat Ther in Geriatr,* 5(3), 41-51.

Hyde-Robertson, B., Pirnie, S.M., and Freeze, C. (1994). A Strategy Against Elderly Mistreatment. *Caring,* 40-44.

American Nursing Association Code of Ethics. Retrieved August 24, 2003 from http://www.nursingworld.org/ethics/code .

American Bar Association Commission on Legal Problems of the Elderly (adopted as policy 2002). Report to the House of Delegates. Retrieved on September 5, 2003. http://www.abanet.org/aging/elder_abuse.pdf.

National Center on Elder Abuse. Retrieved on October 2, 2003 from http://www.elder-abusecenter.org.

Jogerst, G.J., Dawson, J.D., Hartz, A.J., Ely, J.W., and Sweitzer, L.A. (2000). Community Characteristics Associated With Elder Abuse. *J Am Ger Soc,* 48(5), 513-518.

Johnson, T.F. (1991). *Elder mistreatment: Deciding Who is at Risk.* New York, NY: Greenwood Press.

Lachs, M.S., Williams, C.S., O'Brien S, Pillemer, K.A., and Charlson, M.E. (1998). The Mortality of Elder Mistreatment. *JAMA,* 280(5), 428-432.

Marshall, C.E., Benton, D., and Brazier, J.M. (2000). Elder Abuse. Using Clinical Tools to Identify Clues of Mistreatment. *Geriatrics,* 55(2), 45-53.

Nadworny, S.W. (1994). In the Best of Families: Crossing the Line into Neglect. *Caring,* 46-48.

National Center on Elder Abuse. (1998). National Elder Abuse Incidence study(NEAIS): Final Report. The National Center on Elder Abuse at the American Public Services Association in Collaboration with Westat, Inc.

Omnibus Reconcilliation Act 1987.

Pillemer, K., and Finkelhor, D. (1988). The Prevalence of Elder Abuse: A Random Sample Survey. *The Gerontologist*, 28(1), 51-57.

Physical Therapist Code of Ethics, Alexandria, Va: American Physical Therapy Association; 1999.

Reay, A.M., and Browne, K.D. (2001). Risk Factor Characteristics in Carers Who Physically Abuse or Neglect Their Elderly Dependants. *Aging and Mental Health*, 5(1), 56-62.

Sengstock, M.C., and Barrett, S.A. (1993). Abuse and Neglect of the Elderly in Family Settings. In J. Campbell and J. Humphreys (Eds.), *Nursing Care of Survivors of Family Violence* (pp. 173-208). St. Louis, MO: Mosby.

Swagerty, D.L, Takahashi, P.Y., and Evans, J.M. (1999). Elder Mistreatment. *Am Fam. Phys*, 59(10), 2804-2808.

Teaster, P.B. (2000). A Response to the Abuse of Vulnerable Adults: The 2000 Survey Of State Adult Protective Services. The National Center on Elder Abuse; The National Committee for the Prevention of Elder Abuse, The National Association of Adult Protective Services Association; Adult National Association for State Units on Aging.

Wieland, D. (2000). Abuse of older persons: An Overview. *Holistic Nurs Prac*, 14(4), 40-50.

U.S.C. § 1395i-3 (Medicare) and 42 U.S.C. § 1396r (Medicaid).

U.S.C. §§ 3001-3058ee (1994).(Older Adults Act)

Wolf, R.S. (1997). Elder Abuse and Neglect: Causes and Consequences. *J Geri Psych*, 30(1), 153-174.

Wolfe, S. (1998). As America Ages: Look for Signs of Abuse. *RN*, 61(8), 48-51.

Woodtli, M.A.,and Breslin, E.T. (2002). Violence-Related Content in the Nursing Curriculum: A Follow-Up National Survey. *J Nurs Educ*, 41(8), 340-348.

5

UNDERSTANDING ELDER ABUSE IN MINORITY POPULATIONS

Paulina Ruf

THE AGING OF MINORITY POPULATIONS IN THE UNITED STATES

According to the 2000 U.S. Census, there are approximately 35.0 million people 65 years of age and over in the United States, representing 12.4 percent of the total population (Hetzel and Smith, 2001). The Census Bureau projects that the population age 65 and older will exceed 70 million by 2030 (Hollmann et al., 2000). The "graying" of the U.S. population has received a great deal of attention in the past decades. Until recently, however, this attention was focused on the White, non-Hispanic population. The increasing numbers of racial and ethnic minorities in the United States—what Henry (1990) called "the browning of America"—has significantly changed the composition of the elderly population (Angel and Hogan, 1992; Hayes-Bautista et al., 2002). Currently, about 16 percent of those 65 years of age and over are members of a racial/ethnic minority group. In the future, this percentage is expected to increase significantly. For instance, by 2030, the older minority population is expected to reach about 26 percent of the total 65 years old and over population in the United States (Day, 1996).

The youthfulness of the Hispanic population tends to overshadow the growing number of Hispanics 65 years of age and over (Gelfand, 1994). In 2002, there were 37.4 million Hispanics in the United States, 5.1 percent of whom were 65 years of age and over. In contrast, approximately 14.4 percent of the White, non-Hispanic population was 65 years of age and older. The highest proportion of individuals 65 and older was among Cuban Americans (22.6 percent), and the lowest was among Mexican Americans (4.0 percent) (Ramirez and de la Cruz, 2003). In addition, the number of elderly Hispanics is expected to quadruple by the year 2020 (Andrews, 1989).

African Americans are now the second largest minority group in the U.S. after Hispanics. In 2002, there were approximately 36 million African Americans in the U.S., 8 percent of whom were 65 years of age and over (McKinnon, 2003). Often referred to as the "model minority" (Hurh and Kim, 1989), the Asian and Pacific Islander population numbered 12.5 million in 2002, and 7 percent of this group were 65 years of age and over (Reeves and Bennett, 2003). In the 2000 U.S. Census, 4.1 million or 1.5 percent of the population reported American Indian and Alaska Native ancestry (Ogunwole, 2002). Of these 259,663 or about 6 percent were age 65 and over (U.S. Census, 2002).

Over the past decades, we have seen a significant increase in the number of studies involving the older minority population. However, there are still many areas where our understanding of the minority experience of growing old is limited and plagued by misconceptions and stereotypes. One such area is elder abuse. For many years it was assumed that elder abuse could not possibly exist among racial and ethnic minorities because of family dynamics that emphasize respect and solidarity (Anetzberger et al., 1996; Carson, 1995; Sung, 2001).

ELDER ABUSE IN THE UNITED STATES: CULTURAL IMPLICATIONS

Our awareness of the existence and magnitude of elder abuse has increased dramatically in the last decades (Wolf, 2000 and 1988). The best available estimates suggest that between 1 and 2 million people age 65 and over have been mistreated in some way by a care provider (Bonnie and Wallace, 2003). With the baby boom generation approaching 65, we can speculate that the incidence of elder abuse will increase significantly, and that these violations will be reported.

According to the National Elder Abuse Incidence Study (1998), about 551,011 persons aged 60 and over experienced abuse, neglect, and/or self-neglect in homes in 1996. Of these cases, only 21 percent were reported to and substantiated by adult protective service agencies. The same study revealed that people aged 80 and older and women are more likely to be abused and neglected. In terms of race/ethnicity, the findings of this study suggest that although the majority of reported cases involve White, non-Hispanic elderly, African-American elderly are over-represented in neglect, financial/material exploitation, and emotional/psychological abuse. This finding was supported by Dimah and Dimah (2002), who found that 48 of the 107 substantiated elder abuse cases from one elder abuse provider agency in Illinois, involved African American victims.

In a 2000 survey conducted by the National Center on Elder Abuse, 17 percent of reported cases involved African Americans, about 10 percent involved Hispanics, 0.9 percent involved Native Americans, and 0.4 percent involved Asians and Pacific Islanders. Hudson et al. (1999) found that 9.2 percent of African Americans and 4.3 percent of Native Americans reported being abused after age 65. In short, these data suggest that older minority populations may be over-represented among victims of elder abuse (see also Hall, 1987). However, making such generalizations from the findings of these studies is difficult. They generally include small numbers of minority elders, are limited to specific locations around the country, and also differ in the types of elder abuse studied.

The reality remains that the majority of the research studies about elder abuse focus on the white, non-Hispanic population. Further, the authors of the studies that included minority victims did not consider the effect race and ethnicity have on perceptions of elder abuse (Brown, 1989; Griffin, 1994; Hudson and Carlson, 1999; Moon and Williams, 1993). In fact, many states have only recently started collecting race/ethnicity data involving elder abuse cases (Tatara, 1999). In a survey of state adult protective services conducted by the National Center on Elder Abuse (Teaster, 2000), only 24 states responded to the "race/ethnicity of victims" question.

Definitions of abuse and neglect are socially constructed and reflect culturally defined norms and values regarding acceptable and unacceptable behavior. In a diverse society such as the United States, considering the fast-growing older minority population, it is crucial that we clarify how elder abuse and neglect are defined by the different racial/ethnic groups (Brownell, 1997; Chang and Moon, 1997; Davidhizar et al., 1998; Hudson et al., 1999; Williams and Griffin, 1996; Wolf and Donglin, 1999). The few studies that have considered the impact of culture on definitions of elder abuse have found significant differences in the ways racial/ethnic groups define elder abuse (Hudson and Carlton, 1999; Hudson and et al., 1999; Moon and Benton, 2000; Moon and Williams, 1993). For instance, Moon and Williams (1993) found that Korean Americans were more tolerant of abusive behaviors than White, non-Hispanic and African American elderly. Moon and Benton (2000) found that White, non-Hispanic elderly were more tolerant of verbal abuse, while Korean American elderly were more likely to tolerate financial exploitation. In addition, Hudson and Carlson (1999) found that Native Americans rated behaviors as more abusive than African Americans and White, non-Hispanics. Further, some studies have found older minority populations more reluctant to report abuse (Le, 1997; Moon and Williams, 1993; Moon and Benton, 2000; Sanchez Y., 1999; Tomita, 1999).

The studies, then, suggest that cultural norms and values do influence how individuals define abuse. And, although more research is needed, there is sufficient evidence to suggest the need to increase our understanding about the impact of culture on individuals and groups' definitions of abuse. This is particularly important for policy-makers and service providers as they plan and implement services and treatment protocols dealing with elder abuse.

ELDER ABUSE AMONG LATINOS

Although the Latino elderly population is the fastest growing segment of the elderly population, there are still major gaps in our understanding of their aging experiences in the United States. The research is particularly limited in the topic of elder abuse (Sanchez Y., 1999). The National Center on Elder Abuse (1998) found that Hispanic elderly were underrepresented among victims of elder abuse. The most common type of abuse substantiated was neglect, and older Hispanics accounted for 2.7 percent of all these cases. However, researchers speculate that because of language barriers, misinformation, and legal status (i.e., illegal immigrants), the occurrence of elder abuse among Hispanics, like among other non-English speaking populations, is underreported (Otiniano, et al. 1997).

In a study of elder abuse in the Mexican American communities of Carson City, Nevada and Detroit, Michigan, Y. Sanchez (1999) found that 33 percent of the participants reported being aware of at least one incident of elderly abuse among members of their Mexican American community. The most common forms of abuse cited were denial of shelter (40.3 percent) and neglect (22.6 percent). Physical abuse accounted for 11.3 percent of reports of abuse. Also, over 70 percent of the participants stated that they would discuss the problems with family members before contacting the authorities if they were being mistreated by family members. Only 17.9 percent of the Michigan sample and 10 percent of the Nevada sample stated that they would contact authorities under these circumstances. The author found that shame was an important factor in understanding elder abuse in Mexican American families. In this context, shame is accompanied by a sense of "losing face," in that if a family member is the perpetrator of abuse and/or neglect, it brings shame to the whole family. This explains, at least in part, the participants' reduced likelihood of contacting authorities about abuse when the perpetrator is a family member. This lack of reporting also reflects *familismo*, a cultural value that emphasizes family loyalty and integrity, which largely dictates the behavior of individual family members. Thus, Mitchell and colleagues (1999) found that understanding family dynamics is an important step in the provision of protective services to Mexican American clients. Montoya (1997) said it best, "Hispanic culture acts as both an asset that prevents abuse and provides resources to combat it as well as a liability that acts to hide abuse" (p. 16).

According to official statistics cited by C. Sanchez (1999), the number of reports of elder abuse in Puerto Rico increased from 342 reports in 1980 to over 5,000 reports in 1996. In addition, she examined the existing literature regarding elder abuse among Puerto Ricans. The first research study that attempted to assess the existence of elder abuse in Puerto Rico was conducted by Muñoz in 1985 (as cited by C. Sanchez, 1999). This researcher found that neglect was the most common form of abuse, and psychological abuse was the least common form of abuse reported by the participants. In this study, slightly over 50 percent of the abuse was perpetuated by a son or daughter and only 10 percent was perpetuated by a spouse. Muñoz also found a correlation between age and dependency, in that as each of these increased so did the frequency of abuse. C. Sanchez (1999) also discusses research conducted by Arroyo and colleagues in 1992 where professionals and practitioners that provide services to older Puerto Ricans in community centers and home healthcare services were interviewed regarding their experiences and awareness of elder abuse in the Island. About 75 percent of the participants reported at least one incident of elder abuse in the previous 12 months, and like in previous studies, a son or daughter was most likely the perpetrator of the abuse.

However, as with other ethnic groups, the actual number of abuse and neglect cases among older Hispanics is unknown. This is largely due to the older person's unwillingness to report abuse when the perpetrator is a family member, which is most often the case. Very much like within the Mexican family, *familismo* plays a significant role in the unwillingness to report an abusive family member among Puerto Ricans. Another cultural value that appears to prevent Hispanic victims, including Puerto Ricans, from disclosing both the abuse and the abuser is *personalismo*. This value requires that the dignity of individuals is maintained and respected. Also, *personalismo* means that service providers should establish personal, trusting relationships where disclosure of abusive behaviors can take place (Montoya, 1997; C. Sanchez, 1999). For service providers this means that developing trusting, personal relationships with Hispanic clients is very important. It is likely to facilitate the provision of services, and more importantly, increase the likelihood that victims of elder abuse would acknowledge the abuse and perhaps identify the abuser(s).

ELDER ABUSE AMONG AFRICAN AMERICANS

According to The National Center on Elder Abuse (1998), among the reported cases of elder abuse 18.7 percent involved older African Americans and 8.3 percent of substantiated cases of elder abuse involved this population. The most common type of abuse experienced by this population was neglect (17.2 percent), followed by emotional/psychological abuse (14.1 percent), and physical abuse (9.0 percent). As mentioned earlier, older African Americans appear to be overrepresented among victims of elder abuse. However, research on elder abuse among African Americans is limited making any assertions nearly impossible. As with other minority groups, the lack of focus on the impact of culture on definitions of elder abuse is a barrier to our understanding of this experience among African Americans (Cazenave, 1979; Hudson, et al., 1999; Moon and Williams, 1993; Williams and Griffin, 1996).

The few studies that have examined how African Americans perceive elder abuse suggest that there are differences between this population and other groups in how elder abuse is perceived and defined (Anetzberger, et al., 1996; Griffin, 1994; Hudson, et al., 1999; Moon and Williams 1993). For instance, Anetzberger and colleagues (1996), who conducted focus group discussions with middle-aged and older members of four ethnic groups, found that African Americans were more likely to recognize the common forms of elder abuse, and were the only participants to recognize financial exploitation as a form of abuse. Interestingly, Griffin (1994) found that financial exploitation was the most prevalent type of elder abuse. Also, Moon and Williams (1993) found that older African Americans were more likely than others to rate the different scenarios presented to them as abusive. Hudson and colleagues (1999), using a random sample of adults in North Carolina, found that a larger percentage of African Americans (9.2 percent) reported being abused as elders than other groups, supporting the findings of the National Center on Elder Abuse (1998). In addition, these researchers also found that African Americans not only supported the common definitions of elder abuse, but they also considered one occurrence of behaviors defined as elder abuse was sufficient to merit the label. For these participants, older people should be treated with love and respect, and thus elder abuse was unacceptable.

Changes in the family structure among African Americans, coupled with the impact of economic forces, have resulted in an increasing number of older African Americans living with other family members. These increasing numbers of multigenerational households make older African Americans more vulnerable to abuse and exploitation (Benton, 1999; Dimah and Dimah, 2002; Griffin and Williams, 1992). Also, studies suggest that the lack of services available for the caregivers of individuals suffering from dementia and frail older family members is a contributing factor of elder abuse in the African American community (Benton, 1999). These findings, along with the projected growth of the older African American population, indicate that the occurrence of elder abuse in this population will grow in the future.

As in other populations, substance abuse is a risk factor for elder abuse (Galbraith, 1989). In fact, Longres (1992) found that the perpetrator of elder abuse among African Americans was less likely to live with the victim and provide care, and more likely to have substance abuse issues. However, research focusing on the perpetrator of elder abuse among ethnic minority populations is particularly limited. Nonetheless, this finding poses an interesting question for future research, especially if we consider the impact of illicit drug use and abuse among minority populations. Also, Benton (1999) suggests that the high rate of domestic violence among African Americans is a significant risk factor for elder abuse, since the abuse continues as the couple ages.

ELDER ABUSE AMONG ASIAN AND PACIFIC ISLANDERS

According to the National Center on Elder Abuse (1998), older Asian and Pacific Islanders are underrepresented among victims of elder abuse. For this population, the most common types of abuse were emotional and physical abuse, but Asian and Pacific Islanders represented only 0.4 percent of these cases. In 2000, a survey of adult protective service agencies found that 0.4 percent of all substantiated cases of elder abuse involved Asian and Pacific Islanders. However, there is evidence that the occurrence of elder abuse among Asian and Pacific Islanders is significantly underreported. For instance, in 2001 about 10 percent of active cases of elder abuse in San Francisco, California, involved Asian Americans (Manigbas, 2002). The majority of these cases (6.8 percent) involved Chinese Americans. Still, because Chinese culture prevents family members from sharing problems with non-family members, it is speculated that the actual number of elder abuse cases among Chinese Americans, as well as other Asian and Pacific Islander groups, is much larger. Also, Chang and Moon (1997) found that a significant percentage of Korean immigrant elders (34 percent) reported seeing or hearing about at least one incident of elder abuse. For these elders, lack of respect for the elder and not allowing him/her to live with an adult child constitute mistreatment. Hence, abuse was perceived only within family relationships, particularly the parent-child relationship.

Traditional Asian cultural norms emphasize family allegiance and respect for older members. Thus, not caring for one's parents would reflect negatively on the family (Gelfand, 1994; Sung; 2001). However, there is evidence that traditional norms are changing both among Asians in the United States and in

Asian countries. These changes are largely due to the effects of modernization, where adult children live away from parents and women join the paid labor force and are thus unavailable to care for older family members (Gelfand, 1994).

The research examining the impact of Asian and Pacific Islander cultures on perceptions of elder abuse is quite limited. Moon and Williams (1993) found that Korean-Americans were less likely than other groups to both define scenarios as abuse and to seek help, especially from formal service providers. Pablo and Braun (1997) conducted a study in Honolulu where the same scenarios used by Moon and Williams (1993) were utilized. Pablo and Braun found the local Asian American groups provided answers similar to those of the White participants in Moon and Williams' research, which was conducted in Minnesota. Pablo and Braun speculate that the different responses between the two Asian groups may be due to the fact that Asian Americans in Honolulu have access to culturally-appropriate services, whereas the Korean-Americans in Minnesota may not. Because the Asian participants in Honolulu had been in the United States for a longer period of time, the authors speculate that the traditional attitudes and practices of these groups change over time, while at the same time many elders identify with their ethnic background and its traditions.

Le (1997) found that, among a small sample of Vietnamese elderly in California, the most common type of abuse was emotional, followed by verbal abuse. The emotional abuse of these Vietnamese elderly involved being isolated from others, receiving the silent treatment, being threatened with nursing home placement, or being harassed. Because tradition dictates that sons are responsible for the care of their parents, participants reported having problems with their daughters-in-law as well as with their own children. They believed their daughters-in-law were jealous of the filial piety exhibited by their husbands. Chang and Moon (1997) found similar results among Korean immigrant elders, where daughters-in-law were seen as disrespectful and as mistreating their mothers-in-law (see also Sung, 2001). In addition, Le (1997) found that the elders facing abuse were more likely to be newcomers to the United States, and those that came to the country with their children, were less likely to experience abuse. This finding suggests that because of the difficulty of adjusting to a new culture, older family members become very dependent on younger ones, and in turn become more vulnerable to abuse (see also Manigbas, 2002). Like other older ethnic minorities, the Vietnamese elderly in this study were reluctant to disclose abuse and neglect. Doing so would bring shame to the family since it would indicate that filial piety was not observed. Also, Vietnamese culture, like other Asian cultures, emphasizes family preservation and reliance, which contributes to the underreporting of elder abuse (see also Pablo and Braun, 1997; Tomita, 1999).

Tomita (1999) explored domestic violence, including elder abuse, among Japanese Americans. He found that Japanese cultural norms required that individuals place the group above the self, and that the culture emphasized silent suffering and quiet endurance. As a consequence of adhering to these norms, victims of abuse only admitted to the abuse when the abuser was dead or when they were sure no negative consequences could impact the family or the abuser. Hence, service providers might need to use conflict-avoidance and conflict-management techniques. Interventions should emphasize group harmony, safety, and respite, rather than the resolution of the situation which is emphasized by mainstream interventions.

ELDER ABUSE AMONG NATIVE AMERICANS

Despite the growing interest in elder abuse among minority populations, very little attention has been given to Native Americans (Brown, 1999). The National Center on Elder Abuse (1998) found that 0.2 percent of substantiated cases of abuse involved older Native Americans, all of whom experienced physical abuse. In a survey of state adult protective service agencies (Teaster, 2000), the Center found that 0.9 percent of substantiated elder abuse cases involved Native Americans. The issue of underreporting elder abuse among Native Americans is compounded by their social isolation (i.e., residing in remote, rural areas) and their unwillingness to pursue mainstream services (Baldridge, 2001; Carson and Hand, 1999).

In one of the earliest attempts to examine elder abuse among Native Americans, Brown (1989) surveyed older Navajos and their family members, and found that elder abuse clearly existed in this population. The most common type of abuse reported was neglect, and other types of abuse were not found to be very prevalent in this population. Interestingly, the author found that as the elder became more dependent, the family responded by providing more care. However, the care tended to be shared among family members, which tended to result in neglect, largely because no one in particular was seen as responsible for the care. On the other hand, when a single person was designated the primary caregiver (usually a single or widowed daughter with children), the increased burden of the situation usually resulted in neglect and/or psychological abuse.

Maxwell and Maxwell (1992) conducted a study of elder abuse among two Plains Indian reservations. The authors found that the significant economic depravation found in one of the reservations resulted in many cases of elder financial exploitation and neglect. Further, the remoteness of the reservation and the lack of employment opportunities for young people increased their dependence on the elders, many of whom received Supplement Security Income and who owned the best land in the area. These factors exacerbate the risk for elder abuse.

Hudson et al. (1999), using a random sample of adults in several diverse counties in North Carolina, found that Native Americans were more likely to label scenarios as abuse compared to their White and African American counterparts, and that they generally supported common definitions of elder abuse. Like the African American participants, the Native Americans sampled felt that one occurrence of abuse warranted the label. Also, this population indicated that professional assistance should be provided in elder abuse cases, although the authors did not include questions regarding what type of services should be provided or who should provide them. Native Americans elders felt that older people should not only be honored and respected, but they should also receive care if needed.

Similar to other older minorities, becoming dependent and frail increases the risk for elder abuse among older Native Americans (Baldridge, 2001; Brown, 1989). This is of particular concern given the high rates of disability among Native Americans. In addition, the lack of community—and institutionally-based long-term care services for older Native Americans reinforces their need to depend on informal care providers, especially family members that are largely ill-equipped to deal with the elders' failing health (Baldridge, 2001). Because Native American cultures, in general, emphasize family and tribal unity and interdependence, it is crucial that interventions reflect these cultural values. Also, the significant impact of the many social problems that plague Native Americans must be addressed (Brown, 1999; Carson and Hand, 1999).

Much more research is needed to understand the aging experiences and elder abuse among Native Americans. Like Latinos and Asian and Pacific Islanders, Native American nations are very diverse and geographically widespread. Future research efforts should focus on increasing our understanding of how elder abuse is defined by the different Native American nations, it should clarify the types and prevalence of abuse that are common in these populations, and research should also focus on determining if there are significant differences among urban and rural Native American populations. The latter is particularly important for the development and implementation of adequate interventions (Carson and Hand, 1999). Also, increasing our understanding of the experiences of Alaska Natives should be a research priority.

ELDER ABUSE AMONG MINORITY POPULATIONS: DEVELOPING AND IMPLEMENTING SERVICES

A review of the existing literature clearly suggests that the lack of attention on culture is a major problem with current efforts to address elder abuse among minority populations (see Tatara, 1999). The few research studies that have explored the impact of culture on perceptions of elder abuse suggest that it plays a significant role. Cultural norms and values not only impact how elder abuse is perceived but also the likelihood that its victims will seek and/or accept services. Also, the types of services that minority victims accept are determined by culture (Nerenberg, 1999; Tomita, 2000; Wolf and Donglin, 1999).

Efforts to increase awareness and reporting of elder abuse among ethnic minorities have generally taken two approaches (Nerenberg, 1999). An example of a direct approach is found in New York City's "That's Abuse" campaign, where posters depicting abusive situations and diverse ethnic groups have been utilized. San Francisco's "We Are Family" project depicts a nondirect approach. Rather than focusing on abusive behaviors, this project emphasizes the contributions of extended families and ways to support families. The author suggests that it is important to recognize that outreach campaigns consider the target population. For instance, in San Francisco, where the majority of older minorities are Asian and Hispanics, de-emphasizing abuse is probably more effective since these populations are concerned with maintaining the family's honor and integrity (Nerenberg, 1999).

Older minorities that are vulnerable to elder abuse (e.g., those who need assistance) tend to live with relatives. Thus, planning for services and programs that attempt to eliminate elder abuse should not only be sensitive to cultural differences but also focus on interventions that facilitate caregiving responsibilities and strengthen the minority family (C. Sanchez, 1999). Further, Nerenberg (1999) suggests that to the extent that the minority family is experiencing additional stressors such as unemployment, poverty, substance abuse, and racism, the methods utilized by service providers may not be perceived as useful or appropriate, particularly if they are viewed as divisive to family relationships. The author suggests that holistic approaches that address the multiple stressors experienced by many families may be more successful.

Moreover, because the "community" remains of great significance for ethnic minorities in the United States, Quinn and Tomita (1997) suggest that community cooperation is essential for an effective elder abuse system. In this light, Wolf and Donglin (1999) found that socioeconomic status is correlated with the reporting of elder abuse. The authors found that reports of elder abuse were higher in low income areas where the public, many of them minorities, had frequent and direct contact with state and federal agencies which are mandate reporters. Hence, we suggest that the concept of community not only include the ethnic minority group itself, but also other service providers and agencies, including religious organizations, that potential victims of elder abuse come in contact.

Research also suggests that as immigrant groups become acculturated, their attitudes and practices tend to change and may resemble those of the majority population. In this light, although it is important to develop culturally-appropriate services to serve older ethnic minorities, it is also important not to stereotype them and believe all will behave according to their ethnicity (Pablo and Braun, 1997).

Despite increasing awareness of elder abuse in the United States, there are still significant gaps in our understanding of this phenomenon. The preceding sections have highlighted the little we know about elder abuse among ethnic minority groups. However, it is clear that cultural norms and values play a significant role in how we define elder abuse, whether or not we seek help—especially from outsiders—and the types of services that we are likely to accept. The proportion of older minorities is expected to increase significantly in the next decades. Without significantly increasing our efforts to better understand the intersection of aging and culture, we will continue to fail to address the needs of the very groups that have made the United States a culturally rich nation.

REFERENCES

Andrews, H. (1989). *Poverty and Poor Health Among Elderly Hispanic Americans.* Baltimore, MD: Commonwealth Fund Commission on Elderly Living Alone.

Anetzberger, G., Korbin, J., and Tomita, S. (1996). Defining Elder Mistreatment in Four Ethnic Groups Across Two Generations. *Journal of Cross-Cultural Gerontology, 11*(2), 207-232.

Angel, J., and Hogan, D. (1992). The Demography of Minority Aging Populations. *Journal of Family History, 17*(1), 95-116.

Baldridge, D. (2001). Indian Elders: Family Traditions in Crisis. *The American Behavioral Scientist, 44*(9), 1515-1527.

Benton, D. M. (1999). African Americans and Elder Mistreatment: Targeting Information for a High-Risk Population. In Tatara, T. (Ed.), *Understanding Elder Abuse in Minority Populations,* 49-64.

Bonnie, R. J., and Wallace, R. B. (Eds.). (2003). *Elder Mistreatment: Abuse, Neglect, and Exploitation in an Aging America.* Washington, DC: The National Academies Press.

Brown, A. S. (1989). A Survey on Elder Abuse at one Native American Tribe. *Journal of Elder Abuse and Neglect, 1*(2), 17-37.

Brown, A. S. (1999). Patterns of Abuse Among Native American Elderly. In Tatara, T. (Ed.), *Understanding Elder Abuse in Minority Populations,* 143-159.

Brownell, P. (1997). The Application of the Culturagram in Cross-Cultural Practice with Elder Abuse Victims. *Journal of Elder Abuse and Neglect, 9*(2), 19-33.

Carson, D. K. (1995). American Indian Elder Abuse: Risk and Protective Factors Among the Oldest Americans. *Journal of Elder Abuse and Neglect, 7*(1), 17-39.

Carson, D. K., and Hand, C. (1999). Dilemmas Surrounding Elder Abuse and Neglect in Native American Communities. In Tatara, T. (Ed.), *Understanding Elder Abuse in Minority Populations,* 161-184.

Cazenave, N. A. (1979). Family Violence and Aging African Americans: Theoretical Perspectives and Research Possibilities. *Journal of Minority Aging, 4,* 99-108.

Chang, J., and Moon, A. (1997). Korean American Elderly's Knowledge and Perceptions of Elder Abuse: A Qualitative Analysis of Cultural Factors. *Journal of Multicultural Social Work, 6*(1-2), 139-155.

Davidhizar, R., Dowd, S., and Giger, J. N. (1998). Recognizing Abuse in Cultural Diverse Clients. *The Health Care Manager, 17*(2), 10-20.

Day, J. C. (1996). *U.S. Bureau of the Census Current Populations Reports,* Series P-25, No. 1130. *Population Projections of the United States by Age, Sex, Race, and Hispanic Origin: 1995 to 2050.* Washington, DC: U.S. Government Printing Office.

Dimah, A., and Dimah, K. P. (2002). Gender Differences Among Abused Older African Americans and African American Abusers in an Elder Abuse Provider Agency. *Journal of Black Studies, 32*(5), 557-573.

Galbraith, M. W. (1989). A Critical Examination of the Definitional, Methodological and Theoretical Problems of Elder Abuse. In Filinson, R. and Ingman, S. R. (Eds.), *Elder Abuse Practice and Policy,* 126-166. NY: Human Sciences Press.

Gelfand, D. E. (1994). *Aging and Ethnicity: Knowledge and Services.* New York: Springer Publishing.

Griffin, L. W. (1994). Elder Maltreatment Among Rural African Americans. *Journal of Elder Abuse and Neglect, 6*(1), 1-27.

Griffin, L. W., and Williams, O. J. (1992). Abuse Among African-American Elderly. *Journal of Family Violence, 7*(1), 19-35.

Hall, P. A. (1987). Minority Elder Maltreatment: Ethnicity, Gender, Age, and Poverty.

Journal of Gerontological Social Work. Special Issues: Ethnicity and Gerontological Social Work, 9(4), 53-72.

Hayes-Bautista, D. E., Hsu, P., Perez, A., and Gamboa, C. (2002). The 'Browning' of the Graying of America: Diversity in the Elderly Population and Policy Implications. *Generations, 26*(3), 15-24.

Henry, W. A. (1990, April 9). Beyond the Melting Pot. *Time.*

Hetzel, L. and Smith, A. (October 2001). *The 65 years and Over Population: 2000.* Census 2000 Brief, C2KBR/01-10, Washington, DC.

Hollmann, F. W., Mulder, T. J., and Kallan, J. E. (2000). Methodology and Assumptions for the Population Projects of the United States: 1999 to 2100, Population Division Working Paper No. 38, U.S. Bureau of the Census, Issued January 13, 2000.

Hudson, M. F., and Carlson, J. R. (1999). Elder Abuse: Its Meaning to Caucasians, African Americans, and Native Americans. In Tatara, T. (Ed.), *Understanding Elder Abuse in Minority Populations,* 187-204.

Hudson, M. F., et al. (1999). Elder Abuse: Some African American Views. *Journal of Interpersonal Violence, 14*(9), 915-939.

Hurh, W. M. and Kim, K. C. (1989). The "Success" Image of Asian Americans: Its Validity, And its Practical and Theoretical Implications. *Ethnic and Racial Studies, 12,* 512-538.

Le, Q. (1997). Mistreatment of Vietnamese Elderly by Their Families in the United States. *Journal of Elder Abuse and Neglect, 9*(2), 51-62.

Longres, J. (1992). Race and Type of Maltreatment in an Elder Abuse System. *Journal of Elder Abuse and Neglect, 4*(3), 61-83.

Manigbas, M. (2002). Multiservice Organization Combats Elder Abuse in Chinese Community. *Generations, 26*(3), 70-71.

Maxwell, E. K., and Maxwell, R. J. (1992). Insults to the Body Civil: Mistreatment of Elderly in Two Plains Indian Tribes. *Journal of Cross-Cultural Gerontology, 7,* 3-23.

McKinnon, J. (2003). *U.S. Bureau of the Census Current Population Reports,* Series P20-41. *The Black Population in the United States: March 2002.* Washington, DC: U.S. Government Printing Office.

Mitchell, B. M., Festa, N. A., Franco, A. C., Juarez, D., and Lamb, L. L. (1999). Issues in the Provision of Adult-Protective Services to Mexican American Elders in Texas. In Tatara, T. (Ed.), *Understanding Elder Abuse in Minority Populations,* 79-92.

Montoya, V. (1997). Understanding and Combating Elder Abuse in Hispanic Communities. *Journal of Elder Abuse and Neglect, 9*(2), 5-17.

Moon, A., and Benton, D. (2000). Tolerance of Elder Abuse and Attitudes Toward Third-Party Intervention Among African American, Korean American, and White Elderly. *Journal of Multicultural Social Work, 8*(3-4), 283-304.

Moon, A. and Williams, O. J. (1993). Perceptions of Elder Abuse and Help Seeking Patterns Among African American, Caucasian, and Korean-American Elderly. *The Gerontologist, 33,* 386-395.

National Center on Elder Abuse. (1998). *The National Elder Abuse Incidence Study; Final Report.* From www.elderabusecenter.org

Nerenberg, L. (1999). Culturally specific Outreach in Elder Abuse. In Tatara, T. (Ed.), *Understanding Elder Abuse in Minority Populations,* 205-220.

Ogunwole, S. U. (2002). *U.S. Bureau of the Census: Census 2000 Brief,* C2KBR/01-15. *The American Indian and Alaska Native Population: 2000.* Washington, DC: U.S. Government Printing Office.

Otiniano, M. E., Herrera, C. R., and Hardman-Muye, M. (1997). Abuse of Hispanic Elders: A Case Study Review. *Clinical Gerontologist, 18*(1), 39-43.

Pablo, S., and Braun, K. L. (1997). Perceptions of Elder Abuse and Neglect and Help-Seeking Patterns Among Filipino and Korean Elderly Women in Honolulu. *Journal of Elder Abuse and Neglect, 9*(2), 63-76.

Quinn, M. J., and Tomita, S. K. (1997). *Elder Abuse and Neglect: Causes, Diagnosis, and Intervention Strategies* (2nd edition). NY: Springer.

Ramirez, R. R. and de la Cruz, G. P. (2003). *U.S. Bureau of the Census Current Populations Reports*, Series P20-545. *The Hispanic Population in the United States: March 2002*. Washington, DC: U.S. Government Printing Office.

Reeves, T. and Bennett, C. (2003). *U.S. Bureau of the Census Current Population Reports*, Series P20-540. *The Asian and Pacific Islander Population in the United States: March 2002*. Washington, DC: U.S. Government Printing Office.

Sanchez, C. D. (1999). Elder Abuse in the Puerto Rican Context. In Tatara, T. (Ed.), *Understanding Elder Abuse in Minority Populations*, 93-105.

Sanchez, Y. (1999). Elder Mistreatment in Mexican American Communities: The Nevada and Michigan experiences. In Tatara, T. (Ed.), *Understanding Elder Abuse in Minority Populations*, 67-77.

Sung, K. (2001). Elder Respect: Exploration of Ideals and Forms in East Asia. *Journal of Aging Studies, 15*(1), 13-26.

Tatara, T. (Ed.). (1999). *Understanding Elder Abuse in Minority Populations*. Philadelphia, PA: Brunner/Mazel.

Teaster, P. B. (2000). *A Response to the Abuse of Vulnerable Adults: The 2000 Survey of State Adult Protective Services*. Washington, DC: National Center on Elder Abuse. From www.elderabusecenter.org

Tomita, S. (1999). Exploration of Elder Mistreatment Among the Japanese. In Tatara, T. (Ed.), *Understanding Elder Abuse in Minority Populations*, 119-139.

Tomita, S. (2000). Elder mistreatment: Practice Modifications to Accommodate Cultural Differences. *Journal of Multicultural Social Work, 8*(3-4), 305-326.

U.S. Census Bureau. (2002). *Statistical Abstracts of the United States: 2002*. Washington, DC: Public Information Office. www.census.gov/prod/www/statistical-abstract-02.html

Williams, O., and Griffin, L. (1996). Elderly Maltreatment and Cultural Diversity: When Laws are not Enough. *Journal of Multi-Cultural Social Work, 4*(2), 1-13.

Wolf, R. S. (2000). The Nature and Scope of Elder Abuse. *Generations, 24*(2), 6-12.

Wolf, R. S. (1988). Elder abuse: Ten Years Later. *The Journal of the American Geriatrics Society, 36*, 758-762.

Wolf, R. S., and Donglin, L. (1999). Factors Affecting the Rate of Elder Abuse Reporting to a State Protective Services Program. *The Gerontologist, 39*(2), 222-228.

6

INTERNATIONAL/CULTURAL PERSPECTIVES ON ELDER ABUSE

Mary Newman

Elder mistreatment has attracted increasing attention and concern world-wide over the last three decades. As the older population expands in developed, and particularly in developing countries, the urgency for addressing and dealing with these human rights violations mounts. Burston (1975, cited in Yan and So-Kum Tang, 2003), Baker (1975) and Burston (1977) (both cited in World Health Organizations, 2002) published the earliest reports of what they called *granny battering* in British journals. Serious examination of this social crisis began in the United States. Gradually other nations joined in the effort to identify and prevent elder abuse. The number of studies, committees, social service agencies, and laws dedicated to the identification and prevention of elder abuse continues to climb. Many nations recognize a history of elder abuse within their borders. Some, for instance, Norway (Johns and Hydle, 1995) and India (Nagpaul, 1997) see this as a new trend. Either way, increasing numbers of nations and organizations are following the lead of the World Health Assembly and World Health Organization (WHO) (see Krug, Mercy, Dahlberg, and Zwi, 2002; WHO, 2002) in a global effort to prevent mistreatment of older adults. This chapter examines the international literature for defining, identifying and addressing mistreatment of older adults. An effort has been made to point out similarities as well as differences between nations.

DEFINING ELDER ABUSE OUTSIDE THE US

Once the topic of elder abuse had been voiced in the United States, defining abuse posed the first challenge. The American Psychological Association (APA) (2003) provides the following guidelines: *Elder abuse is the infliction of physical, emotional, or psychological harm on an older adult. Elder abuse also can take the form of financial exploitation or intentional or unintentional neglect of an older adult by the caregiver.* The National Center on Elder Abuse (NCEA) (2004) suggests that *such harm refers to any knowing, intentional, or negligent act by a caregiver or any other person that causes harm or a serious risk of harm to a vulnerable adult.*

Defining and identifying elder abuse is difficult enough for those who seek to study and address the problem within the dominant culture of the United States. Take it outside of that culture, and particularly outside the nation, and these challenges are amplified. However, given that similarities and differences in the assessment and identification of abusive behavior have been demonstrated between minority groups and immigrants living in the

U.S., (e.g., Moon, 2000; Chang and Moon, 1997 [cited in Moon, 2000]; see Tatara, 1999, and Chapter 5 of current volume for reviews), similar patterns might be expected between nations. Therefore, scientists endeavored to develop definitions that are general enough to be used in a variety of cultures (e.g., Action on Elder Abuse, 2000; Australian Network for the Prevention of Elder Abuse, 1999; National Center on Aging Abuse 2004; WHO, 2002; Yan and So-Kum Tang, 2003), or to develop measurements specific for particular cultures (e.g., Le, 1997) in order to make comparisons between nations.

Some progress has been made in this regard. The following definitions are representative of those used by many investigators around the world:

The Australian Network for the Prevention of Elder Abuse (1999) proposed that elder abuse:

> "… *is any act occurring within a relationship where there is an implication of trust, which results in harm to an older person. Abuse may be physical sexual, financial, psychological, social and/or neglect.*"

Action on Elder Abuse (2000) (United Kingdom), Australian Network for the Prevention of Elder Abuse (1999), and the United Nations Commission for Social Development (2002) endorsed a very similar definition:

> "*A single or repeated act or lack of appropriate action occurring within any relationship where there is an expectation of trust which causes harm or distress to an older person.*"

The World Health Organization settled on the following guideline:

> *The intentional use of physical force or power, threatened or actual, against oneself, another person, or against a group or community, that either results in or has a high likelihood of resulting in injury, death, psychological harm, maldevelopment or deprivation* (Krug et al., 2002).

Canadians (National Clearinghouse on Family Violence, 2003) aligned their definition with that of the National Center on Aging Abuse (2004), using subcategories of abuse rather than a general definition. Those subcategories include physical, sexual, emotional, and psychological abuse, abandonment, neglect, self-neglect, and financial or material exploitation.

The Secretary-General of the United Nations (2002) provides an extensive list of abuse typologies and examples of each.

Subcategories of Abusive Behavior

Whereas investigators disagree about a comprehensive definition, they generally agree about some aspects of abusive behavior. For instance, there is consensus concerning three categories of abuse: Most recognize that abuse and neglect occur in the home, in institutions, and at the hands of some elders themselves. Similar to the United States (e.g., American Psychological Association, 2003; National Center on Elder Abuse, 1998), a variety of international investigators consider some or all of the following abusive: Verbal, physical, psychological, sexual, legal, and financial abuse, and neglect (e.g., Au Coin, 2003; Hailstones, 1992; Jenkins, Asif, and Bennett, 2000; McCreadie, Bennett, and Tinker, 1998; Nagpaul, 1997; National Clearinghouse on Family Violence, 2003; Perttu, 1996; Reis, 2000; Sharon and Zoabi, 1997; United Nations Secretary-General, 2002; WHO, 2002); and some also include self-neglect (e.g., Krug et al., 2002; National Center on Aging Abuse, 2004; National Clearinghouse on Family Violence, 2003; Sharon and Zoabi, 1997). The World Health Organization (2002) described structural and societal (e.g., government) abuse (United Nations Secretary-General, 2002; WHO, 2002). Kurrle and Sadler (1994) in Australia added social abuse (family or other caregivers limiting an older adult's access to social support and recreation) to the list.

CULTURE AND ELDER ABUSE

One of the factors that impacts the identification and tolerance of elder abuse is culture, meant here to include differences based upon religion, ethnicity, race, sexual orientation, rural versus urban locales, geographic, and national origin. Reports of abuse and neglect are increasingly available for some minorities within the U.S. (e.g., Le, 1997 – Vietnamese immigrants; Moon and Williams, 1993 – Korean-Americans; Nagpaul, 1997 – Asian Indians; Pablo and Braun, 1997; see Moon, 2000, and Tatara, 1999, as well as Chapter 5 of the current volume for reviews), but are still relatively small in number. Far fewer reports are available on a global level. At least five factors probably account for the difficulty in conducting international comparative studies of elder abuse, and the scarcity of information for some regions and populations: 1) Cultural differences in defining and identifying abuse; 2) differential focus of cultures on the individual versus family and community; 3) varying rights and privileges of females and males; 4) differing and changing attitudes toward the elderly; and 5) the failure of some investigators to appreciate cultural differences, to use culturally sensitive means of data collection, and to consider cultural variation in interpreting their findings (however, see, e.g., Le, 1997). Despite the challenges, however, scientists continue to make headway in understanding the phenomenon of elder abuse.

FIRST MULTINATIONAL STUDY OF ELDER ABUSE

Scientists representing the World Health Organization (2002), in collaboration with the International Network for the Prevention of Elder Abuse (INPEA), spoke with focus groups of older persons and primary health care providers in five developing (Argentina, Brazil, India, Kenya, Lebanon) and 3 developed nations (Canada, Austria, Sweden) in the first multi-national study of attitudes about, and perceptions of elder abuse. The purpose of this project was " ... *to raise the awareness among health professionals and the public at large about the problem of elder abuse world-wide, and to develop a global strategy within the context of Primary Health Care for the prevention of elder abuse.*" Data from each of these countries were combined, and primary types of abuse identified: "... *structural and societal abuse, neglect and abandonment, disrespect and ageist attitudes, psychological, emotional and verbal abuse, physical abuse, legal and financial abuse.*"

Findings by the World Health Organization (2002) pointed to differences between cultures, and inequities in the status of the elderly as sources of stress and resulting abuse. In a sample of 48 older adults in Buenos Aires, Argentina, 35% endured some type of abuse. Reports from Kenya, India and Brazil suggested that abuse and abandonment result from lack of health care benefits from the government. Representatives of India, Lebanon and Austria called attention to frequent conflict between women and their mothers-in-law, eventually leading to various types of mistreatment (including physical abuse) and neglect of the older women (WHO, 2002). Similarly, Soeda and Araki (1999) reported that daughters-in-law in Japan were more likely than spouses or adult children to neglect older family members. These reports are consistent with the findings of Le (1997), who interviewed twenty elderly Vietnamese immigrants to the United States. Older women who spoke only Vietnamese were most vulnerable, and daughters-in-law often inflicted verbal and/or emotional abuse. For Vietnamese elderly, being ignored, or given the silent treatment was the harshest form of punishment, even more devastating than physical abuse. Overall, elders from all eight nations suggested that disrespect, which was inflicted by family members as well as governmental and commercial institutions, constituted the worst form of abuse, and was the root of all other forms of abuse. Women (particularly widows and those without children) and poor elders were reported to be most vulnerable. The investigators noted the reluctance of elderly participants to discuss elder abuse. Members of the focus group in India actively avoided the topic of "physical abuse" but acknowledged "mistreatment" of older persons.

PREVALENCE OF ELDER ABUSE

The relative incidence and reporting of these different types of abuse varies somewhat between nations and between studies. For instance, in the United States (e.g., American College of Obstetricians and Gynecologists, 2003; National Center on Elder Abuse, 1998) and in Japan (Soeda and Araki, 1999), neglect is reported to be the most common form of abuse. In Canada, Wolf and Pillemer (1989) and Podnieks (1992) reported that financial abuse occurs more frequently than other forms of mistreatment. In contrast, Au Coin (2003) found that physical abuse is most common in Canada. Results of one study in England suggest that older adults suffer verbal abuse most often; physical abuse is second to that, followed by financial abuse (Ogg, 1993). Verbal abuse occurred most frequently in a Dutch study (Comijs et al., 1998, cited in Bonnie and Wallace, 2003), and in a Canadian institutional study (College of Nurses of Ontario, 1993). Jenkins and colleagues (2000) in the United Kingdom, Perttu (1996) in Finland, and Nagpaul (1997) studying Asian Indians found evidence that psychological abuse was more prevalent than other types. Differences in results may be attributed to variations in language, culture, and research methodology.

Despite the challenges of conducting research on this topic, estimated rates of mistreatment in some, but not all, developed countries are remarkably similar. The World Health Organization (2002) reports abuse and neglect in the U.S. of approximately 4-6%. Estimates of abuse in other countries are comparable. For instance, Podnieks (1990) estimates an abuse rate of 4% based upon a Canadian national survey. Other Canadian studies (e.g., Podnieks and Pillemer, 1990; Podnieks, 1992) suggested a 3-5% abuse rate. An Amsterdam study revealed that 5.6% of older adults were abused (Comijs, Pot, Smit and Jonker, 1998, cited in Bonnie and Wallace, 2003). Ogg and Bennett (1992) found a similar abuse rate in Great Britain. In a small Finnish town, Kivela, Kongas-Saviaro, Kesti, Pahkala, and Ijas (1992; cited in Bonnie and Wallace, 2003) found a 5.7% rate of abuse. Australian figures also indicate a rate of approximately 4.6% to 5.4% (Sadler, Kurrle, and Cameron, 1992).

However, there are studies from some regions that provide evidence of much higher rates of abuse and neglect. For instance, Yan and So-Kum Tang (2001) learned that 20.8% of older Chinese adults in Hong Kong had been verbally abused (e.g., insults, swearing, intimidation), and two percent reported physical abuse (e.g., being hit, burned, physically restrained). The United Nations Secretary General (2002) gathered information on developing nations from crime and news reports, welfare reports and small studies, and concluded that 20% of a sample of 50 older adults from rural India suffered neglect, and 45% of a sample of older adults in Argentina reported abuse, frequently psychological abuse.

The data from these and other projects should be interpreted with caution. It will be necessary to interpret the data in cultural context; to verify the validity and reliability of the data given variability in definitions and methodology; and to determine the level of reliability of these reports given customs in cultures as diverse as Argentina (Hurme, 2002; South Africa (United Nations Population Fund, 2002), and Vietnamese (Le, 1997), and Chinese populations (Yan, So-Kum Tang, and Yeung, 2002) to deny or hide mistreatment of elderly persons. More extensive research is required before any genuine differences between cultures can be more clearly identified. Another caveat regarding these statistics: Most studies have been conducted in urban areas and in developed countries (Nelson, 2002; WHO, 2002). In one of the few studies of rural populations, the rate of abuse in northwest New South Wales was estimated at 5.5%, similar to the findings in urban areas (Cupitt, 1997). The United Nations Secretary General (2002) estimated physical abuse in a rural area of India to be approximately 4%, whereas a 20% neglect rate was found in an urban area. In a study of 120 abused and 120 non-abused Arabs living in Israel, Sharon and Zoabi (1997) found a significantly lower incidence of abuse (including self-neglect) at 2.5%. Persons over 65 years of age comprise only 3.7% of the Arab population living in Israel. These authors reported higher rates of abuse in urban areas and lower rates in rural areas. A project in Western Australia suggested an abuse rate of less than 1% (Centre for Research into Aged Care Services, 2002). Despite limitations in the volume and interpretation of existing research, there is little doubt that violation of the rights of older adults to adequate care and freedom from mistreatment is a worldwide problem. Awareness of the abuse and commitment to its prevention began slowly, but continue to grow due to the efforts and dedication of local, national and international organizations around the globe.

Several international organizations and campaigns provided the impetus and guidance this movement needed. The World Health Assembly released a report in 1996 calling attention to the problem of violence, including elder abuse, worldwide. This organization set as its goal the prevention of violence. The declaration of 1999 as the International Year of Older Persons by the United Nations helped to raise awareness of the plight of the elderly. The United Nations (1999) drafted the *Principles for Older Persons*. The intention of this document was *to add life to the years that have been added to life*, based upon the U.N.'s *Declaration on the Rights and Responsibilities of Older Persons*. The United Nations Economic Council promoted the worldwide recognition of, and attention to the mistreatment of older adults by providing a report on definitions and types of elder abuse in anticipation of the World Assembly on Ageing (United Nations Secretary General, 2002). This report discussed a number of categories of abuse such as those listed above, as well as specific examples of abuse and neglect within those categories. That same year, the World Health Organization followed up with the first report of its kind, the *Global Campaign on Violence Prevention* (see Krug, Mercy, Kahlberg and Zwi, 2002), hoping to gain support at all levels of society from local to international, with particular involvement of public health professionals. Thirty-plus nations subsequently joined in the dialogue, some developing policies addressing the problem, and launching their own campaigns against violence (WHO, 2002).

As motivation and guidance increased at the international level, individual nations were inspired to follow suit for the protection of their older citizens. For instance, Kuwait adopted its own *Declaration on the Rights of Elderly* at the 12th Medical Juristic Symposium on the Rights of Elderly from an Islamic Perspective (1999). Numerous other countries have also adopted policies and formed organizations for the support and protection of their older citizens. Those actively involved in the movement include New Zealand (Age Concern New Zealand, 2004), New South Wales (1996), Australia (Prevention of Elder Abuse Task Force, 2001), Canada (Canadian Network for the Prevention of Elder Abuse; International Network for the Prevention of Elder Abuse), Japan (Japanese Center for the Prevention of Elder Abuse), Latin America (Latin American Committee for the Prevention of Elder Abuse), just to name a few. As these and other nations reveal their findings, victimization of older adults becomes increasingly visible.

WHO ARE THE PERPETRATORS AND VICTIMS?

The National Center on Elder Abuse published a report in the United States (1998) that outlined typical characteristics of the victim and perpetrator. Risk of abuse increased dramatically with age. Particularly vulnerable were those individuals with the lowest incomes, those who required more care, or who suffered from depression or confusion. Approximately equal numbers of men and women were perpetrators, although women were much more likely to neglect their victims, and men were guilty of other types of abuse. Perpetrators tended to be younger than their victims, and most were family members (mostly adult children) or spouses.

Much speculation concerning a profile of the typical perpetrator and victim appears in the international literature. Conflicting reports suggest some difficulty in characterizing these two groups (e.g., Jenkins et al., 2000; National Clearinghouse on Family Violence, 2003; Reis, 2000; Reis and Nahmiash, 1995; National Center on Elder Abuse, 1998) Estimations regarding the relative number of male versus female perpetrators vary. Some of this variability depends upon the caregiving practices and traditions of individual cultures. After examining phone calls made to a free helpline in the United Kingdom, Jenkins and colleagues (2000) claimed that females were just as likely to be abusive as males. A review by Hurme (2002) summarizes reports on elder abuse from nations present at a Nongovernmental Organizations (NGO) Forum workshop. These reports reflect cultural differences in mistreatment of older persons. In Japan women do most of the caregiving, and so most perpetrators are female. In contrast, men are responsible for the greater majority of abuse in Spain.

Women are usually the victims of mistreatment according to reports from the United States, Spain, and Japan (Hurme, 2002), and the World Health Organization (2002). Victims calling the United Kingdom helpline (Jenkins et al., 2000) were much more likely to be female. Although callers to the hotline are self-selected, these findings are consistent with the report from Hurme, and the findings of Kivela in a small town in Finland (1992). Studies of Chinese people living in Hong Kong, (Yan and So-Kum Tang, 2001), and elderly in Boston, Massachusetts (Pillemer and Finkelhor, 1988) revealed equivalent vulnerability of older men and women to abuse. (See Pritchard, 2001, for a study of male victims of elder abuse in the United Kingdom.)

Consistent with the findings of Jenkins and colleagues (2000), Reis and Nahmiash (1995) (cited in Reis, 2000) validated a checklist of factors that are frequently associated with abuse. They found that the combination of these factors reliably predicted the presence of abuse with 78-84.4% accuracy, and the absence of abuse with 99.2% accuracy in a sample of 341 adults 55 years of age or older. Characteristics and financial dependence of caregivers, as well as lack of knowledge concerning the nature of the care recipients' physical and/or mental limitations, increased the risk that a caregiver would become abusive. Families with a history of abusive behavior, particularly directed toward the care recipient, demonstrated increased incidence of elder abuse.

The degree of social support available for the care recipient also contributed to the risk of abuse. These conclusions were supported by the findings of Reis (2000). Contrary to the findings reported by Cupitt (1997), the National Center on Elder Abuse (1998) and the National Clearinghouse on Family Violence (2003), Reis emphasizes that some sources of stress (e.g., amount of assistance needed by the care recipient, as well as his/her mental and physical health) do not distinguish abusive from non-abusive relationships.

THE CHALLENGE OF PREVENTING ELDER ABUSE

Some investigators blame urbanization of developing nations (e.g., Litwin and Zoabi, 2003), or changes in the status of older adults in traditional societies, for elder mistreatment and neglect (e.g., Nagpaul, 1997; Sharon and Zoabi, 1997; Soneja, 2001; Yan, So-Kum Tang, and Yeung, 2002). Violations of long-standing cultural traditions (e.g., respect for elders, filial piety and responsibility) increase as younger adults emulate their peers in developed cultures. Older adults, raised to believe that family problems should remain within the family, and that the welfare of the family supercedes the good of the individual, are reluctant to report abuse.

ADDRESSING THE HUMAN RIGHTS OF
OLDER PERSONS WORLDWIDE

Although there is variability between studies and between nations, in the end, similarities outnumber the differences. Overall many nations acknowledge that 1) elder abuse is a significant social problem; and 2) defining and addressing the problem is difficult. Additionally some recognize the individual's right to have some say in deciding what is and what is not abusive, and what may or may not be done about interceding in individual abusive situations.

Numerous nations and organizations across the globe initiated efforts to understand and address violations of older adults' human rights. Many have generated recommendations for an approach to the problem. The World Health Organization leads the way in raising awareness concerning elder abuse, and recommends the active involvement of the public health sector (Krug et al., 2002). Suggestions from WHO (2002) include increasing awareness and education about mistreatment of old adults; attempts to improve intergenerational relationships; training of professionals on the topics of aging and elder abuse; enabling older adults to act on their own behalf; gaining the cooperation of the media in attending to the images they portray the elderly; advocating for laws to protect the older population, and health care plans suitable for their needs; and finally, this report points out the need for more research on mistreatment of older adults in particular cultural contexts.

REFERENCES

Action on Elder Abuse (2000). Listening is Not Enough: An Analysis of Calls to Elder Abuse Response—Action on Elder Abuse's Nation Helpline. http://www.elder-abuse.org.uk/documents/reportsetc/listen.htm.

Age Concern New Zealand (2004). *Promoting the Rights and Well-being of Older People and Those who Care for Them—A Resource Kit About Elder Abuse and Neglect.* Wellington, N.Z. http://www.ageconcern.org.nz/?/advocacy/elderabuse.

American Psychological Association (2003). Elder Abuse and Neglect: In Search of Solutions. http://www.apa.org/pi/aging/eldabuse.html.

Au Coin, K. (2003). *Family Violence in Canada: A Statistical Profile.* Canadian Centre for Justice Statistics, Catalogue Number 85-224-XIE, 21-26.

The Australian Network for the Prevention of Elder Abuse Working Definition (1999). Contact Aged Rights Advocacy Service, 45 Flinders St, Adelaide 5000.

Baker, A. A. (1975). Granny Battering. *Modern Geriatrics, 5,* 20-24.

Bonnie, R. J., and Wallace, R. B. (Eds.) (2003). *Elder Mistreatment: Abuse, Neglect, and Exploitation in an Aging America.* Wash. D.C.: National Academies Press.

Burston, G. (1975). Granny Battering. *British Medical Journal, 6,* 692.

Burston, G. (1977). Do Your Elderly Patients Live in Fear of Being Battered? *Modern Geriatrics, 7,* 54-55.

Centre for Research into Aged Care Services (2002). *Elder Abuse in Western Australia: Report of a Survey Conducted for the Department of Community Development—Seniors' Interests.* WA Government.

Clearinghouse on Abuse and Neglect of the Elderly (CANE) (2002). *Annotated Bibliography: Elder Abuse: A Global Issue.* http://www.elderabusecenter.org/default.cfm?p=cane_global.cfm.

College of Nurses of Ontario (1993). Abuse of Clients by Registered Nurses and Registered Nursing Assistants: Report to Council on Results of Canada Health. *Monitor Survey of Registrants, 1.*

Comis, H. C., Pot, A. M., Smit, H. H., and Jonker, C. (1998). Elder Abuse in the Community: Prevalence and Consequences. *Journal of the American Geriatrics Society, 46,* 885-888.

Cupitt, M. (1997). Identifying and Addressing the Issues of Elder Abuse: A Rural Perspective. *Journal of Elder Abuse and Neglect, 8,* 21-30.

Daichman, L. (2001). Argentina. Report for the World Health Organization. From *Missing Voices: Views of Older Persons on Elder Abuse.* Geneva.

Hailstones, A. (1992) Abuse of Older People in Their Homes. Discussion paper produced by New South Wales Task Force on Abuse of Older People.

Halicka, M. (1995). Elder Abuse and Neglect in Poland. *Journal of Elder Abuse and Neglect, 6,* 157-169.

Horkan, E. M. (1995). Elder Abuse in the Republic of Ireland. *Journal of Elder Abuse and Neglect, 6,* 119-137.

Hurme, S. B. (2002). *Perspectives on Elder Abuse.* American Association for Retired Persons.

Jenkins, G., Asif, Z. and Bennett, G. (2000). Listening is Not Enough: An Analysis of Calls to Elder Abuse Response-Action on Elder Abuse's National Helpline. *The Journal of Adult Protection, 2.*

Johns, S., and Hydle, I. (1995). Norway: Weakness in Welfare. *Journal of Elder Abuse and Neglect, 5,* 139-156.

Kivela, S. L., Kongas-Saviaro, P., Kesti, E., Pahkala, K., and Ijas, M. L. (1992). Abuse in Old Age: Epidemiological Data from Finland. *Journal of Elder Abuse and Neglect, 4*, 1-18.

Krug, E. G., Mercy, J. A., Dahlberg, L. L., and Zwi, A. B. (2002). The World Report on Violence and Health. *Lancet, 360*, 1083-1088.

Kurrle, S., and Sadler, P. (1994). *Assessing and Managing Abuse of Older People: A Handbook for the Helping Professional*. New South Wales: Alpha Biomedical Communications.

Le, Q. K. (1997). Mistreatment of Vietnamese Elderly by their Families in the United States. *Journal of Elder Abuse and Neglect, 9*, 51-62.

Machado, L., Gomes, R., and Xavier, E. (2001). Report on Elder Abuse in Brazil. Report for the World Health Organization. From *Missing Voices: Views of Older Persons on Elder Abuse*. Geneva.

McCreadie, C., Bennett, G., and Tinker, A. (1998). Investigating British General Practitioners' Knowledge and Experience of Elder Abuse: Report of a Research Study in an Inner London Borough. *Journal of Elder Abuse and Neglect, 9*, 23-39.

Moon, A. (2000). Perceptions of Elder Abuse Among Various Cultural Groups: Similarities and Differences. *Generations, 24*, 75-80.

Moon, A., and Williams, O. (1993). Perceptions of Elder Abuse and Help-Seeking Patterns Among African-American, Caucasian American and Korean-American Elderly Women. *The Gerontologist, 33*, 386-395.

Nagpaul, K. (1997). Elder Abuse Among Asian Indians: Traditional Versus Modern Perspectives. *Journal of Elder Abuse and Neglect, 9*, 77-92.

National Center on Elder Abuse (1998). The National Elder Abuse Incidence Study: Final Report. National Center on Elder Abuse at the American Public Human Services Association, in collaboration with Westat, Inc.

National Center on Elder Abuse (2004). NCEA homepage. http://www.elderabusecenter.org/

National Clearinghouse on Family Violence (2003). *Abuse and Neglect Of Older Adults: A Discussion Paper*. http://www.hc-sc.gc.ca/hppb/familyviolence/html/agediscussion_e.html.

Nelson, D. (2002). Violence Against Elderly People: A Neglected Problem. *Lancet, 360*, 1094.

New South Wales Department of Ageing and Disability (1996). *Dealing with Abuse of Clients and Their Carers, A Training Kit*. Ageing and Disability Department, Sydney, NSW.

Pablo, S., and Braun, K. L. (1997). Perceptions of Elder Abuse and Neglect and Help-Seeking Patterns Among Filipino and Korean Elderly Women in Honolulu. *Journal of Elder Abuse and Neglect, 9*, 63-76.

Pillemer, K., and Finkelhor, D. (1988). The Prevalence of Elder Abuse: A Random Sample Survey. *Gerontologist, 28*, 51-57.

Podnieks, E. (1990). *National Survey on Abuse of the Elderly in Canada*. Ryerson Polytechnical Institute. Ottawa: Ontario: Health and Welfare Canada.

Podnieks, E. (2001). *Report on Elder Abuse in Canada.. Report for the World Health Organization*.

Podnieks, E., and Pillemer, K. (1990). National Survey on Abuse of the Elderly in Canada. Toronto: Ryerson Polytechnical Institute.

Poirier, D., and Poirier, N. (1999). Older Adults' Personal Relationships Final Report: Why is it so Difficult to Combat Elder Abuse and, in Particular, Financial Exploitation of the elderly? Submitted to the Law Commission of Canada. Web site: http://www.lcc.gc.ca/en/themes/pr/oa/poirier/poirier_main.asp.

Prevention of Elder Abuse Task Force (2001). *Strategic Plan for the Prevention of Elder Abuse in Queensland.*

Pritchard, J. (2001). *Male Victims of Elder Abuse: Their Experiences and Needs.* Jessica Kingsley Publishers. Reviewed in *Wordbridges* by L. Cook-Daniels, Web site: http://www.wordbridges.net/elderabuse/culture.

Reis, M. (2000, Summer). An Abuse-Alert Measure That Dispels Myths. *Generation, 24,* p. 13-16.

Reis, M., and Nahmiash, D. (1995). *When Seniors Are Abused: A Guide to Intervention.* North York, Ontario: Captus Press.

Sadler, P., Kurrie, S., and Cameron, I. (1992). Dementia and Elder Abuse. *Australian Journal on Ageing, 14,* 36.

Shah, G., Veedon, R., and Vasi, S. (1995). Elder abuse in India. *Journal of Elder Abuse and Neglect, 6,* 101-110.

Sharon, N., and Zoabi, S. (1997). Elder Abuse in a Land of Tradition: The Case of Israel's Arabs. *Journal of Elder Abuse and Neglect, 8,* 43-58.

Sijuwade, P. O. (1995). Cross-Cultural Perspectives on Elder Abuse as a Family Dilemma. *Social Behavior and Personality, 23,* 247-252.

Soeda, A., and Araki, C. (1999). Elder Abuse by Daughters-in-Law in Japan. *Journal of Elder Abuse and Neglect, 11,* 47.

Soneja, S. (2001). *Elder Abuse in India. Report for the World Health Organization.* From *Missing Voices: Views of Older Persons on Elder Abuse.* Geneva.

Tatara, T. (1999). *Understanding Elder Abuse in Minority Populations.* Levittown, PA: Brunner/Mazel.

United Nations (1999). *United Nations Principles for Older Persons.* http://www.un.org/esa/socdev/iyop/iyoppop.htm.

United Nations Secretary General (2002). Abuse of Older Persons: Recognizing and Responding to Abuse of Older Persons in a Global Context. United Nations Commission for Social Development: Report presented at the Second World Assembly on Ageing, Madrid, Spain.

Wolf, J., and Pillemer, K. (1989). National Survey on Abuse of the Elderly in Canada. *Journal of Elder Abuse and Neglect, 4,* 45-58.

World Health Organization (2002). *Missing voices: Views of Older Persons on Elder Abuse.* Geneva.

Yan, E., and So-Kum Tang, C. (2001). Prevalence and Psychological Impact of Chinese Elder Abuse. *Journal of Interpersonal Violence, 16,* 1158-1174.

Yan, E., So-Kum Tang, C., and Yeung, D. (2002). No Safe Haven: A Review on Elder Abuse in Chinese Families. *Trauma, Violence, and Abuse, 3,* 167-180.

Acknowledgement: The author extends sincere thanks to Jean-Pierre Ruiz, STD, St. John's University, for his assistance with this project, and Anita Evangelista, MSN, RN, Southwest Missouri State University, for her thoughtful review of, and commentary on this manuscript.

7

THE MORAL AND ETHICAL IMPLICATIONS OF ELDER ABUSE

Dawn Oetjen and Reid Oetjen

In the past three decades, much attention has been paid to issues of domestic violence and child abuse; however, the United States has been slow to focus on comparable issues regarding the elderly (Moskowitz, 2003). According to findings from the National Elder Abuse Incidence Study (NEAIS), more than 500,000 Americans over the age of 60 were victims of domestic abuse in 1996. Another statistic that is equally astounding is that only six percent of the abusive situations are referred for help, leaving the overwhelming majority hidden. America's increasing elderly population is affecting every segment of the social, political, and economic landscape (NEAIS, 1999).

The impetus for directing attention and resources toward elder abuse does not stem from the size of the problem, but rather from the ethical principles that are part of the fabric of American society. Elderly citizens, like others, are entitled to live in safe environments and to be treated with respect. A unique aspect of elder abuse, unlike other issues afflicting the elderly, is that it is both treatable and preventable (Pillemer and Finkelhor, 1988). Thus, an understanding of the ethical underpinnings of elder abuse is important because it can assist the provider in choosing and developing intervention strategies, as well as shaping the provider's evaluation of the success of the chosen strategy.

Another argument for the serious investigation into the problem of elder abuse stems from the dramatic shift in thinking about basic health care values. In the last twenty years, there has been a shift from paternalism, the idea that the provider decides what the patient needs and provides it, to autonomy, in which the patient determines what he/she needs. Although medical decision-making was guided by ethics, the quality of care was judged to the extent to which it met professional standards, rather than the needs and objectives of the patient (Shuman and Bebeau, 1994).

The evolving emphasis on patient self-determination places new responsibilities on providers. Aside from the standard duties of using technical expertise to diagnose and treat illness, providers are now expected and required to inform patients adequately regarding their care and gain consent from the patients for treatment. Informed consent is the process by which a competent and unimpaired patient can participate in choices about his/her health care. It originates from the legal and ethical right the patient has to direct what happens to her body and from the ethical duty of the physician to involve the patient in her health care. If the patient is impaired, which is often the case with elderly patients, this respect of self-determination is not considered lost; only its implementation during the decision-making process differs (Marsh, 1986). Due to the requirement of informed consent, the ethical obligations of fidelity and honesty have assumed new importance in the physician-patient relationship.

Coinciding with this shift toward the patient's right to self-determination in health care, there has also been a shift in societal attitudes and values regarding the right to health care. Until the 1960s, medical care was considered a privilege; however, due to the growing concern of the social problems caused by this disparity in health care, a new philosophy based on equity and cost containment has emerged. Due to this increased emphasis on justice and the coinciding efforts to eliminate barriers to health care, providers will continue to be confronted with new ethical dilemmas (Shuman and Bebeau, 1994).

In order to aid detection, it is necessary for providers to be aware of the many types of elder abuse. Three overarching categories of elder abuse are: physical abuse (includes neglect), financial abuse, and psychological abuse. A less common category of abuse is the violation of rights, also referred to as social abuse (Lau and Kosberg, 1979; Valentine and Cash, 1986).

Social abuse is the denial of a senior's fundamental rights; the same rights afforded to all citizens under state and federal law (such as the Bill of Rights, and in health care, the Patient Bill of Rights). This can include ignoring an elderly person's right and capability to make their own decisions, especially about private matters such as health care or living arrangements. Other examples include withholding of information, denial of privacy, denial of visitors, restriction of liberty, or mail censorship.

No one has the right to deny the human rights of another person, including the rights of an elder, unless that person has agreed or is certifiably incompetent. When a person is denied their human rights, it not only affects their self esteem and confidence, but also affects their morale.

PREDOMINANT ETHICAL VALUES OF HEALTH CARE

Webster's Dictionary defines ethics as "a set of moral principles and values; the discipline dealing with what is good and bad and with moral duty and obligation." Definitions of ethics and elder abuse vary among cultures, subcultures, political jurisdictions, and even among members of the same professional discipline. Each looks to ethics as a means of preserving and protecting older adults' rights. When viewed this way, ethics is a part of every aspect of life whether personal or professional (Johnson, 1995).

Ethical conduct is based on values—words or phrases that signal what one "ought to do or be." The predominant principles of medical ethics that providers value are the same ethics that come into play with elder abuse. These main ethical principles are: (1) nonmaleficence, which is encapsulated in the Hippocratic Oath as "do no harm"; (2) beneficence, which implies a duty to promote the patient's welfare; (3) justice, which means ensuring that all individuals have an opportunity for health equal insofar as possible to the health of others; (4) autonomy, meaning that we respect one another as autonomous beings that are free to make choices that do not violate other basic ethical requirements; (5) honesty, defined as integrity; sincerity; truthfulness; freedom from fraud or guile; (6) fidelity, the obligation to keep promises; and (7) respect for persons, which implies treating others with respect, dignity, and compassion insofar as this is compatible with the other basic principles to which individuals are bound (Beauchamp and Childress 1994; Cameron 1995; Jonsen, 2000; and Veatch, Bartels, and LeRoy, 2001).

Beneficence and Nonmaleficence

The principles of beneficence and nonmaleficence are the guiding ethical principles that require providers to intervene when elder abuse is occurring or predicted to occur. Providers are ethically bound to halt this behavior by recognizing the stress limits of the caregiver, educating the caregiver, performing a risk assessment, and if necessary, removing the victim from the harmful environment. (Benton and Marshall, 1991).

An ethical rule derived from the principle of beneficence is to remove harm, to prevent harm, and to provide benefits. Mandatory reporting laws attempt to satisfy the principle of beneficence by stopping elder abuse. Although, there is no evidence to show that these laws have stopped elder abuse, they have alerted health care professionals to the problem (Salend, Kane, and Satz, 1984).

Mandatory reporting statues are beneficent because they may help to prevent harm. These statutes may provide data that will illuminate the problem of elder abuse and thus justify funding for research. Once the issue of elder abuse is fully understood, effective programs can be developed to prevent its occurrence (Gilbert, 1986).

Lastly, the statutes are beneficent because the majority of states provide services to the reported victim. In fact, protective services have been defined as systems of preventive, supportive, and surrogate services for the elderly living in the community to enable them to maintain independent living to avoid abuse (Regan, 1978).

The principle of nonmaleficence includes the infliction of intentional and unintentional harm, as well as acts of commission and omission (Beauchamp and Childress, 1994). Statutes derived from nonmaleficence require that health care professionals do no harm intentionally or unintentionally by acting or by failing to act. The rationale for mandatory reporting statutes is to eliminate the possibility that health care professionals will permit continued infliction of harm on elders by failing to act unless required to do so.

Justice

The principle of justice ensures that all individuals have an opportunity for health that is equal, insofar as possible, to the health of others (Beauchamp and

Childress 1994; Cameron 1995; Jonsen, 2000; Veatch et al., 2001). Often, the distribution of various resources in society is governed by different philosophies: to each according to their need, their merit, or their "worth" to society; to each an equal share; or to each according to their contribution. Health care in the United States is a limited resource and is distributed to its citizens in a complicated manner governed by competing philosophies of justice.

As it applies to elder individuals, the principle of justice suggests that each elder has a right to expect an equal effort on his/her behalf. From a social perspective, elder justice means assuring adequate public-private infrastructure and resources to prevent, detect, treat, understand, intervene in and, where appropriate, prosecute elder abuse, neglect and exploitation. From an individual perspective, elder justice is the right of every older person to be free of abuse, neglect, and exploitation.

Just because a person has become older, may need medical care, or has lost the ability to live on his/her own, does not mean they have forfeited any of their rights as citizens – a point often lost on the abuser. The principle of justice demands that all citizens are entitled to and afforded the same rights, regardless of age, physical ability, and health. Abusers often diminish an elder's right to citizenship and rationalize abuse by the fact that the elder is no longer a full citizen because he/she requires assistance.

Autonomy

Autonomy is defined as self rule, and describes the principle that competent adults have the right to make decisions for themselves, as long as those decisions produce no serious harm to others. Autonomy emphasizes an individual's right to his/her own values, which may or may not be held by others. Autonomy applies to those who are deemed "competent" to exercise self determination and has some limitations for adults who are totally or partially "incompetent."

In the health care context, the principle of autonomy exists to protect an individual's right to accurate and complete information from which he or she can choose medical interventions. In the physician-patient relationship, this principle leads to the necessity of fully disclosing information to patients (the concept of informed consent). Without informed consent, patients cannot make fully informed choices.

Autonomy also leads to confidentiality issues. Patients have the right to determine to whom they want to disclose personal information. Providers have a role in helping patients with difficult decisions, but autonomy mandates that patients reserve for themselves the final decision-making authority.

Autonomy is a particularly sensitive issue to elders due to the potential risk of them losing the ability to choose for themselves; this could be due to, for example, the illnesses and/or weaknesses that sometimes accompany aging, or because of well-intentioned efforts of others to limit the activities of the elders. Autonomy is also important to elders because it is an important predictor of their subjective well-being and successful aging.

Honesty

Honesty, defined as integrity, sincerity, truthfulness, and freedom from fraud or guile, is a basic tenet of all codes of ethics. Common ethical values dictate that individuals are inclined to establish reputations for being honest and trustworthy. Nothing would jeopardize an individual's reputation more than fraudulent, deceptive, and dishonest practices.

Honesty becomes even more important as individuals age. Most elderly come from a generation where a handshake meant something, and honesty was a quality you could assume others upheld. Too often, the elderly are the victims of abuse due to their trusting nature. Proof of abuse preying on elders' trustfulness is supported by numerous news headlines about scams that target the elderly population.

Fidelity

Fidelity is defined as: the duty to keep promises; the duty to be true and loyal to others; faithfulness; loyalty or devotion. Individuals are social beings who engage in and pursue joint or common activities, in which they seek to realize common or individual goals. They require the respect, recognition or tolerance of others, and these individual acts can have an impact on others. Relationships among individuals can take the form of either domination, subordination, or reciprocity (Gould, 1983).

In the context of elder abuse, relationships between the elderly and the abuser take the form of subordination and domination—there is little or no reciprocity in the relationship. Wolf (1998) found that the nature of the relationship and interaction between the elder and the caregiver affected the probability of abuse. Relationships often become strained when the dependent person is perceived to be unappreciative, makes unreasonable demands, fails to help the caregiver, or tries to manipulate the caregiver (Wolf, 1998). Steinmetz (1998) found that abusive behavior by elders was not a reaction to the caregiver's abuse, but rather part of an ongoing, well-established method of behavior in the relationship. Unfortunately, abusive behavior by the elder has been noted to lead to an escalation of elder abuse by the caregiver (Pillemer, 1986).

Respect

Respect is defined as the polite attitude shown toward someone or something that you consider important. Respect recognizes the fact that all individuals have a place in the community, their voices must be heard, and the individual's free will must be honored. There is a normative boundary to respect within the scope of justice as solidarity which comes from the burden of reciprocity: "as one demands respect from other, so one ought to show respect for others" (Sturm, 1998).

In elder abuse, there is a loss of respect for the elder. The dynamics of the abuse are related to the abuser's need to gain and maintain control over the victim. The abuser demands respect, but does not show respect to the abused. Pillemer and Finkelhor (1988) state that victims are not dependent on the abuser for care – rather, the abusers are dependent on the victim. Many abusers are adult children still living at home, who rely on the resources of the parent. Many abusive husbands or male partners believe women are responsible for taking care of them and responding to their every desire. The abusers dependence may be financial, emotional or simply practical. Many victims of elder abuse are independent and not physically or cognitively impaired; they are older adults experiencing family abuse that is similar to abuse of young, battered spouses (Pillemer and Finkelhor, 1988). In these instances, there is a lack of respect for the needs and desires of the elderly person who is being abused.

ETHICAL ISSUES SURROUNDING ELDER ABUSE

It is critical that providers embrace these basic tenets of medical ethics and ensure that their patients receive ethical care. Although only four percent of elder abuse is perpetrated by health care professionals, most would agree that the basic ethical values of health care also apply to greater society. Thus, whether it is the health care provider or informal caregiver, the above ethical principles apply to elder abuse.

Table 1: Relationship Between Type of Abuse and Ethical Principles

Healthcare Value/Ethics Violated	Type of Elder Abuse			
	Physical Abuse	Psychological Abuse	Financial Abuse	Social Abuse
Beneficence	X	X	X	X
Nonmaleficence	X	X	X	X
Justice	X	X	X	X
Autonomy	X	X	X	X
Honesty			X	X
Fidelity	X	X	X	X
Respect for Persons	X	X	X	X

According to Benton and Marshall (1991), the type of abuse present often predicts the most applicable ethical principle. This is illustrated in the following cases and Table 1. Table 1 demonstrates the relationship between the four types of elder abuse and the ethical principles. Many of the same ethical principles are violated in each type of abuse as shown on the table and in the following cases.

The cases discussed in this chapter illustrate both potential and actual cases of elder abuse. The cases represent issues of physical, psychological, financial, and social abuse. The cases are intended to represent the types of mistreatment characterized by elder abuse that elders may encounter when interacting with both professionals and informal caregivers. Any similarity to actual cases is strictly coincidental.

Physical Abuse

John is an 82-year-old man who is morbidly obese and bedridden due to complications from a stroke; his stroke left him partially paralyzed on the right side of his body and he has diminished speech and motor functions. After, recuperating from his stroke, John attempted to live independently with a home health aid checking in daily on him; however, due to a co-morbid condition of diabetes, John languished at home alone, rarely left his bed, never bathed, erratically took his medications and continued to gain weight. The once-a-day visits from the home health aid were not enough. Additionally, due to his inactivity and diabetes, John developed severe ulcers on both of his lower legs and was admitted to the hospital for care. As a result of this self-neglect, both of his legs required below-knee amputations.

After recovery from his double amputation, John was released to the custody of his daughter, Susan, whom he depends on for his care. John is now completely non-ambulatory and cannot move from his bed to his wheelchair without assistance. John has severely impaired speech, thus communication for him can be challenging. Susan works full-time at home and feels obligated to take care of her father.

Initially, Susan was devoted to the care of her father; however, after several months, she has grown frustrated and resentful of this burden. Susan is unwilling to admit that she is incapable of caring for her father, which adds to her feelings of frustration. As a result, John often remains in his room for days at a time. Susan frequently verbally assaults John for being a burden and calls him demeaning names while caring for him. John's decreased verbal ability further frustrates his daughter and the verbal insults often turn into physical abuse when Susan is overwhelmed by her responsibility of caring for her father. Susan's latest attack has left John with two fractured ribs, as well as several cuts and bruises. Additionally, continued neglect with regard to care has led to John developing more ulcers, similar to those that led to his amputations.

A home health care nurse is called in to assess John's ulcers and provide wound care. During the visit, the nurse notices that John is very withdrawn and depressed. Upon physical examination, John's fractured ribs, cuts, and bruises are uncovered. John is quick to tell the home health care nurse that he felt dizzy one day and fell out bed when trying to get into his wheelchair. He asked the nurse not to address these concerns with his daughter because he does not want to burden her with his additional health problems. The nurse, however, suspects the truth – that the daughter is physically abusing her father.

What John does not reveal to the nurse is that he is afraid of his daughter and is embarrassed by this, yet he does not want to live the rest of his life in a nursing home, a consequence that would surely happen if the abuse were identified.

This case provides an example of both self neglect, initially, and then physical abuse of the elderly. John's self-neglect while living alone led to his need for supervised care. While receiving supervised care, John was physically abused and neglected by his caregiver, his daughter Susan.

Physically abused elderly may feel ashamed about the abuse. They may believe that providers cannot or do not want to help, but at the same time, they may feel protective of their partner, family member, or friend who is doing the abusing. Or they may fear that telling about the abuse will put them at risk for more violence. In this case, John meets most of these criteria. He is embarrassed by the act, protective of his daughter, and fearful that the abuse will get worse if he allows it to be reported.

Factors that may prevent providers from asking elderly clients about physical abuse include a lack of awareness of the prevalence of elder abuse, a belief that identifying and intervening in physical abuse cases is not part of the provider's role, discomfort with the feelings evoked by hearing about elder abuse, concern about the time involved in asking about and dealing with abuse if uncovered, and feeling helpless or not knowing how to intervene.

The ethical principles of beneficence and nonmaleficence require those who are knowledgeable of the abuse to report it, thereby, removing or preventing harm and providing benefits. In this case, the nurse has conflicting responsibilities: (1) report the abuse and work to have John removed from the abusive setting, or (2) do not report the abuse and respect the confidentiality and wishes of the patient/abused elder.

While most agree in principle that a patient's wishes come before the organization's or provider's desires, providers often confuse what is good for the patient with what the provider believes is good for the patient. At debate is what constitutes good for a patient without infringing on the patient's autonomy or letting the patient come to serious harm. Is it ethical to overrule your patients' preferences?

On the surface, these requirements to notify authorities regarding suspected elder abuse seem to be an innocuous attempt at identifying abuse; however, some observers have criticized such attempts as an ageist response to the problem. These critics contend that older adults who are victims of family violence should have the same rights of younger adults to refuse referral to an investigative agency. Mandatory reporting laws for elder abuse are similar to child abuse statutes and are based on the state's *parens patriae* to protect persons who cannot or will not protect themselves (Aravantis et al., 1993).

Due to the aforementioned issues, mandatory reporting laws can create difficult ethical dilemmas. On one hand, providers are bound by oaths to maintain the confidentiality of the provider-patient relationship, but may be required to violate that trust to comply with state laws. When faced with such a dilemma where clear historical or physical evidence of abuse or neglect is present, but a competent patient requests that a report not be made, how should the provider respond? In such situation, the provider should explain to the patient that he/she is obligated by law to report suspected abuse and strive to maintain a positive provider-patient relationship, while keeping in mind the medical necessity for intervention. (Aravantis et al., 1993). The provider is not only bound by the duty to the victim to report suspected abuse, but also the ethical duty to protect other potential victims.

The underlying rationale for reporting abuse stems from the desire to stop abuse and secure access to help in the form of outside resources, not from the desire to punish the individual and/or his/her family (Aravantis et al., 1993) or from the need of the provider to exert a controlling or paternalistic attitude. However, when faced with dilemmas such as these, providers often cannot help but wield a degree of paternalism, albeit weak or strong, intentionally or unintentionally, in their reporting decisions. According to Beauchamp and Childress (1994), "weak" paternalism implies that the health care provider is protecting the patient when the patient is unable to make decisions due to medical or emotional problems. On the other hand, "Strong paternalism... involves interactions intended to benefit a person despite the fact that the person's risky choices and actions are informed, voluntary, and autonomous" (Beauchamp and Childress, 1994). Further complicating matters may be differences in state regulations as to what constitutes impairment, thus presenting new ethical dilemmas for providers when caring for patients with impaired decision-making.

The principles of beneficence and nonmaleficence also apply to the daughter, even though she is an informal caregiver. The role of caregiver implies that one will provide care with the intent of helping or healing, and protecting one from harm or abuse. The daughter clearly violates this social contract and the principles of beneficence and nonmaleficence when she physically abuses her father and allows his physical condition to deteriorate.

Furthermore, the daughter violates the ethical principle of fidelity, because acceptance of the role as caregiver, binds the daughter to provide care and comfort to her father. The daughter unmistakably does not uphold this ethical principle, when she crosses the line and lashes out in anger and physically strikes him.

Justice is the right of every person to be free from abuse, neglect, and exploitation. Also implied in the ethical principle of justice is freedom from alienation, which is frequently a byproduct of elder abuse. Alienation is an integral part of elder abuse because much of the mistreatment of elders occurs in the family setting and thus, the elderly person is often simultaneously embarrassed by the abuse, fearful of future mistreatment, and paradoxically protective of the abuser (Moskowitz, 2001). Much of this abuse occurs primarily in private residences, such as in the preceding case, against persons who have limited contact with outsiders (Moskowitz, 2001) and to people who are isolated from the community, therefore compounding their alienation from society (Pillemer and Finkelhor, 1988).

Providers are often confronted with the ethical dilemmas of: (1) the patient's right to choose the extent of harm or the level of abuse in a particular environment or situation; and (2) the right to decide on a placement decision that appears hazardous from the provider's perspective. Autonomy requires people to respect the self-determination of others and to cease from constraining others' self-governing actions and choices (Beauchamp and Childress, 1994). Rules derived from the principle of autonomy are to act only with consent and to protect confidentiality. Herein lies the problem; the principle is often not applicable to elders because they may not be in a position to act autonomously due to incompetence. Many of the mandatory reporting laws require that the consent of the abused person be obtained; however, many elders refuse to consent due to shame, fear of reprisal, guilt, and fear of institutionalization. Thus, when the principle of autonomy and mandatory reporting statutes interact, ethical dilemmas often arise.

The principle of autonomy is central to the case involving John. Is John competent enough to make the decision to remain in this abusive environment? Should the nurse report the suspected abuse by Susan to the authorities? If the abuse is reported, is John's right of self-determination being violated?

Another area of elder abuse that is ripe with ethical dilemmas involving autonomy is that of self-neglect. The phenomenon of self-neglect is subject to the imposition of the observer's values, thus damaging the self-determination of the individual. Given the fact that older adults are ethically entitled to refuse treatment, even if such a refusal results in death, they are equally entitled to make less life-threatening choices regarding other parts of their lives, including personal habits such as eating, grooming, dress, and other lifestyle choices (Katz, 1980). Similarly, an older adult is entitled to subject himself/herself to a hazard that many would not legitimately choose. Thus, the grounds for not obtaining consent from older or self-neglected adults are tenuous (Gilbert, 1986).

In the preceding case, John initially developed bed sores as a result of improper care attributed to self-neglect. As a result of this self-neglect, medical action was taken, and he was placed with his daughter for supervision and care. John's self-neglect continues as more bed sores develop. Should John's autonomy be challenged by the nurse due to his continued self-neglect, or should John be able to continue with this detrimental lifestyle?

Confidentiality is equally questionable when considering autonomy and mandatory reporting statutes. Because people have the duty to respect the self-determination of others, it follows that others have the right to privacy about their actions and unauthorized reporting (Beauchamp and Childress, 1984). By definition, all mandatory elderly abuse reporting statutes involve making information known outside the provider-patient relationship, thus opening a host of ethical conflicts. The provider must balance the self-determination of older adults and adherence to the mandatory reporting requirements of elder abuse statutes.

In the foregoing case, confidentiality comes into play as John's right to confidentiality regarding his personal life is challenged by the provider duty to report the suspected abuse. Which ethical principle has priority – confidentiality or the right to self determination? Is John competent to make his own decision about his environment and maintain the right of self-determination?

Brandi (2000) states that some caregivers or family members hurt older people to exert power and control. Many abusers harm older people to get their own needs met, believing they are entitled to use any means necessary to achieve their goals. Respect for the needs of the elderly person who is being abused is non-existent. In this case, Susan is exerting control over the situation that she is frustrated with by physically abusing her father when he does not act in a manner acceptable to her.

Psychological Abuse

Sam was a 78-year-old man with Alzheimer's disease who recently had been admitted to a nursing home. Although, he was confused, there were also times when he seemed lucid. Because of his Alzheimer's disease, Sam often soiled the bed during the night, at which time he would use his call button to summon help from a certified nursing assistant (CNA).

Marie, a CNA on the midnight shift, was responsible for caring for Sam, as well as 23 other residents. Marie also worked part-time at a retail store during the day in order to support her three small children. Most of the residents under her care slept through the night, except for Sam.

When Marie first started working at the nursing home, she was very attentive and caring towards her residents; however, as time wore on, she became verbally abusive to the residents that she labeled as "trouble-makers."

Sam was one of her "trouble-makers." When he would soil himself and ring his call bell, she would make him wait 15-20 minutes before she would respond. She would then chastise and taunt him with statements such as, "What are you, a baby?" "Even my babies are toilet-trained. You must be stupid" and "I'm not your mama or your babysitter. Use the toilet like a grown man should." She would then threaten him by telling him that if he kept doing this, she wouldn't change his soiled clothes and he could stay that way till morning.

On other occasions, Sam would cry during the night because he was scared and confused. Marie continually berated Sam for being a baby and causing her extra work. As his crying was waking up the other residents, she threatened him with physical violence if he continued to act out, stating "I'll give you something to cry about!"

Marie continued to verbally abuse Sam every night. Because it was known that Sam had no family that regularly visited and that he had Alzheimer's Disease, Marie justified his complaints of psychological abuse to her supervisor as an episodes of dementia.

This case shares many of the same ethical principles and dilemmas that are present in the case of John and Susan. The characteristics of physical and psychological abuse and the underlying ethical principles are similar. The principles of nonmaleficence, beneficence, justice, autonomy, fidelity, respect for persons are present; thus, the similar ethical dilemmas exist.

It can be argued that the abuse in the preceding case is less acceptable because it is being perpetrated by a health care provider. Most health care providers abide by professional codes of ethics that denounce such abusive behavior and all such actions that unintentionally or intentionally harm patients. Health care providers are entrusted with the health and well being of their patients, thus they have a higher moral duty than informal caregivers to uphold this obligation.

The integrity in the relationship between Sam and Marie in the previous example has deteriorated to the point of disaster. The caregiver burden model suggests that abuse occurs because caring for the victim is too difficult and blames the victims for being too needy, thereby, relieving the perpetrator of the responsibility for abusive behavior (Brandi, 2000). Elder abuse victims are frequently given the message that if they would just try harder, the abuse would stop, but abusers often change the rules and find new faults that continue the battering. In the preceding case, Marie initially chastises Sam for his incontinence; however, she then criticizes him regarding his episodes of crying, adding a new rule for Sam to violate and, thus, continuing the cycle of abuse.

Only abusers can take responsibility for their actions and therefore end the abuse cycle (Brandi, 2000). Most abusers do not lose control when they abuse another; they choose how and when to respond in anger. They respond when it is most beneficial to them (Brandi, 2000). As a result of the pressures in

Marie's personal and professional life, the duty to care for Sam and her other patients has become too much. Although it appears that Marie is not in control of her emotions, she clearly chooses to target Sam because of his dementia, knowing that if the abuse were brought to the attention of others, it could easily be discounted.

Financial Abuse

Mary and her adult son, Bart, live in the same small house that he grew up in. Mary has been widowed for over twenty years and enjoys the company of her son, especially since her other three kids live out of state. Bart is physically impaired due to a childhood episode of polio and relies on his mother for care and financial support. Bart previously worked as a dispatcher for the local sheriff's department, but received a medical discharge when his condition worsened. The small stipend that he receives each month from social security/Medicaid is not enough for him to live independently. Mother and son have lived together for the past fifteen years and enjoy the symbiotic relationship. Mary is fulfilled because she has a purpose in life, to care for Bart; Bart is well-taken care of by Mary, is financially secure, and assists his mother by driving her on her errands.

As time progresses, Mary grows older and her physical and mental health deteriorates. At one point, Mary is hospitalized with pneumonia. While in the hospital, Mary attempts to walk to the bathroom without assistance and suffers a fall due to low energy levels. A hip replacement surgery is performed and eventually Mary is discharged to a nursing home for rehabilitation therapy until she fully recovers. Mary seems to be progressing well physically; however, she suffers from frequent bouts of dementia and associated memory lapses.

Meanwhile, Bart is worried about his financial future. Without his mother's social security check, he is unable to maintain the household. Bart visits his mother in the nursing home to see when she will be able to return home and is advised by the facility's medical director that, due to her hip therapy and the need for personal hygiene care, it is best that Mary stay in the nursing home for an undetermined amount of time.

Unable to live without his mother's financial resources, Bart convinces his mother to appoint him as her Power of Attorney in case her mental capacity further deteriorates, putting him in charge of her property and finances. Mary is reluctant, but concedes when Bart promises that he will consult her regarding any financial decisions that arise. The Power of Attorney status allows Bart to sign the deed to the house over to himself, as well as access to his mother's savings account; therefore, securing his financial future. Bart continues to drain Mary's financial savings in order to finance his lifestyle, without consulting his mother.

Several weeks pass and Mary's physical condition has improved; however, her mental state has declined and she need's increased assistance with her activities of daily living. Meanwhile, finances are tight for Bart and he decides to remove her from the nursing home in order to receive her social security check. He signs her out against medical advice.

Concerned with his mother's health, Mary's oldest son Dan visits to survey the situation. Dan finds that the house is messy and unkempt, his mother is bed-ridden, and she has developed bed sores which require immediate medical attention. Dan is upset with his brother for taking advantage of his mother, and feels that she should be readmitted to the nursing home until she is able to take care of herself. Despite Dan's urging to return to a skilled nursing facility, Mary defends her son Bart and says that he is doing the best he can and that she loves him.

Financial abuse is similar to other forms of abuse in that it can be devastating to the victim and is frequently traced to family members, trusted friends, and caregivers. But unlike the other forms of abuse, financial abuse is often done with the tacit knowledge and consent of the elder and can be more difficult to detect and establish (NEAIS, 1999).

Financial abuse occurs when a caregiver or elder misuses money, property, or possessions, as illustrated in the case above, or blocks access to these material goods. Frequently, in the case of financial abuse, the abuser is a spouse, family member (often adult child), caregiver, friend, or a trusted person in the elder's life. Financial abuse is often associated with the other forms of elder abuse, such as emotional abuse, physical abuse, and the denial of rights. In the above scenario, the live-in son Bart engages in financial as well as physical abuse. By preventing / withholding needed medical care, he is indirectly physically abusing his mother.

Financial abuse is also characterized by abrupt changes in a will or other financial documents and the unexplained sudden transfer of assets to a family member or someone outside the family. In the above case, Bart exerts his power and exploits their close relationship when he coerces his mother into signing the Power of Attorney. Bart seizes Mary's financial assets by preying on his mother's emotional and mental instability. Thus, financial abuse is closely related to psychological abuse.

Bart violates the principles of beneficence and nonmaleficence that are implicit in a custodial relationship of caregiver and patient, not to mention violation of trust between a parent and child. Due to Bart's actions to seize his mother's assets, he further violates the principle of nonmaleficence by infringing on his sibling's potential right to these same assets.

In issues involving financial exploitation, an individual's justice, or what they perceive to be their justice, may be violated. In the preceding case, Mary's justice is violated because her right to proper health care is denied by her son's actions. Justice also provides that persons should be free from exploitation, abuse, and neglect. Bart's manipulative and exploitive actions towards his mother are clear examples of the violation of the principle of justice.

Furthermore, Bart violates his mother's autonomy over her personal assets by coercing her to assign Power of Attorney to him. By virtue of the fact that he now controls his mother's estate, he has denied her the ability to make decisions about her financial future and severely limiting her fight to self-determination.

Honesty is also an ethical value that is breached because Bart fails to communicate with his siblings regarding his mother's finances and care. He also is dishonest in his actions to control his mother's assets when he convinces his mother that the motive for his action is based on her mental wellbeing and he will consult with her prior to making any financial decisions.

Bart also violates the tenets of fidelity and respect for person by way of his actions. As caretaker of his mother and her financial assets, he ought to do what is in his mother's best interest. Clearly, Bart's actions to seize Power of Attorney and remove her from the nursing home can only be construed as self-serving.

Social Abuse

Walter, age 78, was a successful businessman in the community in which he lived. Walter was always active in local politics, church and community affairs. Walter was married to his wife Sandy for forty years and had one son, who struggled to find a career. Walter reluctantly retired at age 70 at the urging of his wife and sold his insurance company due to a bout with prostate cancer. The couple had always dreamed of traveling extensively when Walter retired. Unfortunately, shortly after recovering from prostate cancer, Sandy was diagnosed with ALS. After a tough, but losing battle, Sandy died, leaving Walter alone.

Although, Walter was a successful businessman, he always relied on his wife for many of the household chores. Walter attempted to live by himself; however, was unable to live independently and cope with the daily responsibilities of caring for himself and his house. His son hired a housekeeper to take care of household affairs; however, this solution was short lived, as Walter was often combative due to the early stages of Alzheimer's disease.

Walter's son, Andrew, moved home after a failed marriage to take care of his father. Walter moved into the basement suite in order to accommodate his son. Shortly after moving in, Andrew had the phone disconnected, so that his father would not be "disturbed" by friends calling to see how he was doing. Andrew had cellular phone service with an unlisted number that he purposely kept hidden away from his father. He would not allow his father to use the telephone.

Despite the early stages of Alzheimer's disease, Walter was mostly alert, lucid, and mentally capable of handling social affairs. Andrew started laying the groundwork for his father's mental incapacity. When family, friends, and neighbors stopped by to visit, Andrew would turn them away saying that his father wasn't seeing anyone due to his poor health. Andrew further isolated Walter from society by no longer taking Walter to church, selling his father's car, and destroying any personal correspondence that came in the mail. He also gave away most of his father's personal belongings (books, family photo albums, and golf clubs) to the local Goodwill, telling his father that he wasn't capable of using them anymore. Andrew told his father's friends that his father had destroyed these possessions in a fit of anger, often associated with advanced stages of Alzheimer's. Andrew also told visitors that he may have to seek legal counsel to become his father's legal guardian to more effectively take care of his father.

Andrew told his father that in his present mental condition he was lucky to have someone help him at all. Andrew would often yell and treat his father roughly when Walter would not do what he was told. Concerned about Walter's withdrawal from society and his son's excuses for why family and friends could not visit, his friend Joe contacted Adult Protective Services. A social worker investigated the situation and was only allowed entrance into the home after threatening to seek a court order. Walter appeared frail, depressed, and malnourished; however, refused help from the social worker. When pressed further, Walter admitted to the social worker that Andrew often yelled at him and denied him from seeing his friends. Despite these feelings of resentment, Walter defended his son saying that Andrew was under a great deal of stress due to his recent divorce. Walter felt badly that his son had to take care of him and that it was not right for a child to have to take care of their parents.

A psychiatric evaluation was ordered and it was deemed that Walter had the mental capacity to understand the situation he was in and able to make informed decisions, and was mildly depressed; however, Walter did not require treatment. Despite the fact that Walter often felt like a prisoner in his own home and became depressed at his current lifestyle, he felt obligated to his son and he felt that his role as a father took precedence over concerns for his own personal safety and happiness. Walter was offered the option of moving into an assisted living facility; however, Walter decided to stay at home with his son as his caregiver.

The case of Walter and Andrew is not uncommon. Like the preceding cases, the ethical issues in this case of social abuse include beneficence, nonmaleficence, justice, autonomy, justice, honesty, fidelity, and respect for persons.

Victims of elder abuse often choose to stay in abusive environments, even when offered less abusive environments. The principles of beneficence and nonmaleficence call for the removal and/or prevention of harm. The abuse reporting laws that most states have in place were developed with these principles in mind. Therefore, an obvious response to our case example would be for the social worker who visited Walter and Andrew to report the activities she suspected as abusive, and question Walter's competency by his desire to stay in the abusive environment. This would most likely result in the placement of Walter in an assisted living facility, an option he refused when offered due to his belief about familial responsibilities. Would more harm be done to Walter by forcing him to move against his will and reporting Andrew or by letting him remain in an abusive environment?

While in some states abuse reporting laws may support the right of others to intercede on behalf of those who are victims of abuse, issues with regard to justice may surface. The resources to prevent, detect, treat, understand, intervene in and, where appropriate, prosecute elder abuse, neglect, and exploitation, may be limited.

When victims of elder abuse exercise their right of autonomy in ways that seem reasonable to others, their choices are seldom questioned. However, when the victim makes a choice to remain in an abusive environment, such as in the above case, the ethical dilemma of the individual's right to choose versus society's obligation to protect is broached. As adults, the elderly have the right not to report any actions taken against them. The elder is the only one who can determine the limits of behavior that are acceptable for him or her and give permission for intervention. However, reporting laws in most states require reporting of physical and other forms of abuse based on suspicion, rather than tangible knowledge of the abuse.

The ethical mainstay of honesty is obviously violated by the abuser, Andrew, many times throughout the case. Andrew was dishonest with his father and violated the trust his father had bestowed on him when allowing him to move in and look out for his father's best interests. Andrew was dishonest with his father's friends and visitors about his father's health and mental status.

The implied new relationship between Walter and Andrew is one in which Andrew was supposed to care for Walter and, in return, Andrew was allowed to move into Walter's home after his divorce. Fidelity requires one to do what he or she has promised to do. Andrew blatantly disregards this ethical principle when he does not uphold his promise and, instead, exerts his power to the benefit of himself, disregarding the social, psychological, and health needs of his father.

In this case, and in elder abuse in general, there is a loss of respect for the elder. The dynamics of the abuse are related to the abuser's need to gain and maintain control over the victim. Andrew illustrates this through his disconnecting Walter's phone, his isolation of Walter from the friends and family that came to visit, and his selling of Walter's possessions without permission. In these instances, there is a lack of respect by Andrew for the needs and desires of Walter, and Andrew utilizes these methods to keep Walter from seeking help.

Many of the issues in the four types of elder abuse are similar. In each case illustrated in this chapter, there may be one prevalent ethical issue, such as autonomy, but it is not mutually exclusive of the other ethical issues. When the principle of autonomy is violated, beneficence and nonmaleficence are violated as well. In the same vein, when discussing the types of abuse, rarely do the different types occur in isolated instances; often, when physical abuse occurs, psychological abuse occurs as well.

Understanding the underlying ethical issues surrounding elder abuse will enable health care providers and informal caregivers to better recognize how abuse violates ethical principles. This knowledge will provide them with the ability to intervene, when they or someone else crosses the line, in order to protect the rights of the elderly.

REFERENCES

American Medical Association (AMA). (1990). White Paper on Elderly Health: Report of the Council on Scientific Affairs. *Archives of Internal Medicine*, 150: 2459-2472.

Aravantis, S. C., Adelman, R. D., Breckman, R., Fulmer, T. T., Holder, E., Lachs, M. O'Brien, J. G., and Sanders, A. B. (1993) Diagnostic and Treatment Guidelines on Elder Abuse and Neglect. *Archives of Family Medicine*, 2(4): 371-388

Beauchamp T. L. and Childress, J. F. (1994). *Principles of Biomedical Ethics, 4th ed*. New York: Oxford University Press.

Benton, D. and Marshall, C. (1991). Elder Abuse. *Geriatric Home Care*, 7(4), pp. 831-845.

Brandi, B. (2000). Power and Control: Understanding Domestic Abuse in Later Life. *Generations*, 24(2), 39-45.

Cameron, N. M., (1995). The Christian Stake in Bioethics: the State of the Question. In J.F. Kilner, N. M. Cameron, and D. L. Schiedermayer (Eds.), *Bioethics and the Future of Medicine: A Christian appraisal* (pp. 3-13). Grand Rapids, MI: William B. Eerdsmans Publishing Company.

Gilbert, D. A. (1986). The Ethics of Mandatory Elder Abuse Reporting Statutes. *Advances in Nursing Science*, 8(2), 51-62.

Gould, C. (1983). Private Rights and Public Virtues: Women and Democracy. In Carol C. Gould, ed., *Beyond Domination: New Perspectives on Women and Philosophy*. Totowa, NJ: Rowman and Allanheld

Johnson, T.F. (1995). Ethics and Elder Mistreatment: Uniting Protocol with Practice. *Journal of Elder Abuse and Neglect*, 7(2-3).

Johnson, T.F. (1986). Critical Issues in the Definition of Elder Mistreatment. In Pillemer, K.A. and Wolf, S. (eds): *Elder Abuse: Conflict in the Family*. Dover, Auburn House Publishing, 1986, 167.

Jonsen, A. R. (2000). *A Short History of Medical Ethics*. New York: Oxford University Press.

Katz, K. D. (1980). Elder Abuse. *Journal of Family Law*, 18: 695-722.

Lau, E. E. and Kosberg, J. I. (1979) Abuse of the Elderly by Informal Caregivers. *Aging* 299(10).

Marsh, F. H. (1986). Refusal of Treatment. *Clinical Geriatric Medicine* 2:511.

Moskowitz, S. 2003. Golden Age in the Golden State: Contemporary Legal Developments in Elder Abuse and Neglect. *Loyola Law Review.* 35(2). 589-666.

Moskowitz, S. 2001. Reflecting Reality: Adding Elder Abuse and Neglect to Legal Education. *Loyola Law Review,* 47(1). 191-229.

NEAIS. (1999) United States Department of Health and Human Services. *The National Elder Abuse Incidence Study.* Retrieved September 29, 2003, from http://www.aoa.gov/eldfam/Elder_Rights/Elder_Abuse/ABuseReport_Full.pdf

Pillemer, K. 1986. Risk Factors in Elder Abuse: Results From A Case-Control Study. In Karl Pillemer and Rosalie Wolf, Eds, *Elder Abuse Conflict in the Family.* Chapter 10, 239-263, Dover, MA: Auburn House Publishing Company.

Pillemer, K. and Finkelhor, D. (1988). The Prevalence of Elder Abuse: A Random Sample Survey. *Gerontologist,* 28(51): 51-57.

Quinn M.J., and Tomita, S.K. (1997). *Elder Abuse and Neglect: Causes, Diagnosis, and Intervention Strategies.* New York, Springer Publishing, 1986.

Regan, J. J. (1978). Intervention Through Adult Protective Services Programs. *Gerontologist,* 18: 250-254.

Salend, E., Kane, R. A., and Satz, F. M. (1984). Elder Abuse Reporting: Limitations of Statutes. *Gerontologist,* 24(10), 61-69.

Shuman, S. K. and Bebeau, M. J. (1994). Ethical and Legal Issues in Special Patient Care. *Dental Clinics of North America,* 38(3).

Steinmetz, S. (1988). *Dutybound: Elder Abuse and Family Care.* Newbury Park, CA: Sage Pubications.

Sturm, D. (1998). *Solidarity and Suffering: Toward a Politics of Relationality.* Albany, NY: State University of New York Press.

Valentine, D. and Cash T. (1986). A Definitional Discussion of Elder Maltreatment. *Journal of Gerontology,* 9(3):17.

Veatch, P.M., Bartels, D.M., and LeRoy, B.S. (2001, April). Ethical and Professional Challenges Posed by Patients with Genetic Concerns: A Report of Focus Group Discussions with Genetic Counselors, Physicians, and Nurses. *Journal of Genetic Counseling* 10(2): 97-119.

Wolf, R. (1998). Caregiver Stress, Alzheimer's Disease and Elder Abuse. *American Journal of Alzheimer's Disease.* 13(2), 81-83

8

HIDDEN WITHIN THE GOLDEN YEARS: INTIMATE PARTNER VIOLENCE AND ABUSE AGAINST OLDER WOMEN

Bonnie Fisher, Therese Zink, and Saundra Regan

Mrs. S is 68 years old. She married right after graduation from college and quickly became a stay-at-home mother. From the beginning of their marriage and throughout their marriage, her husband made all the decisions–where they would live, what car they would buy, where she could go, whom she could see, how much money she could spend, and even what clothes she wore and how she cut her hair.

Mr. S was a successful executive who was very active in the community and church. He was handsome, charming, kind, and well respected by everyone. Then he would come home. Mr. S has hit, kicked, slapped, and choked Mrs. S. He called her insulting names, told her she was ugly and fat and that no one would ever want her if he ever left her.

Early in her marriage, she attempted to leave him. Her mother told her that her place was with her husband. How would she ever raise five children on her own? Her doctor said that sometimes men are just like that and she needed to be patient and try to ignore his behavior. Her minister told her that God believed her place was with her husband and children because that is what a good wife does. She would certainly be rewarded in heaven.

Mr. S is retired now. He has developed a heart condition. Mrs. S has diabetes and arthritis, which makes it difficult for her to move around. The children are grown and gone and it is just the two of them. The physical violence stopped several years ago but the verbal abuse and control still occurs on almost a daily basis.

Mrs. S questions what would happen if she left him now? Being alone is terrifying to her as she does not drive and has no money of her own. Their children are adults with their own families. Who would take care of him she wonders? With no satisfactory answers, she decides to stay with him.

Mrs. S is not a fictional character. You may know her. She is an older married woman who lives next door or down the block. If you do not personally know her, you may have seen her as she shops at the neighborhood stores and routinely attends religious services. You may not know her by name but Mrs. S's story is a compilation of common themes that run throughout the stories of older women who have experienced and continue to experience intimate partner violence and abuse[1] (IPVA) (Fisher, Zink, Rinto et al., 2003).

Mrs. S is similar to almost all women born before World War II who were socialized primarily into domestic roles. When they did work outside the home, they were often limited to low-paying occupations. This often resulted in financial and social dependence on their husbands. In addition, powerful cultural and social norms existed (and in some places, still exist today) about the privacy of what took place within the home. Her abusive and violent experiences are most likely hidden from the society and, most notably, have generally been overlooked by "natural" advocates, including the domestic violence[2] (DV) and aging communities.

There are a variety of reasons for their collective oversight of IPVA against older women. First, Vinton (2003) attributes this oversight to several "isms in our society:" ageism, sexism, beautyism, and sometimes racism and classism. She argues that convergence of these multiple "isms" of oppression have largely made older women invisible to the general public. Second, within the DV community, the primary service and program emphasis has been on the needs of younger battered women, especially those with children. For example, the shelter movement, which began in the late 1970s, was a grassroots effort led by feminists to provide safe havens for women and their children away from their abusers. Even the DV research community prior to 1990 rarely mentioned the experiences and needs of older battered women (Vinton, 2003). Third, within the aging community, elder abuse advocates have historically not focused on older women's experiences with violence by intimates but have rather focused on elder abuse and neglect by caregivers or self-neglect.

The scant research, advocacy and practitioner materials addressing IPVA against older women are disturbing when one considers the importance of violence and abuse, and in particular acts committed by spouses/partners, against women as a national problem that was acknowledged by Congress

---

[1]We adopted the phrase "violence and abuse against women" as per the U.S. Department of Health and Human Services (2000) suggestion that it become the standard phrase used in research and practice. In this chapter, we will use the term to refer to the combination of all five of the following major components of a range of maltreatment against women: 1) physical violence, 2) sexual violence, 3) threats of physical and/or sexual violence, 4) stalking, and 5) psychological/emotional abuse (U.S. Department of Health and Human Services, 2000, pgs. 6-7).

[2]Domestic violence is a broad term that can include any family member such as a spouse, child, cousin, or non family member that is an intimate partner (male or female).

and President Clinton in the passage of the Violence Against Women Act in 1994 and 1998 (VAWA) (*Thomas: Legislative information on the internet,* 2003). The VAWA goals coupled with recent Census counts that show that older persons, in particular women, are plentiful makes the lack of attention given to older women even more disturbing. The number of older people in the U.S. has continued to increase rapidly. There are now approximately 56 million people age 55 and over, with almost 31 million of them being women (US Census Bureau, 2001). This number will continue to increase substantially over the next 10 years as the baby boomers move into these older age categories. The baby boom cohort aged 36 to 54 in the 2000 census make up 28% of the U.S. population and the age category 50 – 54 was the fastest growing segment of the population with an increase of 55% in the last decade (US Census Bureau, 2001). There is no denying that a substantial proportion of North Americans are aging!

Possibly heightened by the realization that in the coming decade there will be a dramatic increase in the number of older women, there are some signs that both the aging and DV communities' attention may be turning to issues concerning older women and IPVA. In the early1990's the American Association of Retired Persons (AARP) Women's Initiative held a special forum that focused on the differences between abused elders and older battered women (AARP, 1992). During this forum, participants acknowledged that elder abuse and DV of older women were two very different areas in definition and in the scope of service provision. Among the recommendations was to identify the types of violence so that prevention and service strategies could be tailored to the type of violence. Throughout the 1990s a small group of vigilant advocates and researchers across several disciplines were persistent in their efforts to document the experiences of older battered women. Their results stimulated the development and implementation of innovative programs and services tailored to the needs of these women (Brandl and Raymond, 1997; Seaver, 1996; Tatara, 1993; Vinton, Altholz, and Thea, 1997). Efforts have continued into the next century, but still only a handful of publications concerning IPVA against older women exist in comparison to the numerous publications that examine violence against all women, and more salient to our interests, DV against older women (Brandl and Cook-Daniels, 2002; Fisher, Zink, Rinto et al., 2003).

More fully understanding IPVA against older women is one step toward educating interested parties as to its scope. The next step is to address the specific needs of these older women and prevention of such acts. In the first section of this chapter, we highlight what is known about the extent and nature of IPVA against older women from a variety of sources, including older women telling their stories of violence and abuse. Also included is a discussion of methodological limitations inherent in this young field of research. The first section provides a backdrop for the second section that addresses the lack of preparedness by those most likely to serve older women who are experiencing IPVA, their physicians and domestic violence shelters. In the last section, a discussion of future directions is presented. Here, three important points are discussed for researchers, advocates and practitioners from both the aging and domestic violence fields to develop into an agenda for action.

VIOLENCE AGAINST OLDER WOMEN

Available data from various sources suggest that violence and abuse against women are substantial public health and criminal justice problems (Rennison, 2001; Tjaden and Thoennes, 1998a; US Department of Health and Human Services, 2000). For example, across every victim age category for age 12 and over, females were more likely than males to be murdered by an intimate partner in 1999. In fact, intimate partners murdered 1,218 women during 1999 (Rennison, 2001). Point estimates regarding non-lethal violence vary depending on the self-report survey and its context. However, the pattern across two widely cited national-level surveys is consistent. First, findings from the Violence Against Women Study (VAWS) revealed that 22,254,037 women had in her lifetime been physically assaulted by an IP. The most common type of IP assault was being pushed, grabbed, or shoved (18.1% of the women), followed by being slapped or hit (16%). The VAWS also estimated that 7,753,669 women had been raped by an intimate partner in their lifetime (Tjaden and Thoennes, 1998a). Eight percent of women had been stalked at some point in their life, with 4.8% of these women having been stalked by an intimate (Tjaden and Thoennes, 1998b). Second, the National Crime Victimization Survey estimates that in 1999 671,110 rapes/sexual assaults, robbery, simple assaults and aggravated assaults were committed against females by intimate partners, a rate of 5.8 per 1,000 females age 12 years and older (Rennison, 2001).

Estimating violence and abuse can be a daunting challenge under "ideal" research design conditions (Fisher and Cullen, 2000). For example, there is a lack of standard definitions of violence and abuse that is consistently used across studies (Brandl and Cook-Daniels, 2002; US Department of Health and Human Services, 2000). Consequently, comparisons across studies are difficult, if not impossible due to the lack of standard definitions for the different forms of violence (including the crime of rape/sexual assault) and abuse (see Fisher and Cullen, 2000; U.S. Department of Health and Human Services, 2000).

Providing violence and abuse estimates for older women is further challenging for several methodological reasons specific to an older population. First, older women are typically undersampled in "big" national-level empirical studies. Therefore older women, say 55 or older or even those 65 and older, are either overlooked as a separate age grouping or grouped with younger women (for example, those 50 and older) because their numbers are so small in the sample, reliable estimates of the extent of victimization are not possible (Vinton, 2003). In some surveys, for example the NCVS, women 65 years and older were combined with women 50–64 years old because the number of sample cases of women age 65 years and older were too small to produce reliable estimates (Rennison, 2001). Second, when a study has been designed to include older persons or women, such as The National Elder

Abuse Incident Study, IPVA was not among the primary focus of the study, so the reporting of such results are limited. Related is the issue of researchers not reporting a separate victim-perpetrator category for partner/spouse but rather having a general "family member" category (Teaster, Roberto, Duke, and Kim, 2000). Even when the victim-perpetrator relationship includes spouse, there may be no reporting of this relationship by sex of the victim (Tatara, 1993). In all these examples, estimates of IPVA against older women cannot be produced. Third, some studies report estimates based on "official" data sources, such as by Adult Protective Services (APS). Other studies are based on a probability sample that was drawn from either a community-dwelling population or a clinical-based population (Fisher, Regan, Zink, and Pabst, 2003; National Center on Elder Abuse, 1998). A comparison of estimates from these different populations becomes challenging, if not, impossible to accurately do. And last, there is much variation across the age requirement to be designated "older." For example, some studies include women 50 and older while other studies use age 55 as the criteria and still others use age 60 (Tatara, 1993; Teaster et al., 2000). Related, across studies the age categories vary, too. For example, some researchers have measured age in terms of decades: 50–59, 60–69, and 70–79 years old (Mouton, 2003) while others used a five-year category (e.g., 60–64, 65–69, etc.) (National Center on Elder Abuse, 1998). Other studies employed 10-year age categories as well but did not cluster the age dispersion by decades. For example, Fisher and her colleagues (2003) used 55- 64, 65 – 74 and 75 and older as age categories. Still others used a gross age category such as 55 and older (Rennison and Rand, 2003).

As with any newly emerging field of research, the IPVA and older women studies are at an early stage of scientific rigor and as such, there are methodological differences and limitations that will need to be addressed by future researchers. Putting these issues aside for the time being, there is a growing body of research that sheds much insight into the extent and nature of IPVA against older women. These methodological differences cannot be ignored; they will need to be addressed as the measurement of IPVA against older women research matures into a field of scientific study.

Below we discuss results from the growing body of research that has examined the extent of IPVA against older women. In this section we also highlight the gaps in the body of knowledge.

THE EXTENT OF THE PROBLEM

Estimates of elder abuse and violence against women abound from several sources, yet the measurement of IPVA against older women is a relatively young and fragmented field. The measurement of IPVA against older women, nonetheless, is growing both within the more general elder abuse and DV fields (Fisher, Zink, Rinto et al., 2003). There is some hint that an interdisciplinary view of IPVA is emerging among a new generation of researchers, many of whom have been influenced by the new research and practices developed as a result of the VAW Act (Fisher, Regan et al., 2003).

Only a handful studies have been conducted about elder abuse from which we can extrapolate some baseline information about IPVA against older women. One study was executed over 15 years ago by Pillemer and Finkelhor (1988). Their landmark study was designed to produce reliable estimates of abuse (physical violence, verbal aggression, and neglect) against both male and female elders in a community-dwelling population. Prevalence abuse data from a stratified random sample survey of 2,020 elders age 65 and over living in metropolitan Boston revealed that physical violence was the most widespread form of abuse against older women. They reported that 13 per 1,000 female elders had experienced physical violence since turning 65 compared to 9 per 1,000 female elders having experienced verbal aggression and 5 per 1,000 suffering from neglect. Noteworthy is that their results suggest that the largest proportion of elder female abuse, is in fact, spouse abuse. To illustrate, in 17% of the physical violence cases, the perpetrator-victim relationship was husband to wife. In 10% of these cases the son was the perpetrator and in only 3% of the cases the daughter was the perpetrator. Similarly, in 27% of the chronic verbal aggression cases the perpetrator was the husband compared to 8% of these cases where the perpetrators were the son or the daughter, respectively.

Surprisingly, it took almost a decade for Pillmer and Finkelhor's IPVA against older women results to capture the attention of a national-level agency, in particular The National Center on Elder Abuse. Their sponsored national-level study, The National Elder Abuse Incidence Study (NEAIS), collected data from 20 counties in 15 states from Adult Protective Service agencies and sentinels (banks, law enforcement agencies, hospitals, public health departments, home care agencies, senior centers) in 1996 (National Center on Elder Abuse, 1998). The NEAIS is groundbreaking because it provides, for the first time, national-level incidence estimates of different forms of abuse: physical abuse, sexual abuse, emotional or physical abuse, financial or material exploitation, and abandonment, neglect, and self-neglect among elders.

Females aged 60 and older comprised 58% of the total national elderly population at the time of the NEAIS study. However, the NEAIS results showed that women were over-represented compared to their portion of the total elderly population. The results revealed that 76.3% of the victims of emotional/psychological abuse were women. And 71.4% of the older women had experienced physical abuse. For our interest in IPVA, the NEAIS did not break down the victim-offender relationship by sex of the victim. What can be gleaned from this study is that perpetrators of emotional/psychological abuse were more likely to be the children of the victim (53.9%), followed by the victim's spouse (12.6%). The same pattern is evident in physical abuse: 48.6% of the perpetrators were a child of the victim compared to 23.4% who were the victim's spouse.

One explanation for the discrepancy the results reported by the NEAIS and Pillmer and Finkelhor (1988) is that the later gathered information from the elder and did not rely on "official" cases. The difference may be attributed to several methodological differences. First, elders may not report spousal abuse to authorities, such as the APS, or even if reported, APS staff determined that the case was unsubstantiated. The violence against women research shows only a small percentage of victimizations committed by intimate partner are reported to authorities, such as law enforcement (Rennison, 2001). Second, Pillmer and Finkelhor's randomly selected respondents completed the survey either in person or over the telephone. The responses were self-reporting of experiences. The cases reported in the NEAIS consisted of every reported case of suspected abuse during the data collection period which lasted 2 months in every county sentinel agency and APS that was part of the study. Hence, as critics have argued the NEAIS study did not include a large (but unmeasured) segment of older persons who did not come in contact with community services (Brandl and Cook-Daniels, 2002). And yet another reason for the discrepancy could be that the Pillmer and Finkelhor's study was a single site set located in a large urban area whereas the NEAIS's was a nationally-representative sample of 20 counties. We cannot say definitely why the discrepancy in the victim-perpetrator relationship exists, but it does signal the need to further examine the victim-perpetrator relationship in incidents involving older women.

Additional information as to the extent of IPVA against older women can be taken from national-level criminal justice databases. Between 1993 and 1999 the overall rate of intimate partner violence rate reported from the NCVS fell for females age 20-24, 25-34, and 35-49. This downward trend was not evident for women 50 and older (Rennison, 2001). Similarly, the murder rate for women between 50 and 64 and age 65 and older did not decrease between 1993-1999. During this time, the murder rate per 100,000 women age 50 to 64 ranged from 0.5 to 0.8. The murder rate per 100,000 women 65 and older ranged between. 0.5 to 0.7.

Rennison and Rand (2003) examined the extent of non-lethal intimate partner violence (rape, sexual assault, aggravated, and simple assault) from the 1993-2001 NCVS. Over the nine years, they estimated that 117,940 non-lethal violent IP victimizations were committed against women 55 and older. They reported a victimization rate of 2% for women age 55 and older. The authors noted that offenders, as they become older, might reduce the frequency of abuse or commit more psychological/emotional abuse. Noteworthy, is that psychological/emotional abuse is not collected by the NCVS.

Smaller scale studies have contributed to our current body of knowledge about the extent of IPVA against older women. These studies are typically a single community-dwelling sample (Pillemer and Finkelhor, 1988) or clinic-patient sample (Fisher, Regan et al., 2003; Mouton, 2003). Their generalizabilty is limited but given the paucity of research in this area, they contribute to the growing body of knowledge of IPVA against older women.

Supportive of the theme of the national-level studies, the golden years are not golden for many older women. Three studies described the abuse these women have suffered. First, Moutin (2003) studied community-dwelling women, who were involved in a multi-site clinical trial of women's health in San Antonio, Texas. His results showed that of the 1,245 women aged 50-79 years old, 58.5% report exposure to some type of abuse in their adult lifetime by a spouse/partner, with 5.2%-22.8% reporting some type of abuse (physical or verbal) in the past 12 months. Second, using a sample of 998 women aged 55 and older from a patient database located in the Cincinnati, Ohio area, Fisher and her colleagues (2003) found that verbal abuse (40.7% of the women) and emotional/psychological abuse (24.6%) were among the most prevalent among these women. Other forms of violence and abuse while not as prevalent still were experienced by a substantial number of older women. For example, 4.4% of the women suffered control abuse (put on an allowance, routinely checked on respondent in a way that made her afraid, refused to let respondent go to work, social activities or see or talk with friends), 4.2% were physically abused, and 3.2% had been sexually abused since turning 55 years old. Further, they reported, of the women who were victimized since the age 55 a large proportion experienced violence and abuse at the hands of a spouse/partner. Noteworthy, they found that since these women had turned 55 years old, 68% were sexually abused, 56% experienced control abuse, and 37% had been physically abused by their spouse/partner. A third study executed by Grossman and Lundy (2003) of women 55 years old and over who sought services from domestic violence programs in Illinois examined race and ethnicity similarities and differences among White, African Americans, and Hispanics. Across all three groups, almost all the women reported having experienced emotional abuse (White, 97%; African Americans, 96%, and Hispanics, 96%) and physical abuse (71%, 74%, and 77%, respectively). Possibly due to their marital status, a larger percent of older Hispanic women suffered from sexual abuse (17%) compared to Whites (11%), or African Americans (4%).

These studies have begun to bring much-needed attention to the extent of IPVA against older women. Collectively, their results come to the conclusions that IPVA against older women is 1) an emerging critical policy issue, and 2) an important field of scientific inquiry that is in need of more research. As noted, there are methodological limitations in this first generation of IPVA research but with this in mind, researchers can only build more rigorous studies that will broaden understanding of IPVA against older women and fill the gaps in our knowledge. For example, no studies to our knowledge have examined the extent of stalking, the co-occurrence of various forms of IPVA, repeat IPVA victimization, or ethnic differences in IPAV against older women (and violence against older women).

The Nature of IPVA: Victim and Incident Characteristics

Several obvious questions come to mind concerning the IPVA against older women victim and incident characteristics. Below we discuss aspects of older women's experiences with IPVA as reported in the very few studies that have examined the characteristics of these women and their experiences.

One question that comes to mind is the relationship between IPVA victims and their demographic characteristics. Results from the NCVS revealed that black women had the highest rates of non-lethal IPV (56 per 1,000 women age 55 plus), followed by the "other" racial category (52 per 1,000) and white women (42 per 1,000). Caution, however, must be exercised in interpreting these NCVS estimates because two of the racial categories (black and others) had 10 or less sample cases. Older women who were separated had a much higher rate of non-lethal IPV (10.37 per 1,000) than other marital categories (all of which were less than 0.90 per 1,000) (Rennison and Rand, 2003).

The results concerning the relationship between IPVA and income are mixed at best. Mouton (2003) reported no significant differences across income categories and abuse. Rennison and Rand (2003), however, reported that income and non-lethal violence has a U-shaped relationship, with women with annual household incomes of $20,000 and women with an annual household income of $75,000 or more having the two highest rates of victimization (.50 per 1,000 and .92 per 1,000 older females, respectively). Again, the NCVS results must be taken with caution, as small cell sizes are present in three of the four annual household income categories.

Among other questions posed about the nature of IPVA concerns the specific victim-offender relationship. Recall that Pillemer and Finkelhor (1988) were among the first researchers to find that a spouse primarily committed older women's abuse. Rennison and Rand (2003) provide further insight into the nature of this IP relationship. They reported that the perpetrators for older women were the current spouse (62%), current or former partner (26%) and ex-spouse (12%). Interestingly this victim-offender relationship pattern is slightly different from women 25 to 64 years old. The perpetrator for this group of women was the current spouse (44%), current or former partner (38%), and ex-spouse (18%).

Contributing additional insight into our understanding of the victim-offender relationship, Grossman and Lundy (2003) reported that among racial/ethnic groups in their Illinois study, 71% of the Hispanic women reported that their abuser was a husband or ex-husband. Sixty-one percent of White women and 45% of African American clients were abused by a husband or ex-husband.

Unlike younger women in which the majority of the perpetrators are under the influence of drugs and/or alcohol, results from the NCVS show that in 49% of the victimizations the perpetrators of older women were not under the influence of either substance. In 85% of the IPV against older women victimizations, the perpetrator did not have a weapon. In those few cases where a weapon was present, a firearm was the most likely type (Rennison and Rand, 2003).

To date, little is reliably known about the nature of IPVA against older women. This area of inquiry remains a large gap in our IPVA knowledge. Knowing the victim and incident characteristics are critical to understanding differences and similarities within the older women population and between women, especially younger compared to older women. Recognition of these commonalities and difference can then be used as the basis for developing services and programs tailored to the needs of older women (see section below). What is needed are rigorous cross sectional, panel and longitudinal, multi-disciplinary studies that examine the characteristics of older women who have experienced IPVA and the characteristics of their experiences. One step in this direction is listening to oral histories of women who have suffered violence and abuse at the hands of an intimate partner. In the next section, we present oral histories of such women.

IN THEIR OWN WORDS: OLDER WOMEN TELL THEIR STORIES OF VIOLENCE AND ABUSE

The importance of in-depth qualitative information about older women and IPVA is apparent from the current state of research that has reported the experiences of women in their own words. Prior qualitative work has focused primarily on the experience of younger women, although a few studies have included at least one woman over 55 (Hilbert, 1984; Langford, 1996; Lempert, 1996; Merritt-Gray and Wuest, 1995; Moss, Pitula, Campbell, and Halstead, 1997; Newman, 1993). However, to our knowledge, only one qualitative study has focused exclusively on elderly women (Grunfeld, Larsson, Mackay, and Hotch, 1996). In that study, four elderly abused women, ages 63–73, who had received assistance from a hospital domestic violence program, completed oral history interviews aimed at examining the effects of violence on their lives. While the analysis focused primarily on the health-related effects of the abuse, the authors also explored the women's barriers for leaving their relationships. These included: limited financial resources, inability to obtain a divorce, or worry about the effects on their children (Grunfeld et al., 1996).

To further add to the depth of our understanding, Zink, Regan, Jacobson, and Pabst (2003) recruited women over 55 who were currently or had been in an abusive relationship since age 55. Thirty-eight women, ranging from 55 to 90 years old, qualified and participated in an intensive conversation with an interviewer. Eighty percent of the women were white and over half had household incomes greater than $40,000. The length of the abusive relationship was not brief as the median length of the abusive relationship was 23 years. Although a majority (61%) had left their abuser, a large proportion, 39%, had remained in their marriage or relationship

The women's relationships were marked by physical, emotional, social, financial and sexual abuse. Their stories show how extremely complicated these relationships are. Societal ignorance and denial of different forms of family violence (child, domestic, and elder) meant that those women who recognized the abuse as abuse in their domestic lives—and many did, received little social, mental, or financial support from either inside or outside their family. Many women reported that at various times in the relationship they made efforts to seek assistance to stop the abuse. Their experiences were often discounted and they were told to return to the marriage and to make the marriage work—for the children, of course.

Institutions today such as the courts, law enforcement, medical personnel, and social service agencies provide a variety of support services for victims of

IPV. This was not so 30 years ago. When faced with IPV then these institutions, as a whole, upheld the sanctity and privacy of the domestic sphere. Society considered IPV as a family problem that needed to be addressed without any outside interference. It was not the place of the courts, law enforcement, doctors, or the church to interfere in marital affairs.

Reflecting back to previous decades, these older women commented that stricter gender roles had defined their functions and obligations to their husbands. These women described their roles as housewife, mother, and sexual partner. They were expected to submit to the physical and sexual wishes of their husbands. Many of them tolerated abuse because that was the expectation of the times.

Several of the women continue to remain even now because of their own health problems and those of their spouse. Many spoke of the commitment to care for their abusive spouse now that he was in failing health. Other women remained because of their own health conditions, suggesting that they were dependent on their abuser. Despite the abuse, the need to provide or receive care because of failing physical or mental health became fundamental to why they stay with the abuser.

Zink and her colleagues also uncovered that older women face many of the same challenges experienced by younger women in abusive relationships—economics, family attachments, shame, and health. Given the years of abuse and the complex moral dilemmas imposed by their upbringings the risks of older women were magnified. Because of the social culture, older women had less opportunity to develop skills for autonomy and years of abuse and attachment resulted in more to lose if they left. In addition, years of emotional abuse resulted in poor self-image and confidence. As a result, some older women chose to remain in the abusive relationship, the life-generated risks being too great to overcome.

The Zink et al. study is among the first to offer insight into the dynamics of abusive relationships that older women have and continued to experience. More work into these dynamics, especially studies where women provide an oral history, are much needed to provide a life course perspective into both long-term IPVA and that which began at the onset of old age.

RESOURCES FOR OLDER VICTIMIZED WOMEN: DO THEY EXIST?

The Health Care Provider

Who is most likely to see older women outside of their family and friends? In many cases it is their primary care physician (PCP). Research has shown that chronic health problems such as diabetes, arthritis, and hypertension are experienced more often by older women than any other age category (Desai, Zhang, and Hennessey, 1999). These diseases make it necessary for women to see a primary care physician on a regular basis, sometimes as often as once a month. This puts the PCP in a unique position to serve as a gateway to resources about IPVA.

We know from the literature that primary care physicians are doing a poor job of screening women of all ages for intimate partner violence (IOM, 2002; Lapidus et al., 2002; Rodriguez, Bauer, McLoughlin, and Grumbach, 1999). Physicians identify many barriers to screening for IPVA including time constraints, discomfort with the subject, fear of offending the patient, frustration with patient's denial, lack of skills and resources to manage IPVA (Sugg and Inui, 1992; Sugg, Thompson, Thompson, Maiuro, and Rivara, 1999; Waalen, Goodwin, Spitz, Petersen, and Saltzman, 2000). For these reasons, and the fact that physicians do not think of older women as victims of IPVA, screening for IPVA rarely occurs with older female patients (Rovi and Mouton, 1999).

Zink and her colleagues (Zink, Regan, Goldenhar, and Pabst, 2003) conducted focus groups with 47 primary care physicians, nurse practitioners and physician assistants in Cincinnati, Ohio and surrounding suburban and rural areas. They were interested in investigating the level of awareness of IPVA in older women patients, screening behavior for the IPVA, and management, if any, of IPVA once detected.

They reported that PCPs tend to fall along a continuum of screening, identifying, and managing IPVA in older women. One end of the continuum they found that many health care providers are not screening for IPVA among any of their patients regardless of age. Several providers, especially those with suburban practices, clearly stated that they were not screening any patients because they did not believe that IPVA was a problem in any of their patients so there was no reason to screen. Other providers do not believe that IPVA is a medical issue, they do not think there is a medical solution for the problem and consequently do not see a role for the physician to screen, refer, or manage a patient regardless of age.

A second group of providers fell into a middle category. They realized IPVA was a problem but only among younger women. Many stated that unless there was a physical sign such as bruising or broken bone or if the woman brought it up, they would not screen for IPVA. These providers reported calling the police or adult protective services to deal with an obvious case of IPVA especially if it involved an older person. They knew something needed to be done, but were unfamiliar with the range and nuances of resources for older women with IPVA. Providers were identifying and managing their patients only at limited levels. These providers seemed to work primarily with an "acute disease" model—identify and treat the problem and then move on to the next issue. Examples included: treating depression or anxiety, but not exploring the IPVA or providing unrealistic advice such as telling the patient she needed to leave but not offering any suggestions on how she should do that. In addition, some providers did not know the nuances of managing an older victim with IPVA, again seeking simple solutions such as telling them to get a job or telling the husband to come in and the doctor would talk to him.

The last category of providers was at the other end of the continuum—the routine practice of thorough identification and management of older battered women patients. Some providers made sure they saw certain clients on a regular basis as a way of checking on their well-being, monitoring medication, and referring them to counseling. These providers displayed a more "chronic disease" mindset for managing IPVA, ongoing attention to a variety of factors, and understanding the unique challenges of managing the older victim who often needs to seek solutions other than leaving the relationship and the varied capacities of local resources to meet the needs of the older IPVA victim. These physicians showed an understanding of the generational issues faced by older women. They mentioned that many of their older women patients do not want to complain too much and/or are less open about their situation. Since many of these women have been in long-term marriages, the couple's financial, social and emotional lives are intertwined. The physician's experiences had been that those women who had a higher household income may be less forthcoming about an IPVA situation or reluctant to seek outside help because they were embarrassed and took pride in their status. These women feared that by addressing the IPVA a loss of privilege to which they have become accustomed may occur. Those women with lower incomes may have few, if any, resources (e.g., money, insurance, support network) that would allow them to seek counseling or perhaps even to leave their situation. Several providers noted that this is frustrating for them, especially the ones want to provide resources but cannot because they are bound by insurance requirements or other resource constraints.

The Domestic Violence Community

A second resource for older women experiencing IPVA is the networks of domestic violence shelters and crisis lines. The needs of older women IPVA victims are unique compared to those of younger women (Brandl, 1997; Vinton, 1999). For example, since older women have been participating in long marriages many do not want to leave their spouses, they typically just want the abuse to end, their family life to remain intact, and to feel safe at home for their remaining years. The usual assistance for younger women, such as support groups or job training, is not always acceptable to older women (Vinton, 1992; Vinton et al., 1997). Other assistance such as shelters may be filled with children and may not be set up to manage the needs of older women, such as handicap access, medication protocols, or accommodating special dietary needs (Fisher, Zink, Pabst et al., 2003).

A few studies have been undertaken that shed some insight into services and programs the DV community offers to older battered women. Vinton surveyed DV shelters in Florida and nationally about special programming for older battered women. Overall, she found a relative lack of services for these victims (1992, 1998; Vinton et al., 1997). To illustrate, Vinton (1998) reported that only 14.8% of the shelters nationally offered any special programming for older battered women. Outreach and individual intervention were among the most common types of programming, yet only a few shelters, 34% and 19%, respectively, did so.

Extending Vinton's work, Fisher and her colleagues (2003) conducted a survey of all the domestic violence shelters and crisis agencies in Ohio to assess the capabilities for serving older women clients. They reported some very positive results but similar to the results from Zink et al.'s focus groups with the primary care physicians several areas were identified that can be addressed that would improve care to older women experience IPVA. One important aspect of providing services to older women is whether staff members at DVCs are trained about aging. Close to 43% of the DVCs provided training to their staff or volunteers about IPVA and older women. Of these centers however, a little less than a third (32%) conduct routine training.

Fisher and her colleagues (2003) also reported that 36% of DVCs do outreach to women 55 years and older to reach older women who have experienced IPVA. Outreach included brochures given to programs that service older woman, presentations at senior centers, having an advocate at a senior center. A large proportion, 94%, of DVC provided services or referred women to one-on-one/ face-to-face interventions with DV victims/survivors. Nearly 30% of these DVCs provided services or referred at least one woman over 55 years old to one-on-one/face-to-face interventions. Eighty-nine percent of DVCs provided a crisis line, with almost 20% of them having served at least one woman over 55 years old via their crisis line. Eighty-five percent of DVCs ran support groups. Forty percent of these DVC served at least one older woman in their support groups. Nearly 80% of DVC (77%) operate a shelter. Seventy-eight percent of these DVC sheltered at least one women 55 years and older.

Clearly these studies highlight that there are few resources, especially ones tailored to the needs of older women who suffer from abuse and violence. The lack of resources is an opportunity to make suggestions as what needs to be done to improve resources for older women. In the last section of this chapter, we turn to these issues.

FUTURE DIRECTIONS

Although there are only a few studies about older women and IPVA, these studies provide convincing evidence that a significant proportion of older women have experienced abuse and violence at the hands of a spouse/partner and that there is need for further review. In reviewing the state of this body of research, three main themes emerged that researchers, advocates, and practitioners need to pay attention to so that both research and policy can move forward to prevent and respond to the quality of life of older women who have faced or continue to face IPVA. First, one concern that has been confounded in the research is identification of the perpetrator and the labeling of such experience (that is, whether the abuse is intimate partner violence of older women or elder abuse). Discerning between the two can be difficult for the provider but can mean serious consequences for the injured party. Two, once the type of abuse has been identified, the need for appropriate services are extremely important and what is appropriate for younger women may not be appropriate for older women. Three, gatekeepers for younger women experiencing abuse,

such as physicians, domestic violence shelters and service providers for the elderly must be better educated about both older women and IPVA. Each of these
groups must be encouraged to collaborate to create services and programs for
victims. Below we discuss each issue in more detail.

Distinguishing Between Elder Abuse and IPVA Among Older Women

Similar to other states, the state of Ohio's statute on elder abuse/neglect
(Ohio Revised Code, 2000) is for an adult, defined as 60 years of age or older
who is handicapped by the infirmities of aging or who has a physical or mental impairment which prevents the person from providing for their own care
or protection who is being abused physically, sexually, financially, or is being
neglected including self-neglect. Physicians and others who serve older people are encouraged to contact the local Adult Protective Services (APS) in the
area to report this type of abuse. Adult Protective Services focuses on physi-
cal/sexual abuse and neglect and the issue of competence. The law limits APS
in how aggressive APS workers can be about entering a person's home if the
individual seems competent, is unwilling to talk with them and there is no
legal reason to enter.

For many who work with the elderly, Adult Protective Services does little
to protect women who are being abused by a spouse or significant other, as is
the case in IPAV. In many cases, when violence against an older woman is identified, caregiver stress is often considered the primary cause (Pillemer and
Finkelhor, 1988). Even in the case of abuse of an older woman by her husband
it is often thought to be due to an overburdened and stressed caregiver. The
intervention for caregiver abuse is focused on supporting the stressed caregiver with respite assistance, support groups and arranging additional services in
the home for the "patient" (Pillemer and Finkelhor, 1988). This type of response
is not appropriate in the case of an older woman who is being abused. This still
leaves her at the mercy of her abuser without any support for her.

The Violence Against Women Act (VAWA) of 2000 was signed into law by
President Clinton and provided continued funding for many of the programs
that were effective under the Act of 1994. Several other significant measures
passed as part of the final language including that it restored and strength-
ened protections for battered immigrant women; improvements to Full Faith
and Credit provisions; pilot programs for transitional housing and supervised
visitation centers; and programs addressing violence against older or disabled
individuals among other programs such as stalking via the internet. It is
imperative that service providers who work with abused women and those
who work with older women begin to collaborate on education and programming to address this problem.

The Need For Services and Programs Tailored to the
Needs of Older Women

Generational issues make the situations older women face more complicated. There are more years of dependence, more years of control. Providing

support to women who want to remain means that service providers need to think outside the box. The usual systemic responses used with younger abusive couples may not be appropriate. Leaving may not be an option. Attending a support group with younger women may not be helpful to older women who have had a different life experience or may have trouble with transportation or driving in the dark. Residing in a shelter filled with children or that does not accommodate the needs of older individuals (e.g., monitor medications, handicap access, accommodate dietary preferences) may result in an older women returning to her abuser. In addition, the realities of aging, involving both physical and mental incapacities, limits options. Abusive relationships are often marked by isolation from friends and family (Bowker, 1983). One can only imagine how loss of sight or inability to drive may further isolate the victim.

In addition, aging may also limit the ability of the abuser to leave the house, meaning that the victim no longer has any break from the abuse. Mental aging may result in confusion, potentially intensifying the abuse and care required by either partner. Physical abuse declines with age (Harris, 1996), but verbal abuse can be devastating to mental well being (Bowker, 1983). Again, one must ask, how does society support the abusive older couple that seeks assistance or enters the legal, health or social service system because of the abuse? Because of aging, the usual responses may not be appropriate.

What can a community do to support an older woman who is experiencing IPAV? The most frequently given suggestion by physicians, domestic violence shelter advocates and aging agency advocates was community awareness. Public service announcements that Intimate Partner Abuse and Violence is a Life Course phenomenon are crucial. The more that the message can be made public; the less stigma is attached to the abusive act. More information about abuse must be made clear. It is important that people understand that not all abuse is physical, sexual or neglect. The older women, in their own words, made it clear in many cases that the physical abuse had stopped many years ago but the verbal, emotional, psychological and control abuse still took place on a daily basis. More information needs to be made available where older women are more likely to go such as beauty shops, women's clubs, grocery stores, department stores, make-up counters, fabric shops, craft stores, doctor's offices, senior centers, places of worship, and adult day cares.

There must be more facilitation between aging agency advocates and domestic violence advocates. Vinton (2003) describes some very innovative programs between these two types of agencies taking place in Florida. One unique project was the building of a shelter room onto an existing senior center. The room was accessible from a private entrance. It was handicap accessible. People using the senior center and domestic violence advocates were aware of the room's existence. Police and other law enforcement agencies could bring an older woman there where a shelter worker and a caregiving assistant if necessary for personal care would meet them. In another case, certain assisted living agencies volunteered a certain number of days in their facilities for emergency shelter for older women who needed to leave abusive homes. Again, the facilities were handicap accessible, medication could be administered and personal care could be assisted while the woman received assistance from the local domestic violence service agency. And in Ohio, one agency provides foster care for pets. Many times older women who must leave their homes do not want to leave beloved cats or dogs for fear that the abuser may harm them, so a program is set up for the pet to go into foster care with a family until other arrangements can be made.

Most important is dual education by both types of agencies. Domestic violence agencies need to know about aging and aging agencies need to know about the services available for older women experiencing domestic violence. Many times, it is the personnel of aging agencies such as home care workers and meals on wheels deliverers who are in the home on a daily basis and may be good resources for screening for intimate partner violence with the right training by domestic violence advocates. Domestic violence advocates would be helped by knowing about transportation programs, meals on wheels and home care programs. We must continue a move toward a coordinated effort of research, advocacy, and services that seek innovative solutions to identifying, and providing services to older women who are victims of intimate partner violence and abuse.

REFERENCES

American Association of Retired Persons. (1992). *Abused Elders or Older Battered Women?* Washington, D.C.

Bowker, L. (1983). *Beating Wife Beating.* Lexington, MA: Lexington Books.

Brandl, B. (1997). *Developing Services for Older Abused Women.* Madison, WI: Wisconsin Coalition Against Domestic Violence.

Brandl, B., and Cook-Daniels, L. (2002). *Domestic Abuse in Later Life*: National Electronic Network on Violence against Women.

Brandl, B., and Raymond, J. (1997). Unrecognized Elder Abuse Victims. Older Abused Women. *Journal of Case Management, 6*(2), 62-68.

Desai, M., Zhang, P., and Hennessey, C. (1999). Surveillance for Morbidity and Mortality Among Older Adults—United States, 1995-1996. *Morbidity and Mortality Weekly Report, 48,* 7-25.

Fisher, B., and Cullen, F. (2000). Measuring the Sexual Victimization of Women: Evolution, Current Controversies, and Future Research. In David Duffee (ed), *Measurement and Analysis of Crime and Justice, Criminal Justice 2000, Volume 4,* Washington D.C.: U.S. Department of Justice, 317-390.

Fisher, B., Regan, S., Zink, T., and Pabst, S. (2003). *Prevalence and Incidence of Violence Against Women in Women 55 and Older: Results from Ohio.* Paper presented at the Toward a National Research Agenda on Violence against Women, Lexington, Kentucky.

Fisher, B., Zink, T., Pabst, S., Regan, S., Rinto, B., and Gothelf, E. (2003). Services and Programming for Older Abused Women: The Ohio experience. *Journal of Elder Abuse and Neglect, In Press.*

Fisher, B., Zink, T., Rinto, B., Regan, S., Pabst, S., and Gothelf, E. (2003). Overlooked During the Golden Years: Violence Against Older Women. *Violence Against Women, In Press.*

Grosssman, S., and Lundy, M. (2003). Use Of Domestic Violence Services Across Race And Ethnicity By Women 55 And Older: The Illinois Experience. *Violence Against Women, In Press.*

Grunfeld, A. F., Larsson, D. M., Mackay, K., and Hotch, D. (1996). Domestic Violence Against Elderly Women. *Canadian Family Physician, 42*, 1485-1493.

Harris, S. (1996). For Better or for Worse: Spouse Abuse Grown Old. *Journal of Elder Abuse and Neglect, 8*(1), 1-30.

Hilbert, J. (1984). *Pathways of Help for Battered Women: Varying Definitions of the Situation.* Case Western Reserve, Cleveland.

IOM. (2002). *Confronting Chronic Neglect: The Education and Training of Health Professionals on Family Violence.* Washington D.C.: National Academy Press.

Langford, D. (1996). Predicting Unpredictability: A Model of Women's Processes of Predicting Battering Men's Violence. *Scholarly Inquiry for Nursing Practice, 10*, 371-385.

Lapidus, G., Cooke, M., Gelven, E., Sherman, K., Duncan, M., and Banco, L. (2002). A Statewide Survey of Domestic Violence Screening Behaviors Among Pediatricians and Family Physicians. *Archives of Pediatric Adolescent Medicine, 156*, 332-336.

Lempert, L. (1996). Women's Strategies for Survival: Developing Agency in Abusive Relationships. *Journal of Family Violence, 11*, 269-290.

Merritt-Gray, M., and Wuest, J. (1995). Counteracting Abuse and Breaking Free: The Process of Leaving Revealed Through Women's Voices. *Health Care for Women International, 16*, 399-412.

Moss, V., Pitula, C., Campbell, J., and Halstead, L. (1997). The Experience of Terminating an Abusive Relationship From an Anglo and African American Perspective: A Qualitative Descriptive Study. *Issues in Mental Health Nursing, 18*, 433-454.

Mouton, C. (2003). Intimate Partner Violence and Health Status Among Older Women. *Violence Against Women, In Press.*

National Center on Elder Abuse. (1998). The National Elder Abuse Incidence Study.

Newman, K. (1993). Giving up: Shelter Experiences of Battered Women. *Public Health Nursing, 10*, 108-113.

Ohio Revised Code, 5101.61 (2000).

Pillemer, K., and Finkelhor, D. (1988). The Prevalence of Elder Abuse: A Random Sample Survey. *The Gerontologist, 28*(1), 51-57.

Rennison, C. (2001). *Intimate Partner Violence and Age of Victim, 1993-99.* Washington, DC: U.S. Department of Justice.

Rennison, C., and Rand, M. (2003). Non-Lethal Intimate Partner Violence: Women age 55 or Older. *Violence Against Women, In press.*

Rodriguez, M., Bauer, H., McLoughlin, E., and Grumbach, K. (1999). Screening and Intervention for Intimate Partner Abuse: Practice and Attitudes of Primary Care Physicians. *Journal of American Medical Association, 282*(5), 468-474.

Rovi, S., and Mouton, C. (1999). Domestic Violence Education in Family Practice Residencies. *Family Medicine, 31*(6), 398-403.

Seaver, C. (1996). Muted Lives: Older Battered Women. *Journal of Elder Abuse and Neglect, 8*(2), 3-21.

Sugg, N., and Inui, T. (1992). Primary Care Physicians Response to Domestic Violence: Opening Pandora's Box. *JAMA, 267*(23), 3157-3160.

Sugg, N., Thompson, R., Thompson, D., Maiuro, R., and Rivara, F. (1999). Domestic Violence and Primary Care: Attitudes, Practices, and Beliefs. *Archives of Family Medicine, 8*, 301-306.

Tatara, T. (1993). Understanding the Nature and Scope of Domestic Elder Abuse with the Use of State Aggregate Data: Summaries of Key Findings of a National Survey of State APS and Aging Agencies. *Journal of Elder Abuse and Neglect, 5*(4), 35-57.

Teaster, P., Roberto, K., Duke, J., and Kim, M. (2000). Sexual Abuse of Older Adults: Preliminary Findings of Cases in Virginia. *Journal of Elder Abuse and Neglect, 12*(3/4), 1-16.

Thomas: Legislative Information on the Internet. The Library of Congress. Retrieved October 01, 2003, from the World Wide Web: http://thomas.loc.gov/home/thomas2.html

Tjaden, P., and Thoennes, N. (1998a). *Prevalence, Incidence and Consequences of Violence Against Women: Findings from the National Violence Against Women Survey* (NCJ172837), Washington DC: US Department of Justice: National Institute of Justice/Centers of Disease Control and Prevention.

Tjaden, P., and Thoennes, N. (1998b). *Stalking in America: Findings from the National Violence against Women Survey.* Washington, DC: National Institute of Justice.

U.S. Census Bureau. (2001). *United States Census, 2000.* Washington, DC: US Department of Commerce.

U.S. Department of Health and Human Services. (2000). Building Data Systems for Monitoring and Responding to Violence Against Women. *MMWR, 49*(RR-11), 1-16.

Vinton, L. (1992). Battered Women's Shelters and Older Women: The Florida Experience. *Journal of Family Violence, 7*(1), 63-72.

Vinton, L. (1998). A Nationwide Survey of Domestic Violence Shelter's Programming for Older Women. *Violence Against Women, 4*(5), 559-571.

Vinton, L. (1999). Working with Abused Older Women from a Feminist Perspective. *Journal of Women Aging, 11*(2-3), 85-100.

Vinton, L. (2003). A Model Collaborative Project Toward Making Domestic Violence Centers Elder Ready. *Violence Against Women, In Press.*

Vinton, L., Altholz, J. A., and Thea, L.-B. (1997). A Five Year Follow Up Study of Domestic Violence Programming for Older Battered Women. *Journal of Women and Aging, 9* (1/2), 3-15.

Waalen, J., Goodwin, M., Spitz, A., Petersen, R., and Saltzman, L. (2000). Screening for Intimate Partner Violence by Health Care Providers. *American Journal Preventive Medicine, 19*(4), 230-237.

Zink, T., Regan, S., Goldenhar, L., and Pabst, S. (2003). Intimate Partner Violence: Physicians' Experiences with Women Over 55. *Journal of General Internal Medicine, In Press.*

Zink, T., Regan, S., Jacobson, J., and Pabst, S. (2003). Cohort, Period, and Aging Effects: A Qualitative Study of Older Women's Reasons for Remaining in Abusive Relationships. *Violence Against Women, In Press.*

9

VERBAL ABUSE AND COMMUNICATION NEGLECT IN THE ELDERLY

Helen Sorenson

What you are speaks so loudly that I cannot hear what you say.
Ralph Waldo Emerson

As the population of older adults increases, so will the interaction between those over age sixty-five and the younger generation. While intergenerational blending can be a positive experience, it can also lead to misunderstanding. Frustrations that arise based on the old vs. the new way of doing things can result in conflict. When conflict is acted out, it becomes abuse.

This chapter focuses on a narrow but common aspect of abuse: verbal abuse. Comparatively, verbal abuse occurs four times as often in nursing homes as physical abuse. Communication neglect, while not a visible form of mistreatment, can be equally damaging to older adults. An awareness of what constitutes verbal abuse and communication neglect may foster a better communication environment between health care professionals, patients and families.

COMMUNICATION DEFINED

Communication as a global concept is an exchange of information. Within most species communication is innate. Whether with spoken words, a growl, chirping or flattened ears, even between species some forms of communication are universally understood. Communication implies two things; the message has been delivered and the message has been understood. Because there are two components to this process, it is possible and even probable that at times they are independent of each other.

To facilitate the relaying of information there are many forms of non-verbal communication. Tone of voice, body language, facial expressions and gestures are effective in getting the message across. In our society today we have also become dependent on symbols to inform us when to safely cross the street, to alert us when approaching a railroad crossing and even when to refrain from smoking. It would seem that the overabundance of ways to exchange information would avert most discrepancies in delivering a message. Unfortunately, this is not always the case. For many older or infirm adults, communication is difficult. When transmission of vital information is at risk, so is optimal patient care. The new paradigm, patient-centered care, relies on the patient and care provider working as a team. Good teamwork depends on good communication.

Training in effective communication skills is important, not only for health care professionals, but also for the elderly and their families. Enhancing the communication environment for older adults will ultimately affect their quality of life. Providing for an improved environment however requires understanding some of the potential barriers known to hinder effective communication.

BARRIERS TO COMMUNICATION

The most obvious barriers to conversing with many older adults are age or disease related hearing loss, stroke related aphasia, Alzheimer's disease and dementia. There are varying degrees of miscommunication related to:

- Message delivered, not heard
- Message delivered, partially heard
- Message delivered, heard but nor understood
- Message delivered, message understood, response not physiologically possible
- Message delivered, message heard, message ignored

It cannot be presumed that because a conversation has taken place in the presence of an older adult, that any understanding or comprehension of the message was received. The most obvious barrier to communication is hearing impairment or hearing loss. Current data estimates there are as many as 28 million hearing-impaired individuals in the USA, with 75 percent being older than age fifty-five. Prevalence varies greatly with age and gender, ranging from 10 percent in females aged 48 to 52 years to 97 percent in males over age eighty. Presbycusis, the bilateral symmetric loss of auditory function, begins in middle age and progresses with age. It is also possible that accumulated earwax or ototoxicity, defined as hearing loss associated with some pharmaceuticals, play a role in hearing impairment. Aphasia accounts for the disconnect between hearing and understanding. Loosely defined, aphasia is the loss of ability to speak and/or comprehend language as a result of brain cell damage. More specific forms of aphasia; expressive, fluent, non-fluent, receptive, sub-clinical and global, in varying degrees, limit communication. Even after rehabilitation, chronic aphasia presents a challenge, however a recent study revealed that over time, communication for adults with aphasia does improve. Older adults, as a result of both age-related and disease related decremental change, face situations in which they are unable to communicate effectively. The inability to be connected to a family member, a friend, a caregiver or a health care professional can leave older adults very frustrated. This frustration can lead to self-imposed seclusion, feelings of self-pity and even anger. Negative emotions, projected by the older adults unfortunately are communicated quite effectively to those around them, leading to a cycle of more rejection and more anger.

Communicating with older adults can be complex. The collective nature of age and/or disease related physical and functional impairment, coupled with a dependency vs. autonomy struggle, could result in dysfunctional dialogue. Elderly individuals who have led very independent lives may choose to be reticent rather than risk speaking ineffectively. A lifetime of independence may also be projected as an "I don't need help from anyone" attitude, which can stop conversation before it starts. Lack of social opportunity, both in the community and in health care environments is another barrier to communication. While not usually considered a major problem, the insidious lack of verbal contact with another human can be quite harmful.

A relatively recent barrier to communication is lack of technology knowhow. A textbook published in 2001 addresses the need to design computer programs for older persons and train them to be computer literate. The book is based on presentations from an international conference, which linked German and American scientists working in the area of communication and technology.[4] For older adults with communication impairments, being able to adapt to the new technology may be a critical component in improving interactions. Email allows for a social connection and relationships that were not available a decade ago.[5] Defining the barriers to communication and proactively looking at ways to circumnavigate the obstacles is an important task, given the growing population of older adults. The saying "the elderly need so little but they need that little so much" should be a central theme related to communication in the elderly.

Depression, which is estimated to affect 5% to 9% of community dwelling older adults [6], and be three to five times more prevalent in nursing homes [7], produces it's own intricate web of communication malfunction. According to Blazer, depression is perhaps the most frequent cause of emotional suffering in later life and significantly decreases quality of life.[8] Although more prevalent in nursing homes and long-term care facilities, depression is often under diagnosed and untreated. A study of depression in older nursing home residents revealed that of all the residents who had been diagnosed as having an active clinical condition, identified on the Minimum Data Set (MDS) only 55% were receiving antidepressant therapy.[7] Even when medication is available, not all older adults are compliant with the scheduled drug dosing, leading to variable moods and response patterns.

Patients who do not respond when greeted by caregivers are often just categorized as non-responsive to verbal stimuli. All too often it is presumed that the patients are sleeping or too tired to visit. Because of the prevalence of age related hearing impairment, non-responsive patients may not be given the attention they deserve. If when more aggressively assessing the level of awareness of the patient, caregivers notice sad facial expressions, frequent tears, or flat affect, the patient's physician should be notified.

COMMUNICATION NEGLECT

Defining specific categories of elder abuse has not been easy. Referred to as the "definitional disarray" by Pillemer and Finkelhor,[9] the difficulty seems related to the development of definitions from different perspectives. Elderly abuse victims, physicians, social workers and law enforcement officers may all have distinct definitions of elder abuse based on personal feelings, professional codes and agency policy.

Communication neglect may be classified as a form of psychological insult inflicted on another individual. In the health care setting this can occur when caregivers avoid talking to, touching or having any social contact with a patient. Whether as an unintended oversight or a deliberate withholding of any form of communication, both situations may be interpreted and/or defined as abuse.

Unintentional Communication Neglect

Occasionally, the health care professional's concern for efficiency overshadows the patient's need for social contact of some sort. Taking an extra 5 to 10 minutes to chat with a lonely older adult does not alleviate busy schedules and high patient loads. Taking the chance that a "good morning, how are you?" question, may result in a long and detailed response instead of a simple "fine, thank you" is not something we are always willing to risk.

Struggling to communicate with an older adult, whose stroke resulted in aphasia, may be very time consuming and frustrating for both parties. Knowing this, it is sometimes easier not to even start a conversation. These are not examples of willful disregard for humanity, they are the unfortunate consequences of learned behavior. Even when communication does take place, body language may not match the spoken word. Herodotus, ca. 484-425 BC wrote, "we are less convinced by what we hear than by what we see." Asking someone how they feel while simultaneously looking at a chart, checking the phone number on a pager, and/or conversing with someone out in the corridor speaks volumes. Could this be a consequence of a hectic schedule? Most likely, yes. However, when a message is delivered and the response is not acknowledged, a neglectful barrier to communication has been created. Unintentional neglect does not imply lack of concern or caring, but it can be interpreted as such by the elderly patient. Even facial expressions can relay unintentional messages. A caregiver's quick glance at the patient as he/she pass through the hallway, without any attempt to verbalize a greeting may be perceived as punishment for some unknown deed. Without stereotyping all older adults as worriers, it is possible that given enough time to ponder the reasons why no greeting was forthcoming, some older patients may presume that somehow they were at fault.

The term unintentional implies a lack of purposeful deliberation. Health care professionals may be unaware that some of their unplanned actions or lack thereof are causing adults under their care to feel neglected. Interventions to avoid unintentional communication neglect will be covered in another section of this chapter.

Intentional Communication Neglect

Much more harmful to older patients or elderly residents of long-term care facilities, is being on the receiving end of intentional communication neglect. This is akin to using the "silent treatment" as a form of punishment. The deliberate withholding of warmth and caring by performing tasks in a cold, detached manner could be classified as abusive. Setting a food tray down on a patient's bedside table or taking the morning vitals on an alert patient without uttering a single word is neglectful. Another form of communication neglect is demonstrated by talking about, not to a patient in their presence or referring to the patient in terms of their disease of prosthesis. An example of this might be casually asking a coworker to "hold the elevator, I need to take this trach down to radiology for a swallow study." Being referred to as an object is dehumanizing and could precipitate or further deepen depression. Something seemingly as innocent as inquiring, "has the liver transplant's lab work come back yet?", if overheard by a patient or family member, sends a detrimental message.

It is difficult to navigate around the new federal regulations for maintaining patient confidentiality in any institutional setting. Health care professionals must sustain vigilance in preserving patient anonymity in a public hallway without sacrificing the personal dignity of those under their care.

VERBAL ABUSE

Verbal abuse is an extreme example of ineffective and inappropriate communication. Because it is so common, mention of the possible causes need to be addressed. In recent years, research on verbal abuse in nursing homes has determined that the following situations are more often associated with increased incidence of abuse:

- Failure of State laws and agencies to provide adequate oversight and protection of patient's rights
- Managers and administrators failure to create and enforce policies supportive of caregivers and residents
- Inexperienced personnel in crisis prevention and intervention
- Improper staff training in how to prevent verbal abuse
- Staff members under work related stress who are approaching " burnout"
- Employees who have a history of solving problems by resorting to violence
- Employees who harbor negative attitudes toward patients
- Staff members who are provoked by combative or verbally aggressive patients.

Addressing many of these situational eventualities during an educational in-service and emphasizing that professional health care providers must take personal responsibility for their attitudes and behavior, regardless of the circumstances can positively enhance the communication environment.

Unintentional Verbal Abuse

"Why on earth have they decided to CODE this patient, he's been a DNR for days and he's dying." Is this an atypical statement made in frustration in front of a seemingly unconscious patient? Unfortunately, no. A careless remark, often made to no one in particular, and with no harm intended, can indeed be injurious. The terminally ill person hears very well. They may know that they are dying, but to hear a comment similar to the one above would dash all hope. Anything that causes the patient anguish or distress is abuse. Another example of unintentional verbal abuse often relates to odors. Older adults hospitalized for medical reasons and on a variety of prescription drugs, are often incontinent. The room may smell terrible, but calling attention to that fact, in a crude, or even joking manner may be embarrassing or humiliating for the patient. There are many benefits to the use of humor in a health care setting, but care must be taken not to make jokes at the expense of particular patients. Those who work around older adults should be aware that some words like idiot, deaf, and blind elicit strong negative feelings. Even calling an elderly patient by a pet name, if permission has not been forthcoming, is inappropriate.

Many assumptions are made about older adults. The actual prevalence of hearing loss, visual impairment and disease related cognitive changes could lead one to falsely believe that these losses are always consistent with the aging process. While it may be easier to converse with family members present in the room about the patient's condition, to do so is generally insulting. Even when signs of frailty are evident, maintaining eye contact and speaking directly to the geriatric patient is important.

Intentional Verbal Abuse

Much more malignant in nature are the cruel threats and intentional barbs directed at older adults. Verbal abusers attempt to control behavior by using threats of violence or threats of neglect, as in these examples: "If you wet the bed one more time tonight, you'll just have to sleep on soggy sheets." "If you don't eat all your supper, you are not getting any breakfast or lunch tomorrow." " If you don't stop crying I'll give you something to cry about." "If you push that call light one more time tonight, you'll be sorry." If said in a threatening manner, by a caregiver with a scowl on their face, patients will take these statements seriously. Unfortunately, some older adults have been on the receiving end of both verbal and physical abuse. When intimidated and given an ultimatum, they may see compliance as their only option. The helpless and hopeless attitude that develops may become so ingrained that even when kinder and gentler staff ask questions about how they are being treated, they remain silent. Many older adults have no other residential options besides institutional care. Once the pattern of abuse has been set, the elderly are more likely to acquiesce than to rebel against unjust treatment.

Even making fun of patients or playing humiliating practical jokes on an older adult is a form of verbal abuse. Patients in their 30s and 40s may welcome some good-natured bantering as a means of lightening their day. Elderly patients may seem amused, but may internalize the joking as something other than what was intended.

Because verbal abuse and communication neglect are so prevalent, particularly in long term care institutions, the prevention of any type of abuse or neglect is the responsibility of every employee. In order to clarify what the different forms of abuse and neglect look like from all points of view, educating the staff is a necessary component of a continuing education program.

TOXIC TALK

Another form of unhealthy communication in the health care setting is referred to as toxic talk. While not intended to intimidate or frighten patients, toxic talk conveys an attitude of disrespect for person's humanity, the right to privacy and self-determination.

It can be characterized by an attitude, a tone of voice or style of speaking. Toxic talk includes conversations that may or may not happen in the vicinity of the older adult being discussed. As opposed to many types of verbal abuse, toxic talk may not be conducted with negative intent. Although harm is not intended, toxic talk does insinuate that the individual or situation being discussed is not worthy of polite conversation. For example, toxic talk may consist of:

- Using "baby talk" to communicate with an older cognitively impaired older adult
- Using a frustrated tone of voice to call attention to a predicament;
- "Are you wet—again?" "What's your problem today?"
- Discussing a patient and/or situation outside of the room, presuming the patient cannot hear;
- "Have you seen his family? They are all idiots"; "Her whining is just driving me nuts!"; "How can anyone let themselves get so fat?"
- Discussing patients in a detrimental or condescending manner when giving report to the next shift;
- "Be careful when you go into the room—he's got a foul mouth and he's not afraid to use it";
- "She need to be admitted to the psych ward—she's 'loony tunes'."

Although this type of information passing may have a semblance of truth, it is also judgmental and can influence others the attitudes prior to even coming into contact with the older patient. The following case study (a true story) is an example of how communication, both positive and negative examples, can affect a patient's outcome.

"It's not Funny Gracie"—A Case Study

Elmer, a 72 year-old homeless man was involved in a pedestrian-vehicle accident. He was transported to a trauma center via ambulance. Upon arrival at the ER, Elmer said very little, except to repeat over and over "I got hit by a damn truck."

Patient assessment revealed numerous cuts and abrasions on his face, arms and torso. The X-rays showed a fractured arm and two fractured ribs. Based on his injuries, coupled with the fact that he was dehydrated and malnourished, Elmer was admitted to the general floor. Two days after admission, by looking at lab work and diagnostic testing results, internal bleeding was confirmed. Elmer was taken to surgery and his spleen was removed. His recovery was hindered by a number of physical and psychosocial issues, but most harmful was his apparent lack of desire to get well. His face had been "turned to the wall." In the intensive care unit, on a ventilator, Elmer received no visitors. No get-well cards or signs decorated the walls of his room. No one seemed surprised that he was becoming ventilator dependent. Elmer's condition had become somewhat of a joke in the report room. Morning after morning someone would ask; "what happened to Elmer," and a chorus of staff members would reply, "He got hit by a damn truck."

One morning while my students and I were doing routine patient assessments and ventilator checks, Elmer's nurse asked me a question. "Do you think we could cut Elmer's hair"? Elmer had been disheveled and unkempt when admitted, but now, even though cleaned up he still looked pretty shabby. I replied, "We would need his permission." We agreed to ask Elmer if he would like us to cut his hair, and if he did not respond negatively, we would take that as permission. A "no" response was not forthcoming, so we proceeded. The shampoo and haircut was followed by another question; "Elmer, it is OK if we shave off your whiskers"? In the absence of a negative response, we continued.

After finishing the grooming session, and putting the shampoo, razor, and comb in his bedside table, we discovered his glasses, tucked away safely in the drawer. We decided to put his glasses on, sit him up and turn on the television. Then it hit us both at about the same time. Elmer looked just like George Burns. The resemblance was so remarkable that we called in other caregivers to see the results of our hospital makeover.

An amazing thing happened as we stood there smiling at Elmer—he smiled back at us. After that his recovery was amazingly quick. Within days he was weaned off the ventilator. He gave Social Services the name and phone number of his brother who lived in a nearby town. His brother visited him in the hospital and less than two weeks later, the two of them walked out of the hospital, together.

There are two issues related to this case study. The first is toxic talk. The joking banter in the report room, while not audible to the patient or any other caregivers, did affect the attitude of therapists caring for Elmer. Toxic talk, as previously discussed, is harmful. Because of the serious nature of working in an intensive care unit, comic relief is sometimes necessary, but should not involve or be centered on any particular patient or family member.

The other issue is communication neglect. Why did it take 10 days to discover that Elmer wore glasses? If that wonderful nurse had not gone above and beyond her job that morning, would Elmer have survived? It is easy now to look back on that incident and see how valuable and necessary her interventions had been. However, given the fast-paced nature of our jobs where time at the bedside is limited, do we really take the time to communicate with our patients?

CONSEQUENCES

The consequences of verbal abuse and communication neglect are far reaching. First and foremost is the harm inflicted on the patients. It would be difficult to measure the degree of damage, as all people respond differently, but if elders are being abused, they are being affected. There will also be an impact on the family members. Not understanding why grandma has become so quiet and withdrawn could lead to self-recrimination; family members might presume that they had somehow caused this new behavior. Health care providers not involved in the abusive treatment, or unaware that it was taking place may presume it is a new medical problem, and subject the older adult to additional painful testing.

Communication has a positive effect on a person's emotional and psychological well-being. Lack of communication, or deviant forms of communication will have a negative effect. There is a wealth of medical literature linking patient and/or family dissatisfaction with the health care provided, to a failure in communication. The consequences of abuse in older adults however has not received as much attention in published articles. Depression, learned helplessness, mortality and post-traumatic stress are some of the likely outcomes that are being investigated.

DETECTION AND INTERVENTION

Detecting verbal abuse and communication neglect is a complex paradox. Symptoms exhibited by an older adult may indicate some form of abuse, but when questioned he/she may adamantly deny everything. Some of the recognized signs of psychological abuse, including verbal abuse and communication neglect are:

- Being extremely withdrawn, non-responsive or non-communicative.
- Demonstrating unusual behavior often attributed to dementia, such as sucking, biting or rocking.
- Being emotionally upset or agitated.
- Actually verbalizing that they are being abused

Because some of these signs are also consistent with depression, dementia and cognitive impairment, it becomes difficult to base an assumption of abuse on signs/symptoms alone. Unless witnessed by reliable supervisors and or co-workers, abuse is often disavowed by both by the older person and the perpetrator. Abused elderly, for fear of retaliation, shame and/or the stigma of being labeled, fail to report inappropriate treatment. Cognitively and physically challenged older adults may be unable to voice a complaint, which unfortunately puts them at higher risk for being abused. In order to intervene early and diffuse situations before serious harm ensues, there needs to be recognition that a problem exists. Physicians and emergency room personnel are on the front line in detecting signs of physical abuse, but verbal abuse is subtler and leaves no visible scars.

Over the past decade, efforts have been made to create instruments/techniques to identify abuse and abusers. Profiles of those likely to engage in abusive behavior have been developed. Nursing homes and long-term care facilities have become more vigilant in screening prospective employees for evidence of past abusive tendencies. Since the 1970s regulatory safeguards have been enacted to protect residents of long-term care facilities. These safeguards include mandatory criminal background checks of all employees, and ombudsman programs to hear complaints of abuse and neglect. Components of the 1987 Omnibus Budget Reconciliation Act included resident's rights provisions. There have been changes in adult protective legislation and even advances in creating protocols for detection and intervention, but there is more work to be done.

A recent study conducted in assisted living facilities examined decision-making ability and awareness of abusive situations among elderly residents. Videotapes with scenarios of physical, verbal, financial and neglectful abuse were shown to the residents. While the majority (54%) of residents could identify the abusive situations, the study suggested that the residents were poorly informed about options available through adult protective services. Many could recognize abuse on the videotapes, but were uncertain about what to do if they were actually the recipients of such treatment. Although this study had a small sample size, it raised important questions.

Some interventional models have been developed to increase identification of elder abuse, improve care planning and promote prevention. Among these are; education on what constitutes abuse, training of caregivers in communication skills, the use of "volunteer buddies" to listen and monitor for abuse, the formation of a victim's empowerment group and the creation of a handbook for caregivers to self-assess risk for elder abuse and to identify community resources. Many of these interventions have been successful and have not been cost-prohibitive in implementation.

Unfortunately, those who are under their care direct some of the verbal abuse in institutional settings at caregivers. Older adults with aphasia occasionally repeat inappropriate phrases. Patients with dementia can lash out with very offensive language. When caregivers are met with a constant barrage of profanity, they sometimes retaliate in kind. Education on the appropriate way for caregivers to respond is imperative. A cooperative communication intervention for nursing home staff and family members of residents was successful in improving family-staff relationships. While outside the scope of the study to determine the effect that improved staff-family communication had on the residents themselves, this might be an area where future research is needed.

COMMUNICATING WITH ELDERLY PATIENTS

The following are examples of positive communication interventions. Older adults are not always going to respond to questions, comments or even a generic greeting. Our role as caregivers is not to make them talk, but rather to provide a safe environment, which allows them the opportunity to talk if they so desire.

Communication Tips

- Be accessible
- Listen and try to understand
- Invite rapport by exhibiting a smile and a friendly manner
- Give the patient your full attention—show them they are important
- Provide privacy if possible when talking about personal health
- Express an interest in their comments, both by facial and verbal expression
- Talk with a reassuring non-threatening, non-authoritarian tone of voice
- When talking to someone with a hearing impairment, keep lips visible
- If patients are visually impaired, verbal instructions are imperative
- Maintain eye contact to see if patient appears puzzled or confused
- Avoid talking in "medical speak"
- Repeat instructions if needed, using short explanations to reinforce the message
- Reinforce verbal explanation with written instructions (14 font, double-spaced black print on white paper)
- Give patients the opportunity to ask and re-ask the same question
- If patient appears confused, ask if there is a family member who can be contacted
- Empathize - and treat every patient as if they were your elderly loved one

FUTURE DIRECTIONS

In less than ten years, the leaders of the baby-boom wave will reach age sixty-five. Numbers of older adults will swell. Increased awareness of disease risk factors, life-style modifications, an improved attitude toward staying fit and active, and new technology in health care will result in a healthier cohort of elderly. Older adults are also becoming more independent. We live in a society that values autonomy. It is difficult to project how these factors will affect the prevalence or incidence of elder abuse in the future. For now, education, a heightened awareness of what constitutes abuse, and an improvement in communication skills seem to be the best weapons to guard against verbal abuse and communication neglect directed at our elderly. Finding answers does not rest merely on the shoulders of the researchers; detection of abuse is not the sole responsibility of physicians, adult protective services is not the only organization of interest in addressing abusive situations, it has to be a multidisciplinary collaborative effort. Within a health care setting however, it is the responsibility of every employee, regardless of their job status, to prevent any type of abuse or neglect of those under their care, while they are dependent on our care.

REFERENCES

Anetzberger, G.J., Palmisano, B.R., et al. A Model for Elder Abuse and Dementia. *The Gerontologist*, 2000; Vol 40(4) 492-497.

Blazer, D.G. Depression in Late Life: Review and Commentary. *The Journal of Gerontology Series A: Biological Sciences and Medical Sciences*, 2003; 58: M249-M265.

Brody, D.S., Hahn, S.R., Spitzer, R.L. et al. Identifying Patients with Depression in the Primary Care Setting. *Archives of Internal Medicine*, 1998; 158: 2469-2475.

Brown, M.N., Lapane, K.L., and Luisi, A.F. The Management of Depression in Older Nursing Home Residents. *Journal of the American Geriatrics Society*, 2002; 50: 69-76.

Burgio, L.D., Annen-Burge, R., et al. Come Talk with Me. *The Gerontologist*, 2001; Vol 41(4) 449-460.

Charness, N., Parks, D.C., and Sabel, B.A. (Eds). *Communication, Technology and Aging: Opportunities and Challenges for the Future*. 2001. Springer Publishing Co. New York, NY.

Filinson, R. and Ingram SR (Eds) *Elder Abuse: Practice and Policy*. 1989. Human Sciences Press, New York, NY.

Hazzard, W.R. et al. (Eds). *Principles of Geriatric Medicine and Gerontology, 5th Edition*, 2003. McGraw-Hill Professional, New York, NY.

Hinckley, J.J. Vocational and Social Outcomes of Adults with yhasia. *Journal of Communication Disorders*, 2002; 35: 543.560.

Hintz, C.A. *Communicating with Your Patients: Skills for Building Rapport*. 2000; American Medical Association, Chicago, IL.

National Clearinghouse on Family Violence Publication. Abuse and Neglect of Older Adults: A Discussion Paper. Available at: [http://canada.justice.gc.ca/en/ps/fm/adultsfs.html]

Pillemar, K. and Finkelhor, D. The Prevalence of Elder Abuse: Ayrvey. *The Gerontologist*, 1988; 29(3): 321-327.

Pillemer, K., Suitor, JJ, et al. A Cooperative Communication Intervention for Nursing Home Staff and Family Members of Residents. *The Gerontologist*, 2003; Vol 43 (Supplement 2): 96 - 106.

Reis, M. and Nahmiash, D. When Seniors are Abused: An Intervention Model. *The Gerontologist*, 1995; Vol 35 (5): 666-671.

Ripich, D.N. Communication and Aging: Moving Toward a Unified, Systemic Approach. *The Gerontologist*, 2003; 43 (1): 136-139.

Santo Pietro, M.J. and Ostuni, MA. *Successful Communication with Person's with*

Alzheimer's Disease. 2003; Butterworth-Heinemann; St. Louis, MO.

Wolf, R. Elder Abuse and Neglect: Causes and Consequences. *Journal of Geriatric Psychiatry*, 1997; 30(1): 153-174.

Wood, S. and Stevens, M. Vulnerability to Elder Abuse and Neglect in Assisted Living Facilities. *The Gerontologist,* 2003; 43: 753-757.

10

SEXUAL VIOLENCE AGAINST ELDERLY WOMEN

Joanne Ardovini

OVERVIEW OF THE SEXUAL ABUSE OF ELDERLY WOMEN

Sexual assault is one of the most under-reported crimes identified by the FBI. The public at large, administrators, law enforcement, legislatures, and researchers are unaware of the actual rates at which sexual abuse of elderly women occurs. It is an unsavory thing to think of, yet it occurs and possibly at a much more frequent rate than we know (www.forensicnursemag.com/articles/331feat2.html).

A study surveying 300 women asked them to rank which crime they most feared. The crimes included in the study were murder, burglary, robbery, attempted murder, and rape. Women under the age of thirty-five noted that rape was their number one fear. Women thirty-six to fifty noted that rape was their number two. Women over sixty-six years old ranked rape as their ninth greatest fear (www.archstone.org/usr_doc/silent_suffering.pdf).

While sexual violence against women in general does not appear to be decreasing, our awareness of sexual violence against elderly women does not seem to be increasing. Sexual abuse is thought to be the least perceived, acknowledged, detected, and reported type of elder abuse. Adult Protective Services have reported that sexual abuse constitutes less than one percent of all types of abuse cases reported with the majority of its victims being female (Teaster, Roberto, Duke, and Kim 2000: 1-16). The preliminary findings of a study conducted by Teaster, Roberto, Duke, and Kim found that women constituted 95.2% of all the victims of sexual abuse reported within a three year period in the state of Virginia (Teaster, Roberto, Duke, and Kim 2000: 5). It is acknowledged that lack of reporting is not due to a lack of occurrences but due to the stigma associated with sexual abuse.

DEFINITION OF SEXUAL ABUSE

Sexual assault is a crime of violence that preys on people who are vulnerable. Those who are the most vulnerable are the young and the elderly populations. The National Center on Elder Abuse defines sexual abuse of the elderly as any sexual behavior that is non-consensual sexual contact of any kind with an elderly person (www.elderabusecenter.org/default.cfm?p=basics.cfm). Sexual conduct with any person incapable of giving consent is also considered sexual abuse. It includes, but is not limited to, unwanted touching, all types of sexual assault or battery, such as rape, sodomy, coerced nudity, and sexually explicit photographing (www.elderabusecenter.org/default.cfm?p=basics.cfm). Rape is defined as "unlawful sexual intercourse with a female who did not consent to engaging in the sexual act (www.nursinghomeabuseresourcecenter.com/glossary/r.html). Sodomy is defined as "oral or anal sex without consent (www.nursinghomeabuseresourcecenter.com/glossary/r.html). A major component of these definitions are consent, "voluntary agreement of one who has sufficient mental capacity to make an intelligent choice to do something proposed by another person" (www.nursinghomeabuseresourcecenter.com/glossary/r.html). If the elderly individual does not grant consent then the sexual behavior is seen as being coerced. Coercion is the act of compelling by pressure, threat, or force (www.nursinghomeabuseresourcecenter.com/glossary/r.html).

Sexual assault of elderly women may present itself in a variety of ways. First, a victim of sexual abuse may exhibit physical signs, such as, difficulty walking or sitting, recurring or unexplained injuries, combination of new and old injuries, injuries without underlying diseases, injuries in areas usually covered by clothing (www.keln.org/bibs/mcdaniel.html). A victim of sexual abuse may also experience pain, itching, bruising, or bleeding in the genital area. Other physical signs include an unexplained venereal disease or genital infections (Brandl and Horan 2002:43). The elder sexual assault victims exposed to sexually transmitted diseases, including HIV, may never receive any medical care. In turn, they may not be given any emotional support following the abuse as well. This leads to another sign of sexual abuse.

Second, social-psychological signs may present themselves. These signs include depression or withdrawal, hesitation to speak openly, fearfulness of caregiver or strangers, confusion, and denial. Post-traumatic rape syndrome may also present itself after an assault. Post-traumatic rape syndrome is a recognized phenomenon among sexual assault researchers (www.forensicnursemag.com/articles/331feat2.html). Elderly female victims of sexual assault may experience the impact of this syndrome at a heightened level than female victims of college age, for example. This maybe due to the indigestibility of the nature of the offense and the perception that rape does not occur to women 65 years of age and older. The elderly have the attitude that sexual assault is not going to happen to them. It is not something they are concerned about. This gives elderly women a false sense of security. They don't expect it, therefore; when it does happen, the sexual assault is much more traumatic for them (www.archstone.org/usr_doc/silent_suffering.pdf). These signs of sexual abuse of elderly women are often overlooked or not recognized. This leads to a gross under-reporting of the crime (Tatara and Kusmeskus 1999: 1).

VICTIMS OF SEXUAL ABUSE

Sexual abuse of women can affect women of all ethnic backgrounds and social statuses. However, being elderly compounds the impact of victimization for women. What makes an elder female vulnerable to sexual assault is dependent upon a variety of factors such as social isolation, mental and/or physical impairment, and financial variables. (www.archstone.org/usr_doc/silent_suffering.pdf). Other social factors may also increase an elderly woman's potential for sexual victimization. For instance, poor communication between themselves and their caregiver may impede the victims' ability to express their disapproval of the behavior and the abusers' inability to understand the lack of consent. An elderly female who has abused the caregiver in the past may experience abuse by the caregiver. An elderly female who lives constantly with their caregiver also has an increased potential for victimization (Campbell Reay and Browne 2001: 60). All these variables are factors that give us insight into what makes an older adult female vulnerable to sexual abuse by their caregivers.

OFFENDERS OF SEXUAL ABUSE

In general, abusers of older female adults are both male and female. However, Adult Protective Services has reported that 62.6% of offenders of physical abuse committed against the elderly are males (www.aoa.gov/abuse/report/Gfindings-02.htm). Males also make-up the majority of sexual offenders, who sexually abuse elderly females (Teaster, Roberto, Duke, and Kim 2000: 9). Teaster, Roberto, Duke, and Kim in their study of sexual victimization of older females reported in Virginia within a three-year period found that all of the noted alleged offenders were identified as male (Teaster, Roberto, Duke, and Kim 2000: 9).

The National Center on Elder Abuse has also compiled data concerning the characteristics of an offender of elderly abuse. The NCEA has reported that family members are more often the abusers than any other group. For several years, the data indicated that adult children were the most common abusers of family members. Recent information indicates spouses are the most common perpetrators when state data concerning elders and vulnerable adults is combined (www.Elderabusecenter.org/default.cfm?p=faqs.cfm). However, this data is representative of offenders of elder abuse in general and is not specific to sexual abuse.

Therefore, we must rely on the general characteristics of offenders of elder abuse as potential indicators for sexual abuse. Some of these general characteristics include:

- A caregiver living constantly with their elderly dependents may view the elder as a target for sexual abuse;
- A caregiver who is suffering from relationship conflict and often exhibits hostile, threatening and/or aggressive behavior;
- A caregiver who is subject to high stress, strain, isolation, and lacks community and personal support;
- A caregiver who has a history of mental health problems, sexual abuse (as a victim and/or offender), anxiety disorder, depression, and/or alcohol/drug use (Campbell Reay and Browne 2001:56).

In a study conducted over a three-year period, the researchers found in year 1 , 28.6% of the offenders were family members, 28.6% were facility staff members, 28.6% were residents in the older adult facility, and in 14.2% of the cases the offender was unrelated to the older adult and was not a member of the household or staff member of a facility (Teaster, Roberto, Duke, Kim 2000: 9). During year 2 and 3, the majority of the offenders were residents living in the same facility as the older female adult, constituting 83.3% and 86.7% respectively, of all cases of sexual abuse reported (Teaster, Roberto, Duke, Kim 2000: 9).

Other characteristics were found in the study. During year 1 of the research, 12.5% of the offenders were dependent on the income of the older female victim, 25.0% abused alcohol and/or drugs, and 12.5% suffered from mental illness. Similarly for year 2, 9.1% of the offenders were dependent economically, 18.2% abused alcohol and/or drugs, and 54.5% suffered mental illness. Only 9.1% of the offenders were unemployed. During year 3 of the study, there was little deviation from the previous years findings (Teaster, Roberto, Duke, Kim 2000: 9-11).

RISK FACTORS OF SEXUAL VICTIMIZATION

Possible risk factors that may lead to the sexual victimization of older female include the following:

- Personal Factors = Often relating to a pattern of abuse in the family. The elder female perceives herself as helpless and dependent; sexual victimization only serves to increase these feeling of vulnerability. Often, when the elder female is confused and helpless, the stress on the caregiver is magnified and thus the possibility of random instances of abuse are increased;

- Interpersonal Factors = May include a variety of unresolved past conflicts and lifelong histories of inadequate relationships. The caregiver may feel that he is receiving insufficient gratification for his sacrifices and attention. Power conflicts between the elder female and her caregiver may also exist;

- Situational Factors = the addition of a dependent family member provides increased stress and possible conflict. The middle-aged abuser can be described as being in the "sandwich generation," providing care both to children and to the older female. Other factors include unemployment, substance abuse, marital problems, economic difficulties related to providing care for the victim or other financial stresses, the stress of providing constant care, and medical problems;

- Sociocultural Factors = these may include pervasive, negative attitudes toward older female (Paveza 1997: 2).

PROVIDER ATTITUDE TOWARDS THE SEXUAL VICTIMIZATION

Sexual violence is a significant problem that adversely affects the health and safety of millions of women throughout their lifespan. Given the demographics of aging women and their longer life expectancies, clinicians are increasingly likely to see patients whose injuries or poor health status are caused or affected by abusive relationships (Brandl and Horan 2002: 41). Therefore, providers of elder care, as well as criminal justice professionals and Adult Protective Service Workers, must expand their perceptions of potential victims of sexual abuse in order to be able to identify victimization and establish comprehensive intervention and prevention efforts.

Since the sexual violation of elder females is perceived as taboo, it is often misread. Understanding how various individuals perceive their role in dealing with cases concerning elderly females is important, given the way that the acts have been treated as social problems rather than systemic problems in the past (Curry, Johnson and Sigler 1994:65-71). For example, surveys of law enforcement officers suggested that elderly citizens presented a number of aggravations to police. A study of 180 police department reported that 67% of the police believed that the elderly lacked an understanding of the nature and scope of the police. This same study also reported that 43% of the responding departments indicated that they lacked an understanding of and training concerning the elderly (Blakely and Dolon 2000:73).

The gap in training and understanding of the victimization of elder women is due to a variety of interrelated, systemic issues. The abuse of elderly individuals, including women, has been defined as criminal behavior since the early 1990s. However, research showing the effectiveness of criminalization on the occurrences of sexual abuse is almost unheard of (Payne, Berg, and Toussaint 2001: 607). Therefore, what is needed is not only research in this area, but professional training; coordination among state service systems and among service providers; technical assistance in the development of policy manuals and protocols that outline the proper or preferred procedures; and public education (www.aoa.gov/Factsheets/abuse.html).

PREVENTION

Adult Protective Service programs are designated as the primary agencies in most states to receive and investigate reports of abuse (www.preventelderabuse.org/professionals/professional.html). Adult Protective Service workers, are the "front line" in elder abuse prevention and should receive training on signs of sexual violence. Health and medical professionals also play an important role in the identification of sexual abuse of elderly females. It is important for these professionals to develop trust and respect with their patients (www.preventelderabuse.org/professionals/professional.html). If the victim is comfortable with their health care provider, they are more likely to report abuse. In turn, if the health care provider respects their patient, they are less likely to overlook signs of sexual abuse. This also holds true for law enforcement personnel. These individuals are able to ensure victims' safety and hold perpetrators accountable for their actions (www.preventelderabuse.org/professionals/professional.html.

Researchers have the ability to affect prevention through their work to provide insight into the etiology, rates, and risk factors associated with the sexual victimization of elderly females. The information that is uncovered through research can be critical to professionals working in the field of aging, health care and medical professionals, and law enforcement personnel. Research may also impact the development of legislation which can assist in the establishment of effective interventions and services (www.preventelderabuse.org/professionals/professional.html).

The media, an important agent of socialization, plays a fundamental role in informing the public of the occurrences of the sexual victimization of elderly females. The media also plays a role in the construction of public perceptions. It can enlist the public's help in identifying abuse, educate policy makers about the need for improved services and public policy, direct victims to needed services, and warn abusers about the consequences of their actions (www.preventelderabuse.org/professionals/professional.html).

Concerned citizens can also play a vital role in the prevention of sexual abuse of elderly females. This can be done by reporting potential cases of sexual abuse, helping raise awareness, volunteering at agencies, and advocating for needed services and policies (www.preventelderabuse.org/professionals/professional.html).

As noted, sexual abuse and abuse in general of elderly women is a multidimensional problem that requires broad expertise and a variety of resources. The most common approach to preventing elder abuse is to provide professional and public education programs at the community level. In addition to established federal and state laws designed for reporting elderly abuse neglect, many states also provide informal caregivers and interested citizens with training in eldercare. In most communities, both public and private agencies work collaboratively to ensure the protection of vulnerable elders. Although the causes of elderly abuse are complex and varied, a promising approach to increasing self-determination for the elderly is based on empowerment concepts. The rationale for the application of an empowerment approach to the sexual abuse of elderly females derives from the powerlessness these victims experience based on social reconstruction theory, an orientation specific to older age (Chima 2002:61-62).

Social reconstruction theory provides a perspective that assess planned change at the societal level that will benefit older adults due to its analysis of the breakdown and competence in older age (Chima 2002: 62). As a result of the social reorganization that occurs in later life, older people are devalued, develop negative self-images, and a loss of occupational roles and established networks. Therefore, the empowerment perspective attempts to increase personal, ,interpersonal, and political power so that individuals can take action to improve their life situation (Chima 2002: 62). This is done in a variety of ways:

1) Increasing self-efficiency by impacting one's ability to produce and to regulate events in one's life;
2) Developing group consciousness among the general population and the elderly;
3) Reducing self-blame by attributing their problems to the existing power structure in society;
4) Assuming personal responsibility for change, which counteracts some of the potentially negative results of reducing self-blame (Chima 2002: 62-63).

Another approach to decreasing the sexual abuse of elderly females is the intervention approach. There are three major tenets of this approach. They include: awareness of policies and services, caretaker assistance, and advocacy. Those that take this approach argue that significant attention needs to be paid to the provision of services. Although social workers and care providers often receive clinical training and experience, they lack an awareness of their potential impact in the policy making process. They must evaluate the services that they provide on their impact on preventing abuse and not solely upon their availability (Chima 2002: 64). They work closest with the elderly and are more apt to detect problems and needed resources and policies.

Caretaker assistance is an important aspect of curtailing potential sexually abusive situations. Caretakers can be provided and educated concerning information regarding resources that are available to them (Chima 2002: 64).

While the roles of social workers in the field of aging are increasing, their role as advocate is crucial in responding to the sexual abuse of elderly females. A beneficial guideline for advocacy is the Older Americans Act of 1965 and its amendments, which provide the basis for financial aid by the federal government to assist states and local communities to meet the needs of the elderly. A major objective of this act is to provide advocates with systematic measures and purpose of actions to decrease elder abuse and increase the chances of more elderly needs being met (Chima 2002: 64).

Regardless of the theoretical approach taken when exploring the sexual abuse of elderly females, we must remember that prevention is the goal. Therefore, intervention must be tailored to the needs of the elderly females and the circumstances of the sexual abuse. Success of prevention programs and the development of policies should be based upon the needs of the population it serves and education of the general public.

REFERENCES

Andermahr, Sonya, Terry Lovell, and Carol Wolkowitz 2000. *A Glossary of Feminist Theory*. London: Arnold.

Bell, Christine, Mary F. Ferris, and Laura Criss. 2002. "Sexual Assault and the Elderly: Shattering the Myths." Long Beach, CA: Archstone Foundation, Retrieved

September 10, 2003 (www.archstone.org/usr_doc/silent_suffering.pdf).

Blakely, B.E. and Ronald Dolon. 2000. "Perceptions of Adult Protective Services Workers of the Support Provided by Criminal Justice Professionals in a Case of Elder Abuse." *Journal of Elder Abuse and Neglect* 12:71-94.

Brandl, Bonnie and Deborah L. Horan. 2002. " Definitions and Dynamics of Elder Abuse and Domestic Violence in yfe." Pp. 42-54 in *Domestic ylence and Health Care: Policies and Prevention*, edited by Carolina Reyes, William J. Rudman, and Calvin R. Hewitt. Binghamton, NY: Haworth Press, Inc.

Campbell Reay, A.M. and K.D. Browne. 2001. "Risk Factors Characteristics in Careers who Physically Abuse or Neglect Their Elderly Dependants." *Aging and Mental Health* 5:56-62.

Chima, Felix O. 2002. "Overview of Sources, Prevalence and Intervention Initiatives." *Free Inquiry in Creative Sociology* 30:57-66.

Curry, B.S., I.M. Johnson, and R.T. Sigler. 1994. "Elder Abuse: Justice Problem, Social Problem, or Research Problem." *Free Inquiry in Creative Sociology* 22:65-71.

Katayama, Barbara. 2003. "Sexual Abuse of the Elderly." Forensic Nurse. Retrieved October 10, 2003. (www.forensicnursemag.com/articles/331feat2.html)

McDaniel, Christine. 1996. "Elder Abuse in the Domestic Setting." KELN.org Bibliography.. Retrieved September 10, 2003. (www.keln.org/ bibs/mcdaniel.html).

NA. 2003. "Elderly Sexual Abuse: Nursing Home Resident Sexual Abuse." Nursing Home Abuse Resource Center. Retrieved October 13, 2003. (www.aoa.gov/ abuse/report/Gfindings-02.htm)

NA. 2003. "The Basics: Major Types of Elder Abuse." National Center on Elder Abuse. Retrieved June 30, 2003. (www.nursinghomeabuserresourcecenter.com/glossary/r.html)

NA. 2003. "Frequently Asked Question." National Center on Elder Abuse. Retrieved June 30, 2003. (www.elderabusecenter.org/default.cfm?p=faqs.cfm.)

NA. 2003. "Critical Issues in Elder abuse." National Committee for the Prevention of Elder Abuse. Retrieved June 2, 2003. (www.preventelderabuse.org/ issues/issues.html).

NA. 2001. "Elder Abuse Prevention: Administration on Aging Fact Sheet." Administration on Aging. Retrieved June 2, 2003. (www.aoa.gov/ Factsheets/abuse.html.)

Payne, Brian. K., Bruce L. Berg, and Jeff Tousaint. 2001. "The Police Response to the Criminalization of Elder Abuse: An Exploratory Study." *Policing: An International Journal of Police Strategies and Management* 24:605-625.

Paveza, Gregory. 1997. "Elder Justice: Medical Forensic Issues Concerning Abuse and Neglect." National Institute for Justice. Retrieved September 10, 2003. www.ojp.gov/nij/elderjust/elder_07.html.

Taeuber, Cynthia M. 1996. *Statistical Handbook on Women in America (Second edition)*. Phoenix: Arizona: The Oryx Press.

Tatara, Toshio and Lisa M. Kuzmeskus. 1999. *Types of Elder Abuse in Domestic Settings*. Washington, DC: National Center on Elder Abuse.

Teaster, Pamela B., Karen A. Roberto, Joy O. Duke, and Myeonghwan Kim. 2000. "Sexual Abuse of Older Adults: Preliminary Findings of Cases in Virginia." *Journal of Elder Abuse and Neglect* 12:1-16.

11

HELPING VICTIMS: SOCIAL SERVICES, HEALTH CARE INTERVENTIONS IN ELDER ABUSE

James Anderson and Nancie Mangels

The problem of elder abuse is so pervasive that officials at the Centers for Disease Control (CDC) have already declared it an epidemic in America (see Rosenberg and Fenley,1991).

Elder abuse is a public health issue because of the medical and psychological consequences associated with this type of victimization. This chapter is divided into four parts. Part One presents the epidemiological approach used by the public health community to prevent injuries and premature deaths of the greater population. Part Two provides several theories that explain the causes of elder abuse. Part Three describes social services and health care interventions. Part Four discusses preventions and policy implications that can be used (at the local and state levels) to drastically lower the number of cases while better dealing with victims and offenders. In the final analysis, the chapter argues that elder abuse is a public health issue that can be prevented and those who suffer this victimization can overcome its negative consequences.

EPIDEMIOLOGY AND THE EPIDEMIOLOGICAL APPROACH

Epidemiology is the basic science of public health (Gostin, 2000; Schneider, 2000). It involves the study of epidemics and their impact on the community at-large. While some people are confused about the similarities between public health and medical care, the two are quite different. Medical care is concerned with individual patients. Public health sees the community as its patient. It tries to improve the health of the population. While medicine tries to heal patients who are ill, public health focuses on preventing illnesses (Schneider, 2000). Stated another way, medicine is individualized, while public health is concerned with the quality of health found within the population. Proponents of public health argue that it contributes a great deal more to the overall health of the population than medicine. For example, some researchers contend that the longevity of the population has increased from 45 to 75 years over the past century because of advances in medical technology and efforts of public health. They cite improvements in the quality of public health as being due, in part, to better nutrition, housing, sanitation, and occupational safety. Proponents also argue that one responsibility of public health is to educate the public and politicians about the crucial role that a strong public health system must play in maintaining and improving the health of the public.

Those in the public health community (e.g. clinics, hospitals, local and state health departments, and the CDC, to name a few) use the epidemiological approach to assess the health of the population, diagnose its problems, seek the causes of those problems, and devise strategies to cure them (Gostin,2000; Schneider, 2000). Epidemiology examines the distribution and determinants of disease frequency in human populations (Gostin,2000). Epidemiologists are concerned with disease "frequency." However, they use the term "disease" broadly to mean "health outcome." Epidemiology uses two types of frequency measures: incidence and prevalence. More specifically, incidence rates measure the probability that a healthy person in the population will develop a disease or injury. The rates are useful in identifying causes of a disease or injury. Prevalence is the total number of cases existing in a defined population. Incidence and prevalence are related to each other, but the relationship is contingent upon how long people live with injury or disease.

The public health community is concerned about preventing elder abuse for several reasons. First, violence against the elderly extends beyond the reach of criminal justice. While the health consequences of violence are tremendous, society has generally looked to the criminal justice system to protect its citizens from violence. However, the injuries, disabilities, and premature deaths associated with violence far exceed the resources and expertise of most state criminal justice systems (Donziger,1996). For example, when the perpetrator has been apprehended, arrested, and charged, this does not provide the victim with the treatment that he or she needs to move toward recovery. As a result, the CDC has added a new component called the National Center for Injury Prevention and Control (NCIPC) to reduce the human suffering and medical costs associated with injuries. Officials at the CDC contend that fatal and nonfatal injuries resulting from interpersonal violence have become one of the most important public health problems facing our country. The crime of elder abuse is no exception. Second, the public health community introduces a primary prevention approach to the problem of violence. While criminal justice concentrates on deterrence and incapacitation, the public health approach is focused on prevention (Anderson, Grandison, and Dyson, 1996). Officials in public health do not believe their efforts alone can solve the problem of elder abuse. In fact, they contend that criminal justice must play a crucial role, but the role of public health must be proactive and at the forefront. Criminal justice should take a reactive role to enhance the efforts of the public health system. Scholars contend that the efforts of public health will compliment the work of the criminal justice system (Donziger,1996). Public health officials argue that since its strategies have been successfully used in the past to combat the spread of infectious diseases, premature deaths, and physical illnesses that include lung cancer, heart diseases and motor vehicle crashes, it is believed that they can reach the same results when focusing on preventing elder abuse (Braithwaite and Taylor, 1992; Rosenberg and Fenley, 1991).

The Epidemiological Approach

The public health community uses the epidemiological approach. This approach consists of health-event surveillance, epidemiological analysis, and intervention design and evaluation focused unwaveringly on a single, clear outcome — the prevention of a particular illness or injury. Again, because of its proven track record, experts at the CDC believe that the epidemiological approach can prevent violence – namely, elder abuse, with similar success (see Braithwaite and Taylor 1992; Rosenberg and Fenley,1991). The epidemiological approach is multi-disciplinary in nature. Because of the complexities of infectious diseases and interpersonal violence, the approach draws on the resources of various disciplines to better understand and address the issue of violence. The disciplines included in the epidemiological approach are: (a) biomedical sciences (bacteria, yeast, protozoa caused by micro-organisms), (b) environmental health sciences (preventing the spread of diseases through water, air, and food), (c) social sciences (social environmental impact on behavior), and (d) the behavioral sciences (psychological and mental health) (Schneider, 2000). With these, public health officials can mobilize resources in medicine, mental health, social sciences, and substance abuse services to prevent injuries and premature death (see Rosenberg and Fenley, 1991). Therefore, epidemiologists represent a coalition of professions united by their shared mission and focus on disease prevention and health promotion.

PREVENTION AND INTERVENTION

To prevent injuries and minimize their consequences when they occur, the NCIPC relies on the public health methodology that utilizes five steps to address health issues and injuries. The public health methodology, or the epidemiological approach, includes:

First	defining the injury or health problem;
Second	identifying the risk and protective factors associated with the problem;
Third	developing and testing prevention strategies to control the problem;
Fourth	implementing the interventions to improve the health of the population;
Fifth	monitoring those interventions to assess their effectiveness.

Epidemiologists believe that prevention must come through intervention after a problem has been identified by either the assessment process of a public health agency or through community concerns. The public health system uses several intervention methods: primary prevention, secondary prevention, and tertiary prevention. First, primary prevention seeks to avoid the occurrence of an illness or injury by preventing exposure to risk factors (e.g, preventing the occurrence of the act by being proactive in terms of educating caregivers and the community at-large about elder abuse). Next, secondary prevention seeks to minimize the severity of the illness or injury-causing events once the event has occurred (e.g., quickly getting treatment and counseling for victims and offenders of elder abuse). Third, tertiary prevention seeks to minimize disability by providing medical care and rehabilitation services (e.g., develop emergency and medical services). Epidemiologists view an injury as the result of a "chain of causation" involving an agent, a host, and the environment (Braithwaite and Taylor, 1992).

Prevention is achieved by breaking the chain of causation at any step (see Schneider, 2000). In the case of elder abuse, it could be as easy as removing either the elder or the caregiver from the home or institutional setting and offering treatment to both parties in order to prevent the continuation of the behavior and to alleviate the pain and suffering associated with the behavior. However, in some cases, the criminal justice system will be used to make arrests when caregivers have committed crimes against an elder (Gaines, Kaune, and Miller, 2000). When epidemiologists study patterns of diseases and injuries in human populations and the causative factors that influence these patterns, they detect signals of an emerging epidemic. Epidemiologists look for common exposures or other shared characteristics in the people who are sick or affected by violence in order to seek causative factors. Some questions that epidemiologists typically ask are who, when, and where. They are concerned with: First, who is being injured or contracting the disease under investigation? Second, when is the injury or disease occurring? Third, where is the injury or disease occurring? From this information, epidemiologists can make better decisions about why the injury or disease is occurring. Their main goal is to use this knowledge to control and prevent the spread of injuries and diseases. Stated another way, public health officials believe that it is more important to determine why people become violent and to develop strategies to reduce the risk factors that lead to interpersonal violence (Donziger,1996).

THEORIES ON THE CAUSES OF ELDER ABUSE

In using the epidemiological approach to understanding the causes of elder abuse, experts in public health (especially those in the social and behavioral sciences), examine the impact of the offender's social environment and the quality of their mental and emotional health. The motivation to engage in elder abuse is of interest to officials in public health, criminal justice, community treatment centers, and concerned citizens. In order to prevent the behavior, officials need to be able to identify, explain, and make predictions regarding who is likely to be an offender for these two reasons: First, identification is necessary to prevent offenders from injuring the elderly. Second, it is important to remove and properly treat victims. Therefore, the work of researchers is crucial. At the same time, people, in general, are intrigued by offenders who engage in such activity considering the pain and injury this activity inflicts upon the most vulnerable members of society. Concern exists over the types of life experiences offenders may have endured for their actions to manifest into this behavior. Scholars contend that explanations for engaging in elder abuse may differ from one offender to the next. However, most scholars agree that there are both micro-and-macro level explanations that could explain elder abuse. In epidemiology, researchers focus on common exposures or other shared characteristics in offenders, as well as victims, to isolate the causes of elder abuse. Some of the more widely accepted theories are: the cycle of violence; psychopathology; social exchange; family stress; and the techniques of neutralization, or "drift" (Centers for Disease Control,1997; Reiss and Roth, 1993; Adler, Mueller, and Laufer,2001).

Cycle of Violence Theory

A popular yet controversial theory used to explain elder abuse is the cycle of violence theory. The theory argues that people who have been psychologically, physically, or sexually abused as children have a greater likelihood of becoming violent adults (Simons, Wu, Johnson, and Conger, 1995; Spaccarelli,Coatsworth,and Bowden, 1995). Gelles (1993) suggests that the physical punishment of children is the most effective way to teach violence. Moreover, research finds that people who are victimized at an early age face a higher risk of being arrested for committing crimes as adults (Widom,1992). For example, Spaccarelli et al.(1995) report that young men are more likely to engage in violent behavior if they were the targets of physical abuse and were exposed to violent behavior by someone they knew or lived with. Similarly, Doerner and Lab, (2002) contend that there is evidence that warn that children who watch parents engage in violent outbursts will grow to accept these behaviors as legitimate. Some experts refer to the cycle of violence as the intergenerational transmission of violence. Essentially, they argue that violence is handed down and the chain of aggressive behavior continues generation after generation, because those exposed to violent and aggressive behavior develop a predisposition to use it (see Hunter and Kilstrsom,1979).

A major concern about the cycle of violence is that parents may be unaware that they are perpetuating this behavior. In fact, they may indirectly socialize children into using it as an acceptable response to life's problems. Though many people embrace the cycle of violence argument, Wolf and Pillemer (1989) report that not everyone who commits elder abuse was reared in a home where violence took place. Similarly, Pagelow (1984) along with Gelles and Cornell (1990) argue that though much of the research literature does not support this position, the idea is commonly accepted—the cycle of violence exists. While laypersons readily accept this theory, Wallace (1999) reports that there is no way to prove or disprove the cycle of violence theory. That is to say, violence committed by a family member who is a caregiver is a manifestation of one's acting out violence earlier committed against himself or herself. The inconsistent support of the theory makes the argument controversial.

Psychopathology

While some domestic violence experts may reject the argument of a cycle of violence theory, a segment of scholars attribute family violence in general, but elder abuse in particular, to a psychopathology found within offenders (Wallace, 1999). For example, Young (1974) argues that clinicians and practitioners tend to attribute elder abuse and other forms of domestic violence to sadistic personality traits. Rosenberg and Fenley (1991) find that intraindividual dynamics may explain the cause of elder abuse. They suggest that psychological well-being is related to the quality of the family relationship. In fact, it can serve as a predictor of outcomes in domestic violence situations (Andrews and Withy, 1979; Glenn and Weaver, 1981; Lee, 1978). Research supports that in situations where the caregivers suffer personality disorders, the probability is greater that elder abuse is a likely outcome. Some research even suggests that to cure child abuse, wife abuse, and other forms of interpersonal violence will require targeting and treating emotional illnesses (Gelles, 1974). Moreover, Hickey and Douglas (1981) argue that the manifestations of the disease can be seen in either the physical or verbal abuse targeted at the elder. These experts believe that such offenders may suffer from mental disorders that cause them to engage in abusive behavior. For example, Wolf and Pillemer (1989) contend that abusers suffer a form of flawed mental development. Wolf, Strugnell, and Godkin's (1982) research suggests that a high level of mental illness is common among elder abusers. Similarly, Beckman and Adelman (1992) find that many perpetrators of elder abuse have been hospitalized and diagnosed with serious psychiatric disorders, such as schizophrenia and other identifiable psychoses. In most cases, because psychological theories are based on untestable hypotheses rather than empirical data, psychological explanations for criminal behavior are often considered inconclusive and are therefore accepted with caution (Cleckley,1974; Gaines, Kaune, and Miller, 2000).

Social Exchange Theory

Unlike the cycle of violence and psychopathology theories, the social exchange theory argues that the more dependent the victim is on the abuser, the greater the likelihood that abuse will occur. Stated another way, the social exchange theory suggests that the increased dependency of the victim on the abuser results in acts of abuse (Davidson, 1979). Rosenberg and Fenley (1991) argue that the social exchange theory has led to two separate arguments that relate dependency to elder abuse. The first argument emphasizes that the level of stress experienced by the caregiver may account for violence inflicted on the elder. This suggests that different types of abuse may result from resentment that the abuser feels because he or she is the sole caregiver. Domestic violence experts argue that when adult children invite an aging parent to live with them, they also agree to provide them with the care and attention they need. However, despite what good intentions the adult child may have, this new arrangement could create a strain since caring for the parent could disrupt the adult child's life. The new addition could (1) strain an already troubled marriage; (2) interfere with the caregiver's employment; or (3) obstruct participation in social activities. As a result, the caregiver could resent the parent and abuse him or her accordingly because his or her presence is a constant reminder of the sacrifice that was made to accommodate and assist the aging parent.

The second argument suggests the reverse is true. It holds that the more the abuser depends on the elder for income, the greater the likelihood that abuse will occur. Baruch and Barnett (1983); Cicirelli (1981); and Johnson and Bursk (1977) find that the literature on family relations support the notion that dependency on an older person leads to poor quality relationships with relatives. This research also finds that parents' health is positively linked to feelings of closeness and attachment between parents and their adult children. Furthermore, where abuser dependency is concerned, experts suggest that the feeling of powerlessness is the main factor that explains abuse (see Finkelhor, 1983). Gerontologists suggest that the feeling of being dependent on one's parent is an intense source of strain on an adult child since it violates societal expectations for normal adult behavior (Rosenberg and Fenley,1991). Pillemer and Suitor (1998) report that the dependent's embarrassment about his or her economic situation could be the source of the abuse. Moreover, evidence suggests that mutual dependency exists from both the elder and the caregiver. For example, Wolf, Strugnell, and Godkin, (1982) find that in two-thirds of the cases, caregivers were economically dependent on the victim. Similarly, Hwalek et al. (1989) report that in a case-control study, financial dependency was a high risk factor of elder abuse. Furthermore, Anetzberger (1987) contends that survey data reveal that economically dependent relatives is an important determinant of elder abuse. Domestic violence experts contend that controversy exists in these relationships over who is really dependent on whom.

Family Stress Theory

Another explanation that has gained widespread support is the family stress theory (Steinmetz,1988). The family stress theory suggests that providing care for an elderly person places a tremendous amount of stress on the entire household. The theory holds that family stress comes from multiple angles such as an economic hardship, alterations made to the home, intrusion into the privacy of the family, and sleep deprivation. Experts advise that family stress is a major factor that could cause elder maltreatment. Gelles (1983) argues that some adult children may often forgo job security or greater employment opportunities to provide care for an aging parent or relative. For example, some adult children may refuse to relocate to another state, or accept a promotion that pays more money if it means spending less time in the home with an ill or aging parent or relative. Despite the good intentions of adult caregivers, Gelles also contends that the physical and psychological burden of providing for an elder with declining health can lead to the loss of control and later abuse.

Techniques of Neutralization or "Drift" Theory

The *"Techniques of Neutralization" or "Drift Theory"* can also be used to explain elder abuse (see Tomita, 1990). Sykes and Matza (1957) argued that not everyone abides by laws all the time, but instead, some people have the ability to engage in both conventional and deviant behavior after mastering techniques of neutralization. These people may appear normal and law-abiding, yet they are criminals. Essentially, after perpetrators master denying responsibility, injury, and a victim, along with learning to condemn their condemners, and to appeal to higher loyalties, they also learn to justify, rationalize, and excuse their behavior. The techniques of neutralization allow offenders to live double lives since they can move from being deviant and criminal, to law-abiding. After committing crimes, offenders quickly justify it, and "drift" back into conventional lifestyles with others who are grounded in morality and mainstream values.

Denial of Responsibility

When offenders deny responsibility, they typically argue that the elder abuse occurred because of circumstances beyond their control. For example, the offenders may reason that because they were reared in a dysfunctional home or the father was never present or because they were under the influence of a mind-altering drug at the time of the crime, they therefore, bare no responsibility for having committed the crime. For example, after physically abusing a parent, adult caregivers may not admit responsibility for their actions. They may contend that the physical abuse was a one time occurrence that happened by accident or because of circumstances beyond their control. Offenders believe that they bare no responsibility for committing physical abuse against an elderly parent.

Denial of Injury

When offenders deny injury, they contend that no one suffered as a result of the crime. For example, abusers who neglect or commit sexual abuse against an aging parent or relative often believe that engaging in sexual intercourse has no adverse impact on the victim, physically or psychologically. At the same time, if the caregiver does not give the aged person medication on a regular basis or maintain their hygiene, then no real injury occurred because the elder person does not have any appointments to keep and others are unaware of the neglect. Offenders often argue that because the elder suffers from mental disease, he or she cannot remember. Therefore, no one suffered as a result of their actions and believe no real harm has occurred from the victimization.

Denial of the Victim

When the offenders deny the victim, abusers may feel that the victim got what he or she deserved. He or she may reason that the elder was just asking to be victimized. This is a way of diminishing the personhood of the victim. For example, when people participate in "granny-bashing" or other hate crimes, they reason that elderly persons got what they deserved. From their vulnerability of being physically weak and unaware, the victims were just asking for it. Abusers often feel that victims get what they deserve, or that elders secretly want to relive their youth and fantasize about having sexual intercourse with a younger adult. They often believe that victims were asking to be victimized. This justification allows the offender to dehumanize or diminish the personhood of the elder victim.

Condemnation of the Condemners

After being arrested and charged, adult children or institutional caregivers may retaliate by accusing officials in the criminal justice system. They often argue that police are corrupt, and lawyers and judges take bribes. They argue that everyone is tainted and engages in some type of questionable behavior, yet the focus is on them and their behavior with an elder parent or relative. Elder abusers often view mandatory reporting laws and protective services as unfair and unjust. They contend that such services and laws represent an unfair intrusion into their lives. They condemn social service agencies for interfering with their family.

Appeal to Higher Loyalties

Offenders may justify abuse on the grounds that their behavior benefits others and not themselves. For example, an adult child whose family is experiencing a strain because of the presence of his or her parent, may view their physical abuse and neglect as a way of satisfying an unhappy spouse who opposes the presence of the elder in the home and who is frustrated by the attention and strain that the elder has placed on the family.

Social Services and Health Care Interventions

Family violence experts argue that because of a lack of knowledge about the nature, extent, and dynamics of elder abuse, it has been difficult to create uniform intervention strategies. They also contend that surveillance is limited and the problem remains greatly hidden. Since there is no comprehensive national policy regarding maltreatment of the elderly, states and communities have created their own programs to meet the needs of the victims and families of elder abuse (see Rosenberg and Fenley, 1991). For example, a survey of existing programs reveals a variety of strategies used to assist victims and perpetrators of elder abuse. Programs range from elder protective services to family counseling to legal intervention (Meadows, 2004). However, family violence experts believe that the different interventions adopted by practitioners and policymakers can be categorized into three main areas that include: (1) mandatory reporting laws; (2) protective services programs; and (3) service options (see Rosenberg and Fenley, 1991). While these programs appear to be the most often used in cases of elder abuse, there has been little evaluation research conducted that supports their effectiveness. Therefore, little is known about their ability to deter continued behavior. At the same time, success could depend on the amount of resources devoted to these programs in their respective jurisdictions. As such, it is possible for some states to have success with a program and another state to implement the same program (perhaps without committing adequate resources) and not have the same success. We caution that since there have been few if any evaluations of these programs, any signs of success should be critically evaluated.

Mandatory Reporting Laws

Mandatory reporting laws can be found in every state in America (Kapp,1995; Macolini,1995; and Thobaben,1989). These laws alert social service professionals to the problems of elder abuse so that they can take appropriate actions (Doerner and Lab, 2002). More specifically, mandatory reporting laws generally require that certain groups of people (e.g., health care professionals, case managers, legal guardians, bank tellers, police officers, independent living counselors, rehabilitation counselors, or conservators) report suspicious cases of abuse to the proper authorities. Persons outside these categories do not have a legal responsibility to report suspected cases of abuse. Despite this, experts suggest that anyone who suspects elder abuse should report it to social and rehabilitation services. In most states, the law has been crafted to foster a greater participation by requiring that the reporter's identity remain anonymous (Meadows, 2004). The promise of anonymity is believed by many to ensure successful reporting of the behavior. Mandatory reporting laws serve the twin purpose of identifying seniors who face abuse and allowing for intervention. In fact, supporters of mandatory laws argue that were it not for such laws, many cases of elder abuse would remain hidden, seniors would continue to be subjected to abuse, and may even suffer premature death. It should be noted that because these laws vary from state to state, the definition of abuse also varies, and the agency that is designated to receive the report of abuse is also responsible for conducting the investigation.

Criticisms of Mandatory Reporting Laws

Mandatory reporting laws are considered controversial because of several criticisms. Some experts argue that the criticisms are fourfold. First, opponents of mandatory reporting laws contend that these laws have not yet proven to be effective in alleviating the problem, and that increased reporting could be a product of the increased public attention about the problem of elder abuse (see Davis and Medina-Ariza, 2001). Second, critics also contend that legal penalties are not enforced because agencies fail to report abuse (Blakely and Dolon,1991; Quinn and Tomita,1986; Thobaben,1989). A third criticism is that most states do not take elder abuse seriously. Critics observe that after mandatory reporting laws are passed, states believe that they have done enough and quickly put the issue of elder abuse to rest. For example, most states often fail to provide adequate resources to fund the services that are desperately needed by victims and abusers (Crystal,1986; Anetzberger,1989). A fourth criticism is that the reporting process frustrates the relationship and confidentiality between professionals and clients. Cyrstal (1986) and Macolini (1995) report that these laws require physicians to report suspected cases of abuse. Doctors and public health officials argue this practice violates patient-physician confidentiality. Stated another way, professionals are faced with having to violate the law or breach the trust of a client and conceivably jeopardize a long standing therapeutic relationship with the victim and family. Opponents of these programs say they cannot stand alone and if they are to be effective, they must be accompanied by a commitment of resources from the designated reporting agency.

Protective Services

Protective services are designed to investigate concerns of elder abuse and neglect. Many agencies and organizations are found in many jurisdictions to meet the needs of abused and neglected elderly citizens. These agencies are commonly referred to as Adult Protective Services (APS). Protective service programs are generally supported by state legislation and are connected to agencies such as Health and Human Services Departments. While protective services are primarily concerned with assisting the elderly, they are also involved in activities, such as granting licenses to nursing homes, funding research, and training social service workers to meet the needs of clients (see Doerner and Lab, 2002). The services given to elder abuse victims are also controversial because social workers usually are empowered to serve in a legal intervention role. For example, social workers are those charged with the responsibility for initially investigating cases of abuse followed by attempts at treating the situation by providing services when needed. Protective service programs generally include the use of a legal surrogate option (e.g., guardianship or conservatorship) when the elder is found to be incompetent (Callendar,1982).

Criticisms of Protective Services

Similar to mandatory reporting laws, protective service programs also have their share of criticisms. First, members of the legal community argue that these programs intrude on the civil liberties of elderly citizens and demean them. Critics argue that protective services may inadvertently reduce elders to the status of needy infants or the mentally disabled (Doerner and Lab, 2002). For example, under protective services, guardians can and often do remove the rights and freedom that elderly citizens enjoy. Critics contend that this is usually contrary to what elderly victims desire. Second, the legal community argues that the definition that most states attach to elder abuse is too broad. More specifically, some lawyers argue that such laws intrude in the lives of families that may be experiencing the normal range of human problems (Callahan, 1981). In fact, Dolon and Hendricks (1989) and Fiegener, Fiegener, and Meszaros (1989) argue that because elder abuse is defined in an ambiguous manner, the police or law enforcement is minimally involved as an immediate contact source or aid. They argue that much elder abuse could be a product of self-neglect. As such, many elderly victims have questionable legal status. These critics also contend that one simply does not know whether neglect is self-imposed or is the product of a caregiver. A third and perhaps the main criticism of protective service programs is that they should be designed to reduce tension within the legal community and alleviate the ambiguity of tasks performed by protective service agencies (Bergman, 1989; Bergeron,1989). They suggest protective service programs could be effective if they offered a holistic approach in handling long-term problems instead of serving as a quick-fix solution. More specifically, Bergman (1989) suggests a combination of crisis intervention and protective service strategies, while Bergeron (1989) advocates the integration of adult protective services with human service providers.

Service Options

As stated earlier, because economic resources vary across states their range of service programs to assist the elderly vary also. However, every program is premised on the notion that the elderly experience abuse because they are dependent on the abuser (e.g., a domestic or institutional setting). Consequently, most service programs utilize unclear health and social services that are not specific to abuse. These services are tailored for victims who are functionally-impaired and dependent on the caregiver. In most cases, the abuse is probably caused by the strain that the caregiver faces. For example, experts argue that providing care to the elderly can be overwhelming to some especially when the elderly are in poor physical and mental health (Rosenberg and Fenley,1991). Caregivers are responsible for making sure that the elderly receive medication, are properly dressed and fed, and are assisted to make routine visits to the doctor or receive hospitalization when needed. Again, the responsibility of caring for the elderly can be an overwhelming experience that could lead to abuse. In some cases, service options given to alleviate the burden of care giving have included home care services, such as housekeeping and meal preparation. In other cases, victims can be relatively independent elders who are abused by a dependent relative (Rosenberg and Fenley,1991). In this instance, service options may require different types of intervention—typically those that are often used in spouse abuse situations. For example, some of the services may include increased social support for the elderly or the use of group consciousness raising. Domestic violence experts argue that like battered women, the elderly should be made aware that they have a right to be free from violence and that abuse can never be justified. Advocates, such as gerontologists and members of the American

Association of Retired Persons (AARP) have long argued that efforts should be made to generate social consciousness among the elderly and the lay public about powerless groups in society. Meadows (2004) contends that elders should also be made aware that they have the right to be treated with dignity and respect and to have their personal worth protected.

Another option is the use of safe houses or emergency shelters for elderly victims. This option has been successful in aiding battered women who have had to flee their abusers and seek shelter for their safety and the safety of their children. This option is designed to provide the elderly with an alternative that offers them escape and protection from continued abuse. At the same time, the option sends the message that the victim can live independently of the perpetrator and that he or she will no longer tolerate abuse because there is somewhere to turn for help. A third service option is legal intervention. Some experts argue that criminal justice sanctions can be of invaluable help in cases of domestic abuse. For example, in their seminal research, Sherman and Berk (1984) reported that law enforcement intervention successfully reduced domestic violence. More specifically, in a Minnesota experiment, they discovered that a formal arrest was a more effective method than using an eight hour cooling off period or mediation to prevent continued wife abuse. The study also revealed that since police are usually the first on the crime scene, after they make an arrest, they can direct victims to effective community services. In addition to police departments, some communities have created task forces to provide the elderly with needed services. These groups raise the consciousness of professionals and concerned citizens about the plight and needs of elderly victims of abuse and neglect (Wolf and Pillemer,1989; Hwalek, Hill, and Stahl,1989).

Elder Abuse: A Public Health Issue

Officials at the CDC argue that elder abuse is a public health issue because of the pain, suffering, and diminished quality of life associated with this type of violence. Both gerontologists and epidemiologists agree that the problem is likely to get worse since the elderly comprise an increasing proportion of Americans. Apart from the abuse, the elderly community already depends on the health care community since many suffer from physical problems such as diabetes, amputations, cancer, strokes, altered mental status, high blood pressure, urinary tract infections, syphilis, and congestive heart failure. Some may even require special attention from a nurse or caregiver for being incontinent. Furthermore, because of physical abuse, some elderly victims may need hospitalization and medical attention to recover from injuries sustained at the hands of their caregiver. While experiencing abuse, the elderly may suffer burns, gunshot wounds, punctures, injuries from rape, fractures or broken bones, and stab wounds. Moreover, some caregivers have been known to either intentionally or unintentionally withhold medication from those suffering from diabetes, depression, glaucoma, Alzheimer's, hypertension, arthritis, and shingles. Public health experts argue that elder abuse could lead some victims to depression or even suicide. Elias (1986) argues that sometimes the elderly may sustain debilitating injuries that can place limitations on their already restricted freedom of movement which could take an even greater psychological toll. What is more regrettable is that a segment of elderly victims will experience premature death if health care interventions are not forthcoming. Therefore, the health care community believes that because of the problems associated with injuries, elder abuse is a public health issue since many elderly victims will need both short-and long-term physical, as well as psychological, treatment to aid them in recovery (Braithwaite and Taylor,1992; Rosenberg and Fenley,1991).

Health care contributes significantly in patients' recovery. It often provides needed health care service within the home. It can be used after acute illnesses, hospitalization for chronic illnesses, or injuries sustained from abuse that require the care of a skilled nurse. It is also needed to assist people in accomplishing daily activities. Home health care services may include providing the following:

- A skilled nurse (who assesses the needs of a patient and develops treatment plans);
- Parenteral/enteral therapy (care for intravenous fluids, antibotics, pain control or tube feedings);
- Ostomy and wound care (a comprehensive program to assist patients with ostomies or other skin problems);
- Home health aide (nursing aides to assist with bathing, dressing, skin care, and oral hygiene);
- Physical therapy (exercise, treatment and special equipment to restore viability and decrease pain);
- Speech therapy (assist in the recovery of speaking, listening, and learning new ways to communicate); and
- Social services (assist the patient and family with social and economic problems caused by illness and acts as a liaison with community resource agencies.

In addition to health care services, states such as Missouri and Kansas are implementing senior clinics to care for the elderly. These clinics are designed for homebound seniors and residents of long-term care and assisted living. They were created to meet the challenges posed by health care needs. They provide a comfortable, convenient, cost-effective setting in which patients' special needs can be assessed, diagnosed, and treated by a primary care or specialty physician. Moreover, these clinics provide access to treatment for an improved quality of life, better monitoring through reduced hospitalization, and they allow chronic illnesses and injuries to be monitored for better medical outcomes. Senior clinics provide services for patients who:

- Require diagnostic evaluation;
- Have been recently discharged from acute care to long-term care, and

who need follow-up care from primary and or speciality physicians; or
- Require specialty care services.

Health care professionals are responsible for assessing and treating physical, as well as mental health, problems that are common among the aging population. When the elderly are taken to a hospital for injuries caused by a caregiver, case managers and social workers are duty bound to report incidents of suspected abuse to the appropriate authorities. After the elderly receive treatment and are released, case management workers assess the needs of patients. In most cases, they set up services and speak directly to the caregiver. Case management workers and social workers make inquiries about what type of equipment or service will be needed to aid the patient. They may have to make arrangements for the delivery of special equipment that will be needed for recovery. Depending on the condition of the elderly, such items may include a hospital bed, a wheelchair, a neck brace, bedside commode, or a rolling walker. Moreover, home health nurses typically visit the patient's home several times a week or as often as needed to assess the patient's progress.These nurses usually monitor vital signs, give medication as needed, and teach the caregiver how to provide for the patient. These services are typically paid for by Medicaid and Medicare programs.

Health care professionals argue that elder abuse adds to an already strained health care system. This is especially true for states' existing health care programs, such as Medicaid. Despite this, health experts argue that the elderly poor, unlike those who are affluent, experience unequal access to Medicaid and Medicare (see Julian and Kornblum,1986). In fact, they argue that minorities typically face differences in health and in effective access to health services. Comparatively, they report that middle class elders have greater access to health care and receive better quality of health care services, such as medical attention, medication, and treatments. They argue that this is not the reality for the minority elderly population that is disproportionately made up of African-Americans and Hispanics. For example, Braithwaite and Taylor (1992) contend that many elderly minorities suffer more since they have major obstacles to health that include poverty or a lack of financial resources, fragmented care or a lack of quality care, unemployment, and a lack of qualified staff. What is more alarming is that when the minority elderly are in reasonably good health, it may soon decline because of factors, such as an improper diet, lack of regular medication, medical attention, therapeutic equipments and routine checkups (Braithwaite and Taylor, 1992). Health experts argue that access to the health care system is highly unequal because it is based on the ability to pay (Calhoun, Light, and Keller, 1997).

PREVENTION STRATEGIES AND POLICY IMPLICATIONS

Despite the fact that elder abuse has existed for a long period of time, prevention strategies are in developmental or infancy stages (Doener and Lab, 2002). In fact, experts report that only within the past decade has formal legislation seriously attempted to address the rights and needs of senior Americans. Furthermore, there have been a number of interventions made to alleviate the pain and suffering of elder abuse. Some of these efforts have included the aforementioned programs, such as mandatory reporting laws, protective services, and service options. While these intervention efforts have contributed much in the way of assisting the elderly, some experts report that legal remedies, a comprehensive program, and the creation of more gerontology programs may actually be more effective in preventing elder abuse. In fact, some of these programs can help assist abused victims and put them on the road to recovery.

Legal Remedies (Civil and Criminal)

During the 1980s, most practitioners who worked with elder adults were reluctant to rely on the legal system as a means to protect their clients (Quinn and Heisler, 2002). As a result, the legal system was under-utilized for preventing elder abuse. Today, however, practitioners, as well as senior adults, have embraced the idea that the legal system can be used to protect the elderly's property interests and make perpetrators accountable for their misbehavior towards the elderly. The legal system provides two remedies: civil justice and criminal justice. Essentially, the civil justice system addresses the personal injuries and damages a defendant sustains at the hands of other persons or entities. The criminal justice system addresses the harm committed against persons and property. Both systems strive to restore balance and teach people and entities to obey the law. However, in civil cases, if the plaintiff prevails, he or she is awarded compensation for injuries. In criminal cases, if one is found guilty of a crime, he or she could face a loss of life, freedom, pay a fine, or make restitution to the victim depending on the seriousness of the crime. Sometimes defendants face a combination of sanctions.

Where elder abuse is concerned, Heisler and Quinn (1995) write that civil and criminal justice systems seek remedies to prevent and resolve elder maltreatment. More specially, both justice systems strive to (1) stop the unlawful, improper, or exploitative conduct that is inflicted on the victim; (2) protect the victim and society from the perpetrator; (3) hold the offender accountable for the behavior and communicate the message that the behavior is unacceptable; (4) rehabilitate the offender; and (5) make the victim whole by ordering the perpetrator to pay restitution or return property, as well as make payments for expenses incurred by the victim. Again, legal remedies include the use of the civil justice and criminal justice systems.

The Civil Justice System

Elder abuse or neglect is an issue that the civil justice system addresses. To prevail in a civil proceeding, the elder victim or a surviving family member (the plaintiff) must show the injuries or damages that he or she sustained with a "preponderance of the evidence." Essentially, the elderly victim (injured party) must present more evidence to prove that the injuries were sustained and inflicted or caused by the defendant (caregiver). The party that has a majority of the evidence in his/her favor will win the case. In *Rolando V. del Carmen* (1991), a criminal justice scholar argues that the degree of certainty required to win a civil lawsuit is the establishment of a preponderance of the evidence. This typically requires more than fifty percent of the evidence in one's favor. In other situations, such as a challenge for guardianship or conservatorship, the courts require a higher degree of certainty and the burden of proof is greater. *del Carmen* postulates that the degree of certainty needed to prove that an elder is unable to care for himself or herself is "clear and convincing evidence." This generally requires 80 percent of the evidence. The burden of proof is higher because elderly citizens may lose the freedom to care for themselves and be placed in the custody and care of a guardian or conservator.

The Criminal Justice System

Elder abuse or neglect is also an issue that the criminal justice system addresses. For example, if a defendant is charged with an offense, such as neglect or a crime against an elderly person, he/she could lose freedom and civil rights. He could also be forced to pay restitution. Subsequently, the state has the heavy burden of proving "guilt beyond a reason doubt." Essentially, the prosecutor must take 95 percent of the state's evidence and connect the accused to the crime (*del Carmen*, 1991). If the jury is at least 6 percent sure that the accused did not commit the crime, reasonable doubt exists and therefore, the jury will be instructed to find the defendant "not guilty." Some legal scholars argue that of the two systems, the civil justice system is probably better because the victim or surviving family members can bring a legal action against the accused. These experts argue that this is not the case in the criminal justice system. In criminal cases, the State, or the people, represent the injured party, thus, removing the victim from the process. The prosecutor represents the people. In fact, critics worry that the victim may be removed from the process entirely. In some cases, however, victims may be called as witnesses. Sometimes, the victims are even allowed to give impact statements before a jury pronounces its verdict and sentence.

Changes in the Civil Justice System Affecting Elder Abuse

Reforms have occurred in the civil justice system. Chief among them are enhancement laws that require elder abuse and neglect to be reported to: (1) Adult Protective Services; (2) law enforcement agencies; and (3) other authorities, such as a long-term Ombudsman (Quinn and Hiesler, 2002). Some states, such as California, require cross reporting between these three agencies. Moreover, when law enforcement discovers elder abuse is being committed, they must report the abuse to the appropriate licencing agency. Furthermore, issues are emerging in Medicaid-funded facilities that are being investigated by local prosecutorial agencies. However, some of these cases are being reviewed by federal prosecutors because they cross state lines (U.S. Department of Justice and U.S. Department of Health and Human Services, 2000). Experts also contend that over the years, Adult Protective Services (APS) have expanded in most states (APS is the section of local departments of Human Services agencies responsible for receiving and investigating reports of elder abuse and neglect). Current changes to APS include enhanced worker training and a mandatory response time to each report. Other changes in response to elder abuse include new laws and innovative causes of action (see Quinn and Hiesler, 2002). Some states, including California, offer trial setting preference for cases involving the elderly (see *California Code of Civil Procedure Section 76; Penal Code Section 1048*). Another example comes from the U.S. House of Representatives (2001) which provides that those who engage in nursing home abuse should be made civilly and criminally liable. Some experts argue that a Congressional hearing is needed since many civil lawsuits had been filed against nursing homes. Charges in these suits range from improper billing, failure to provide adequate training and supervision of staff, inadequate care, failure to supervise and protect patients from harm and neglect, and engaging in unfair business practices (see *People v. Casa Blanca Convalescent Homes, Inc, 1984*). Another cause of action that has emerged in California is entitled the *California Elder Abuse and Dependant Adult Civil Protection Act* (see *California Welfare and Institutional Code Section 11567-1167.3*), and provides that victims of elder abuse can recover damages for pain and suffering in addition to actual damages, attorney's fees, costs, and punitive damages from physical abuse, neglect, and fiduciary abuse where the defendant is guilty of recklessness, oppression, fraud, or malice in the commission of the abuse.

Changes in the Criminal Justice System Affecting Elder Abuse

Reforms have also occurred in the criminal justice system to better assist victims of elder abuse. For example, many states have created specialized laws to enhance punishment for crimes committed against elderly citizens (see Stiegel, 1995). Another effort is the creation of special training programs on elder abuse. The programs provide special investigatory techniques to criminal justice personnel. These programs are currently being used in states such as Florida and South Carolina. Some agencies are following these examples by creating special training programs to assist the elderly. They include the Police Executive Research Forum (PERF) and the California Commission on Police Officer Standards and Training (POST) (see Quinn and Hiesler, 2002). Another emerging trend has been the creation of special units within police departments and prosecutorial offices to address the special issues found in elder abuse and neglect cases. Moreover, many states have also created specialty courts with jurisdiction over particular issues in criminal justice. For example, some states now have elder courts. These courts help to remove heavy caseloads from the existing court system and focus primarily on the special needs of elderly victims. They also allow court personnel to become experts (see Gaines, Kaune, and Miller, 2000). Despite the help of legal remedies, Quinn and Tomita (1986) argue that no one legal system can solve the problem of elder abuse. Moreover, they also argue that legal remedies alone may not be enough. Another way to effectively control and prevent elder abuse is to create comprehensive systems.

A Comprehensive Service System for the Elderly and Their Families

A comprehensive service system is needed to meet the needs of victims and their families. Davis and Medina-Ariza (2001) report that elder abuse is a complex problem that goes beyond the resources of one agency or organization. In fact, elder abuse remedies utilize the help of police, prosecution, abuser education, social services for victims and even medical assistance. Despite the assistance provided by each, these components address only a small part of the problem. In fact, experts caution that none alone can provide an effective solution to elder abuse. As such, what is needed is a coordinated effort or a multidisciplinary approach among several agencies. A coordinated strategy could be planned by agencies such as police, prosecutors, counseling organizations, shelters, emergency rooms and hospital, foster families, adult daycare, community education, and the creation and development of gerontology programs. While much is known about how police and the criminal justice system respond to elder abuse, very little is understood about what other agencies can provide the elderly. Therefore, attention is given to emergency rooms and hospitals along with the creation of more gerontology programs.

Emergency Rooms and Hospitals

To help prevent elder abuse, emergency rooms and hospitals can quickly take a proactive or a reactive role. For example, the Massachusetts Office of the Attorney General (1992) provides that as part of a multidisciplinary approach to prevent the continuation of elder abuse, emergency rooms and hospitals can create protocol for abuse and neglect cases. According to the attorney general, as soon as health care professionals recognize the warning signs of physical abuse or neglect, they can question the patient to collect more facts to either confirm or dispel suspicion that abuse is occurring. If their suspicion is corroborated by information from the patient, the emergency room or hospital personnel should immediately notify the proper authorities so that someone can investigate the matter. Experts contend that this will allow for the reduction and elimination of many cases of elder abuse, and aid in the prevention of premature deaths. These experts also criticize emergency rooms and hospitals for not having a standard protocol in place to assist victims of elder abuse.

Increase Gerontology Programs

Some experts argue that the creation of more gerontology programs in the nation's colleges and universities can help to increase awareness of and prevent elder abuse. Gerontology is defined as the study of the aging process and people as they grow from middle age through life (Calhoun, Light, and Keller, 1997). It is a multidisciplinary field that relies on biology, sociology and psychology to understand and assist the elderly. In short, gerontology focuses on the study of physical, mental, and social changes in older people. It also investigates the changes in society that results from the aging population, such as the family, economy, health services delivery, government and private programs, and religious institutions. Those with educational backgrounds in gerontology are referred to as gerontologists.They provide many services to the aging population. For example, gerontologists work in areas such as community and human services, health care and long-term care institutions, federal, state, and local governmental agencies, retirement communities, academic and educational research settings, professional organizations and other areas. Gerontologists work either directly or indirectly with the elderly. Gerontologists have first-hand knowledge about the plight of elders, including issues of abuse. They can use their knowledge to sensitize the public and make it aware of the needs and experiences of elders. For example, gerontologists often use the public health approach by visiting communities where elder abuse is a common occurrence as discovered through health surveillance. They can educate residents on the definition and consequences of elder abuse. They can also enlist the help of police and health care professionals to assist them.

Officials at the CDC argue that while visiting targeted areas where elder abuse is found, gerontologists and health care officials can educate a population on the dangers of this epidemic by citing the sheer numbers of those affected and how others in the environment are also affected by the cycle of violence, exchange, and family stress theories. Gerontologists and health officials can also use visual captions of injuries and even photos of victims who have been killed by abuse. CDC officials believe that this technique can be instrumental in dramatizing the harsh realities associated with elder abuse. Gerontologists can also use their positions to advocate the interests of the elderly population. For example, they can apply their expertise to help transcend the quality of life for elders, speak about aspects of aging in civic and community groups, and influence agencies and organizations that serve the elderly. Most importantly, gerontologists can positively influence legislation and policies that affect the elderly by joining forces with such groups as AARP and similar organizations to lobby elected officials to create better legislation and to vigorously enforce existing laws. As the demographic composition of the U.S. continues to age, the need for gerontologists becomes more apparent. Therefore, colleges and universities around the country would do well to market their gerontology programs to attract and train the next generation of gerontologists to serve in the areas of service provision, administration, health professionals, and educator/ researchers to meet the demands of this emerging population.

Policy Recommendations

Politicians and public health officials agree that elder abuse is a serious problem in the U.S. However, they may be at odds over which approach is the best way to address the issue. In the U.S., there is no national crime or health policy (Donziger, 1996). Each state legislature is responsible for creating its separate policies. The results have been a mixture of liberal to moderate to conservative approaches in dealing with the issue of crime and health care. Experts warn that policymakers must view crime and health policies in the larger context of society. Crime and health policies must make the country safe and healthier and be crafted in a cost-effective manner (Donziger, 1996). Both politicians and public health officials agree that in order for public policy to be effective, they must address some of the causes that are associated with elder abuse. Policy recommendations include the following:

- Public service announcements
- Expand the definition of hate crime to include elder abuse and repeated cases of neglect
- Mandatory standardized protocol used by hospitals
- Publicizing the identity and photo of those who engage in elder abuse
- Better data collection
- Random unannounced inspections of nursing homes
- More social worker contact in high risk abuse cases
- Mandatory certification for home health care workers
- Aggressive enforcement of mandatory reporting laws
- Evaluation research to determine the effectiveness of existing programs.

Public Service Announcements

As part of the public health approach to prevent disease and injury, CDC officials rely on public service announcements to launch campaigns against the dangers of tobacco, teenage pregnancy, child abuse and domestic violence against women. Other health care professionals also use public service announcements to increase social awareness of the dangers of these and other epidemics. These announcements are strategically scheduled to be aired during prime time television viewing. In addition, public service announcements are often made over radio programming and placed on community billboards. Gerontologists and epidemiologists contend that the same strategy can be used to increase awareness and educate the public on the reality of elder abuse. These announcements are used to show the vulnerability of elders and the consequences of abuse on everyone in the household. They may also imply that the behavior is intergenerational.

Expand the Definition of Hate Crime to Include Elder Abuse

Expanding the definition of hate crime to include elder abuse and repeated cases of neglect followed by a sentence enhancement seems a logical policy that may serve to reduce and prevent elder abuse. This seems a logical course of action since other victimized groups in society have been included in its definition. For example, under hate crime laws those who receive protection include: Minorities, women, the handicapped, people with alternative lifestyles, and others who are targeted for crime because of religion. As part of their punishment, offenders should be forced to receive sensitivity counseling and anger management courses prior to being released from confinement. This may serve as an effective strategy since recent crime statistics reveal that hate crimes are actually declining from several years ago (Uniform Crime Reports, 2001).

Mandatory Standardized Protocol Used by Hospitals

Mandatory protocol should be used by all of the nation's hospitals. They should create a uniform set of procedures to be invoked when cases of elder abuse are suspected and confirmed. These cases should also be included in a yearly compilation on the number of visits made by elderly persons. To do so may prevent continued levels of abuse and make offenders more accountable for their behavior. These data can also be used to establish that a hospital did not act in a negligent way or a manner that was "deliberately indifferent" to the plight of an elderly victim. If these data are collected around the nation, they can help determine the nature and extent of the problem.

Publicizing the Identity and Photo of Those Who Engage in Elder Abuse

Shaming has been successfully used in the past as a deterrent to crime, such as theft, prostitution, and child sexual abuse. Therefore, shaming should also be used as a strategy to reduce and prevent elder abuse. States and localities should print the identity and publish photos of offenders found guilty of engaging in elder abuse. This information should be printed in local newspapers and aired on television as a means of exposing this hidden problem. The desired result is that it would force offenders into conformity and reduce levels of recidivism.

Better Data Collection

A national clearinghouse is needed that collects yearly statistics on cases of elder abuse and neglect. This data collection can be similar to other crime data such as the Uniform Crime Reports and the National Crime Victimization Survey. By creating a national data compilation, it will enable an accurate determination of the nature, extent, and dynamics of elder abuse. It will also indicate if the number of elder abuse cases is increasing or decreasing. At the same time, it should allow for an examination of the trends and patterns associated with elder abuse. It may be instrumental in indicating whether resources are achieving their intended objective. If it is discovered that they are not, it may reveal that other strategies are needed to reduce and prevent elder abuse.

Random Unannounced Inspections of Nursing Homes

Health officials should engage in random and unannounced visits of nursing homes to ensure compliance with state standards. In cases where repeated violations occur, the nursing home should have its license revoked and closed. If health officials discover that the administrator had prior knowledge of abuse but failed to discipline, terminate, or take corrective measures against an employee, the administrator should be terminated and prosecuted. Residents should also be immediately reassigned and even allowed to file a tort claim in civil court for damages and injuries sustained. In cases, where abuse is not egregious, the nursing home should simply replace its manager and the residents should be interviewed in an attempt to uncover the extent of abuse and neglect.

More Social Worker Contact In High Risk Abuse Cases

In cases where it has been reported that an elderly person is at high risk, social workers should give priority to such cases by making routine visits to ensure that the elder is safe. Moreover, in such cases, efforts should be made to allow the elder to be more independent by setting up accounts that automatically deposit their social security and retirement funds and to automatically pay bills such as rent, utilities, and phone. This is believed to deter violence that some elderly suffer at the hands of caregivers who have chemical dependency problems (these are the high risk cases).

Mandatory Certification for Home Health Care Workers

An existing problem that appears to be pronounced in elder abuse is that many in-home service providers who assist elderly patients with critical services on a daily basis lack the academic and training credentials to render these needed services. Some experts report that because of the low pay that is given to these workers, this area of employment is attractive to people who lack skills to engage in other endeavors. While it does not appear to be an issue in emergency rooms and hospitals around the country, the problem is found at alarming rates within the context of many individual and nursing homes. In order to ensure quality control and the safety of patients, home health care workers should receive state certification before caring for elderly patients.

Aggressive Enforcement of Mandatory Reporting Laws

Criticisms exist over the lack of enforcement when those authorized to report cases of elder abuse fail or refuse to act. Some advocates contend that if violators were forced to pay a hefty fine or receive incarceration, this would have both a specific and general deterrent effect because it would send the message that compliance is not discretionary, but rather, it is what the law requires. Essentially, it would create an obligation to act when one does not feel compelled to act. Despite what most people believe, mandatory reporting laws can easily be enforced because of the failure to act when there is a legal obligation to act.

Evaluation Research to Determine the Effectiveness of Existing Programs

As stated previously, every state in the country has some type of program in place to assist elderly victims of abuse. These typically include mandatory reporting laws, protective services and service options. However, it is very difficult to determine if these programs are having a positive effect on reducing elder abuse. This is due, in part, to a lack of evaluation research conducted on existing programs. It is vital that research be conducted to determine if these programs are meeting their stated objectives. As of now, it is almost impossible to know if states have genuine concerns about the effectiveness of such programs or if states simply want to say that they have assistance or a response in place to help elder victims of abuse. Moreover, state officials who sponsor programs to assist the elderly should require that funded programs receive evaluation to determine it the funds are being wisely spent. Otherwise the money to defray the costs of existing programs could be better spent on strategies that may be more viable in alleviating the problem of elder abuse.

Elder abuse is a criminal justice, as well as public health, issue in the U.S. As the elderly population rises, the number of victimizations and the magnitude of the resulting health problems will become even more serious. It is critical that the response to elder abuse improves in order to successfully address prevention and treatment issues now and in the future. Currently, states intervene with social services, such as mandatory reporting laws, protective services, and service options. Yet, the effectiveness of these interventions is unknown because of the paucity of program evaluation. As state budgets grow tighter it is increasingly imperative that elder abuse funds are managed wisely. At the same time, the approach to elder abuse needs to be interdisciplinary, since no single program or agency can adequately address prevention and treatment. We believe that the public health approach offers such a strategy. The authors of this chapter suggest the following policies be adopted in order to accomplish prevention and treatment goals: (1) public service announcements; (2) expanding the definition of hate crime; (3) mandatory standardized protocol used by hospitals; (4) publicizing the identity and photo of those who engage in elder abuse; (5) better data collection; (6) random unannounced inspections of nursing homes; (7) more social worker contact in high risk abuse cases; (8) mandatory certification for home health care workers; (9) aggressive enforcement of mandatory reporting laws; and (10) evaluation research to determine the effectiveness of existing programs. At the same time, we argue that the elderly should rely more on the help of the criminal justice and civil justice systems. We caution that a failure to heed our policy recommendations may mean that more cases of elder abuse will continue to go unreported, and unfortunately others may even experience a premature death.

REFERENCES

Adler, F., Mueller, G.O., and Laufer, W.S. (2001). *Criminology and the Criminal Justice System*. Boston:McGraw Hill.

Anderson, J.F., Grandison, T., and Dyson, L. (1996). Victims of Random Violence and the Public Health Implication: A Health Care or Criminal Justice Issue? *Journal of Criminal Justice* 24(5):379-392.

Andrew, F.M., and Withy, S.B. (1979). *Social Indicators Of Well-Being: Americans' Perceptions of Life Quality*. New York: Plenum.

Anetzberger, G.J. (1989). "Implications of Research on Elder Abuse Perpetrators: Rethinking Current Social Policy and Programming." In R. Filinson and S.R. Ingman (eds.). *Elder Abuse: Practice and Policy*. New York: Human Services Press.

Anetzberger, G.J. (1987). *Etiology of Elder Abuse by Adult Offspring*. Springfield, IL: Charles C. Thomas.

Baruch, G., and Barnett, R.C. (1983). Adult Daughters' Relationships with their Mothers. *Journal of Marriage Family*. 45:601-606.

Beckman, R.S., and Adelman, R.D. (1992). "Elder Abuse and Neglect." In R.T. Ammerman, and Hersen, M. (eds.), Assessment of family violence, a clinical and legal sourcebook. Wiley, New York.

Bergeron, L. R. (1989). "Elder Abuse Prevention: A holistic approach." In Filinson, R., and Ingman, S. (eds.). *Elder Abuse: Practice and policy*. New York: Human Services Press: 218-228.

Bergman, J. A., (1989). Responding to Abuse and Neglect Cases: Protective Services Versus Crisis Intervention. In Filinson, R., and Ingman, S. (eds.). *Elder abuse: Practice and Policy*. New York: Human Services Press. Pp., 94-103.

Blakely, B. E., and Dolon, R. (1991). "Elder Mistreatment." In J. E. Hedricks (eds.).*Crisis Intervention in Criminal Justice/Social Service*. Springfield, IL: Charles C. Thomas.

Braithwaite, R.L. and Taylor, S. E. (1992). *Health Issues in the Black Community*. San Francisco,CA: Jossey-Bass Publications.

Calhoun, C., Light, D., and Keller, S. (1997). *Sociology*. (7th ed.). New York: The McGraw-Hill Companies, Inc.

Callahan, J. J. (1981). Elder Abuse Programming: Will it Help the Elderly? Presentation at the National Conference on the Abuse of Older Persons, Boston.

Callendar, W. (1982). Improving Protective Services for Older Americans: A National Guide Series. Portland: Center for Research and Advanced Study, University of Southern Maine.

Centers for Disease Control. (1997). Position Papers from the Third National Injury Conference: Setting the national Agenda for Injury Control in the 1990s. Washington, D.C.: Department of Health and Human Services.

Cleckley, H.M. (1974). *The Mask of Insanity*. (4th ed.). St. Louis: Mosby Press.

Cicirelli, V.G. (1981). *Helping Elderly Parents: The Role of Adult Children*. Boston: Auburn House.

Crystal, S. (1986). "Social Policy and Elder Abuse." In K.A. Pillemer and R.S. Wold (eds.). *Elder Abuse: Conflict in the family*. Dover, MA: Auburn House.

Davidson, J.L. (1979).Elder abuse. In Block, M.R. and Sinnott, J.D. (Eds.). Battered Elder Syndrome: An Exploratory Study. College Park: University of Maryland, Center on Aging.

Davis, R.C., and Median-Ariza, J. (2001). Results from an Elder Abuse Prevention Experiment in New York City. Washington, D.C.: National Institute of Justice.

del Carmen, R.V. (1991). *Civil Liabilities in American Policing*. Englewood Cliffs, New

Jersey: Brady Publisher.

Doerner, W.G., and Lab, S.P. (2002). *Victimology*. (3rd ed.). Cincinnati, OH: Anderson Publishing Co.

Dolon, R., and Hendricks, J.E. (1989). "An Exploratory Study Comparing Attitudes and Practices of Police Officers and Social Service Providers in Elder Abuse and Neglect Cases." *Journal of Elder Abuse and Neglect* 1: 75-90.

Donziger, S.R. (1996). *The Real War on Crime: The Report of the National Criminal Justice Commission*. New York, NY: Harper-Perennial.

Elias, R. (1986). *The Politics of Victimization: Victims, Victimology and Human Rights*. New York: Oxford University Press.

Fiegener, J.J., Fiegener, M., and Meszaros, J. (1989). "Policy Implications of a statewide Survey of Elder Abuse." *Journal of Elder Abuse and Neglect* 1:39-58.

Finkelhor, D. (1983). Common Features of Family Abuse. In Finkelhor D., Gelles, R.J. Hotaling, G., Straus, M. (ed.). *The Dark Side of Families: Current Family Violence Research*. Beverly Hills, CA: Sage.

Gaines, L K., Kaune, M., and Miller, R.L. (2000). *Criminal Justice in Action*. Belmont, CA: Wadsworth/Thomson Learning.

Gelles, R. (1983). An Exchange/Social Control Theory. In Finklhor,D., Hotaling, G., Gelles, R., and Straus, M. ed. *The Dark Side of Families: Current Family Violence Research*. Beverly Hills, CA: Sage.

Gelles, R.J. (1974). "Child Abuse as Psychopathology: A Sociological Critique and Reformulation. In Steinmetz, S. and Straus, M.A. (Eds.). *Violence in the Family*. New York: Dodd, Mead, 109-204.

Gelles, R.J. (1993). "Family Violence." In R.L. Hampton, et al. (eds). *Family Violence: Prevention and Treatment*. Newbury Park, CA: Sage.

Gelles, R.J., and Cornell, C.P. (1990). *Intimate Violence in Families*. (2nd ed.)Beverly Hills: Sage.

Glenn, N., and Weaver, C. (1981). A Multivariate-Multisurvey Study of Marital Happiness. *Journal of Marriage Family*, 40:269-282.

Gostin, L.O. (2000). *Public Health Law: Power, Duty, Restraint*. Berkeley, CA: University of California Press.

Heisler, C.J. and Quinn, M.J. (1995). A Legal Perspective. *Journal of Elder Abuse and Neglect*, 7(2/3): 131-156.

Henslin, J.M. (2003). *Sociology: A Down to Earth Approach*. (6th ed.). Boston, MA: Allan and Bacon.

Hickey, T., and Douglas, R.L. (1981). Mistreatment of the Elderly in the Domestic Setting: An Exploratory Study." *American Journal of Public Health*. 71:500-517.

Hunter, R., and Kilstrom, N. (1979). "Breaking the Cycle in Abusive Families." *American Journal of Psychiatry*. 136 (1320).

Hwalek, M., Hill, B., and Stahl, C. (1989). Illinois Plan for a Statewide Abuse Program. In Filinson, R., and Ingman, S. (eds.). *Elder Abuse: Practice and Policy*. New York: Human Services Press: 196-207.

Johnson, E. S., and Bursk, B.J. (1977). Relationships Between Elderly and Their Adult Children. *Gerontologist*. 17:90-96.

Julian, J., and Kornblum, W. (1986). *Social Problems*. (5th ed.). Englewood Cliffs, New Jersey: Prentice-Hall.

Kapp, M.B. (1995). "Elder mistreatment: Legal Interventions and Policy Uncertainties." *Behavioral Sciences and the Law*. 13:365-380.

Lee, G. (1978). Marriage and Morale in Later Life. *Journal of Marriage Family*. 40:131-139.

Nachman, S. (1991). "Elder Abuse and Neglect Substantiations: What They Tell us

About the Problem." *Journal of Elder Abuse and Neglect*, 3,3: 19-43.

Macolini, R. M. (1995). "Elderly Abuse Policy: Considerations in Research and Legislation." Behavioral Sciences and the Law. 13:349-363.

Massachusetts Office of the Attorney General (1992). "Prevention and Protection: Empowering Elders and People with Disabilities." Boston, MA.

Meadows, R.J. (2004). *Understanding Violence and Victimization*. (3rd ed.). Upper Saddle River, New Jersey: Pearson Prentice Hall.

Nachman, S. (1991). "Elder Abuse and Neglect Substantiations: What They Tell us About the Problem." *Journal of Elder Abuse and Neglect*, 3(3):19-43.

National Institute on Aging. (2003). " Research Goals to Reduce or Eliminate Health Disparities." Bethesda, MD.

Pagelow, M.D. (1984). *Family Violence*. New York: Greenwood Press.

Pillemer, K A.,and Moore, D.W. (1990). "Highlights from a Study of Abuse of Patients in Nursing Homes." *Journal of Elder Abuse and Neglect*. 2(1-2):5-29.

Pillemer, K., and Suitor, J.J. (1993). "Violence and Violent Feelings: What Causes Them Among Family Caregivers?" *Journal of Gerontology*.47(4):165-172.

Pillemer, K., and Suitor, J.J. (1998). "Violence and Violent Feelings: What Causes Them Among Family Caregivers?" In Raquel Kennedy Bergen (ed). Intimate violence. Thousand Oaks, CA: Sage Publications. Pp 255-265.

Quinn, M.J.and Heisler, C.J. (2002). The Legal System: Civil and Criminal Responses to Elder Abuse and Neglect: *The Public Policy and Aging Report*, 12(2): 8-14.

Quinn, M.J., and Tomita, S.K. (1986). *Elder Abuse and Neglect:Causes, Diagnosis and intervention strategies*. New York: Springer.

Reiss, A.J, and Roth, J.A. (1993). *Understanding and Preventing Violence*. Washington, D.C.: National Academy Press.

Rosenberg, M.L., and Fenley, M.A. (1991). *Violence in America: A Public Health Approach*. New York: Oxford University Press.

Schneider, M.J. (2000). *Introduction to Public Health*. Gaithersbury, Maryland: Aspen Publishers.

Sherman, L. W., and Berk, R.A. (1984). Minneapolis Domestic Violence Experiment. Police Foundation Reports, Vol. 1, April.

Simons, R.L., Wu, C., Johnson, C., and Conger, R.D. (1995). A Test of Various Perspectives on the Intergenerational Transmission of Domestic Violence." Criminology 33:141-171.

Spaccarelli, S., Coatsworth, J.D., and Bowden, B.S. (1995). "Exposure to Serious Family Violence Among Incarcerated Boys: It's Association with Violent Offending and Potential Mediating Variables." *Violence and Victims*. 10:163-180.

Steinmetz, S.K.(1988). *Duty Bound: Elder Abuse and Family Care*. Newbury Park, CA: Sage Publication.

Stiegel, L. (1995). Recommended Guidelines for State Courts Handling Cases Involving Elder Abuse. American Bar Association Commission on Legal Problems of the Elderly. Washington, D.C.

Sykes, G. M., and Matza, D. 1957. *"Techniques of Neutralization: A Theory of Delinquency,"* American Sociological Review, 22: 664-70.

Thobaben, M. (1989). "State Elder/Adult Abuse and Protection Laws." In R. Filinson and S.R. Ingman (eds.)., *Elder abuse: Practice and policy*. New York: Human Sciences Press.

Tomita, S.K. (1990). "The Denial of Elder Mistreatment by Victims And Abusers: The Application of Neutralization Theory." *Violence and Victims*, 5(3), 171.Heisler, C.J. and Quinn, M.J. (1995). A legal perspective. *Journal of Elder Abuse and Neglect*,

7(2/3): 131-156.

Uniform Crime Reports (2001). Crime in the United States. Washington, D.C.: U.S. Government Printing Office.

U.S. Department of Justice and U.S. Department of Health and Human Services. (2000). *Institutional Abuse and Neglect: Joining Resources to Combat Institutional Abuse and Neglect. Our Aging Population. Promoting Empowerment, Preventing Victimization, and Implementing Coordinated Interventions*: A Report of Proceedings, June 14.

U.S. House of Representatives (2001). *Committee on Government Reform: Abuse of Residents a Major Problem in U.S. Nursing Homes*. A Report Prepared for Rep. Henry A. Waxman, July 30, 2001.

Wallace, H. (1999). *Family Violence: Legal, Medical, and Social Perspectives*. (2nd ed.). Boston: Allyn and Bacon.

Widom, C.S. (1992). *The Cycle of Violence*. Washington, D.C.:National Institute of Justice.

Wolf, R.S., Godkin, M.A., and Pillemer, K.A. (1986). Maltreatment of the Elderly: A Comparative Analysis. *Pride Institutional Journal of Long Term Home Health Care*. 5(1):10-17.

Wolf, R.S., and Pillemer, K.A. (1989). *Helping Elderly Victims: The Reality of Elder Abuse*. New York, NY: Columbia University Press.

Wolf, R., Strugnell, C., and Godkin, M. (1982). Preliminary Findings From Three Model Projects on Elder Abuse. (University of Massachusetts Medical Center, Worcester, Massachusetts).

Young, L. (1974). In Steinmetz, S., and Straus, M.A. (eds.). *Violence in the Family*. New York: Dodd, 187-189.

Cases Cited

People v. Casa Blanca Convalescent Homes. Inc. (CA., 1984) 159 Cal. App. 3rd 509.

California Laws

California Elder Abuse and Dependent Adult Civil Protection Act
Cal. Welfare and Institutional Code Section 11567-1167.3
Code of Civil Procedure: 76; *Penal Code Section* 1048.

12

CONCLUSION

Randal Summers and Allan Hoffman

We would like to believe that our retiring parents and our beloved grandparents are enjoying the latter part of their lives and receiving the honor and respect that they so deserve. Unfortunately, for millions of elderly, this is only an idealistic figment of imagination. The sobering truth is that a significant number of our elderly are being abused by family members and caregivers in the home or to a lesser extent by the staff and residents in our institutional settings. There are projections that our elderly population 65 years and older will exceed 70 million by the year 2030. A conservative elder abuse estimate of 5% of this population would suggest that there will be over 3 million elders victimized in the U.S alone. This is sad commentary for one of the most educated, wealthy and powerful countries in the developed world.

RECOMMENDATIONS FOR ACTION

Despite this harsh reality, there is hope. We are slowly coming to the realization that much has to be done if we are to stem the tide of elder abuse. Throughout this volume recommendations for action have been identified in regard to the specific topics being addressed.

In regard to Intimate Partner Violence and Abuse (IPVA) and older women the research body of knowledge is at a very early stage of scientific maturity. We need to have a better understanding of and ways for identifying the perpetrators. Currently there are few resources that specifically deal with the needs of older women. We need to identify what constitutes the appropriate services and educate our physicians and shelter service providers.

Very little is known about the offenders in the sexual victimization of our elders. Current research into sexual abuse often overlooks elderly women. We need to help providers of elder care, criminal justice and adult protective service workers expand their perception of sexual abuse in order to more adequately identify and protect victims.

There is a great need for more research on the effectiveness of criminalization and the coordination among statistical service systems and service providers. We have seen advances in adult protection legislation and creating protocols for detection and intervention but more has to be done in this area. In the area of communication, we need to design computer programs for older persons and train them to be computer literate. We should assist nursing home staff and family members with better ways of communicating with the elderly residents. Cooperation from the media is critical if we are to have any influence over prevailing negative attitudes toward the elderly. We need to ensure that the images we portray of the elderly are respectful. More research is needed on the cultural aspects of elder abuse as well as a more accurate international perspective. We should have a better understanding of elder abuse among Native Americans especially in regard to differences between urban and rural situations. This, in turn, will help us to develop more relevant interventions. Since elder abuse is both a criminal justice and public health issue we need to advocate effective laws to protect the older population. There are mandatory reporting laws in most states and protective services but we need to do more research on their effectiveness. There must be more reliance on the criminal justice and civil justice systems and recognize that we must accept an interdisciplinary approach to elder abuse since no single agency can address all aspects of prevention and treatment. In addition, we need to enhance elder abuse awareness through public service announcements, encourage more social work contact in high risk situations, and enhance the competencies of home health care workers. In reference to elder abuse, we are in a state of crisis. All of these actions require the courage and commitment to affect change in a world gone awry. Although the remarks of the Deputy Secretary of Defense Paul Wolfowitz were aimed at terrorism, they are especially poignant in regard to our challenge in the area of Elder Abuse:

"Building a Better World: One Path from Crisis to Opportunity"

Remarks delivered by Deputy Secretary of Defense Paul Wolfowitz, at the Brookings Institution, Washington, DC, Thursday, September 5, 2002.

ADDITIONAL RESOURCES

SeniorCitizens.com: Elder Abuse and Neglect
www.Elder-Abuse-Information.com
www.Elderly-Abuse-Nursing-Home.com
National Citizens' Coalition for Nursing Home Reform
www.nccnhr.org/
www.nursinghomealert.com/
www.oaktrees.org/elder/
www.preventelderabuse.org/
www.eldercare.gov/
SeniorCitizens.com: Elder Abuse and Neglect
In California: Californias Attorney Crime and Violence Prevention Center
http://www.safestate.org/index.cfm?navid=14
National Center on Elder Abuse (NCEA)
    1201 15th Street N.W., Suite 350, Washington , DC
Major source of data and funds the Clearinghouse on Abuse and Neglect
    of the Elderly at the University of Delaware
http://www.elderabusecenter.org

Index

ABOUT THE EDITORS

Allan M. Hoffman, Ed.D. CHES

Allan M. Hoffman, Ed.D. CHES, is a nationally recognized expert on issues associated with violence and violence prevention. He is a frequent guest on radio, television and often quoted in news articles concerning violence issues.

Currently, Dr. Hoffman is Vice President at Hartnell College in Salinas, California. Among his previous positions, he served as Director of the Center for the Prevention of Community Violence and is an experienced educator and human services administrator. He has held executive-level positions in higher education and health care, having served as dean, associate dean, executive officer, and faculty member. Dr. Hoffman has been a visiting scholar, adjunct professor, clinical professor, and professor at several institutions. Dr. Hoffman has published extensively and authored several books including: *Domestic Violence: A Global View* (Greenwood, 2002), *Teen Violence: A Global View* (Greenwood, 2001), *Schools, Violence and Society* (Praeger Publishers, 1996), *Violence on Campus* (Aspen Publishers, 1998), *Teen Violence: A Global View* (Greenwood, 2000), *Managing Colleges and Universities: Issues for Leadership* (Bergin and Garvey, 2000), *Total Quality Management: Implications for Higher Education* (Prescott Publishing, 1995).

He has served on the editorial board or as a manuscript reviewer for the *Journal of Allied Health, Journal of Public Health,* and *Police Practice and Research: an International Journal.* He has provided consulting services to schools, colleges, and business organizations in multinational settings. His consulting efforts focus on violence in schools, colleges, and the workplace and leadership issues. He earned his B.S. magna cum laude from the University of Hartford, and received two M.A. degrees and an Ed.D. from Teachers College, Columbia University where he was named a Kellogg Fellow. He is a Certified Health Education Specialist. Dr. Hoffman is the recipient of numerous awards and honors associated with his teaching and his efforts to prevent violence and resolve conflict creatively. He received a Certificate of Special Congressional Recognition from the Congress of the United States of America and a Special Recognition Award from the Executive Office of the President of the United States, Office of National Drug Control Policy.

Dr. Hoffman lives in Montery County, California, and can be contacted by email at: drallan52@sbcglobal.net

Randal W. Summers, Ph.D.

Currently, Dr. Summers is a principle in the organization effectiveness consulting practice of Summers and Associates. He provides consulting services to schools, colleges, and business organizations in multinational settings. He has served as an internal consultant for a number of Fortune 100 companies in the areas of organization effectiveness and leadership development. His previous academic positions included adjunct faculty member with the Center for the Prevention of Community Violence (Iowa), adjunct professor in Business Administration at the University of Phoenix, adjunct senior professor in Business Administration and Health Care Administration at the University of LaVerne. He has served as a Clinical Psychologist in a large teaching hospital in Canada as well as in private practice. He has developed programs and managed psychologists and social workers in large institutional settings related to youth corrections and the developmentally handicapped; advocating "normalization," transition back into the community.

Dr. Summers has authored several books including: *Domestic Violence: A Global View* (Greenwood, 2002), *Teen Violence: A Global View* (Greenwood, 2001), *Managing Colleges and Universities: Issues for Leadership* (Bergin and Garvey, 2000) and he has been a contributing author in *Schools, Violence and Society* (Praeger Publishers, 1996), *Violence on Campus* (Aspen Publishers, 1998), and *Total Quality Management: Implications for Higher Education* (Prescott Publishing, 1995).

Dr. Summers lives in the San Francisco Bay area and can be contacted by email at: ransum@thegrid.net

ABOUT THE CONTRIBUTING AUTHORS

James F. Anderson is Associate Professor of *Criminal Justice and Criminology* at the University of Missouri at Kansas City. Prior to joining the faculty in 1999, he was employed at Eastern Kentucky University in the Department of Police Studies. He has published several books and articles in the areas of criminological theory, intermediate sanctions, legal rights of prisoners, and crime and public health care. He is currently working on a book for police procedures. Dr. James F. Anderson, University of Missouri at Kansas City, Department of Sociology/Criminal Justice and Criminology, 5100 Rockhill Road, Kansas City, MO 64110; andersonjf@umkc.edu

Joanne Ardovini, Ph.D., Assistant Professor, Metropolitan College of New York, 75 Varick Street, New York, NY 10013-1919

Denise Gaffigan Bender, JD, PT, GCS is an associate professor in the College of Allied Health, Department of Rehabilitation Sciences at the University of Oklahoma Health Sciences Center (OUHSC) in Oklahoma City, OK. She also has an adjunct appointment as clinical associate professor at the OUHSC Donald W. Reynolds Department of Geriatric Medicine. She is certified by the American Board of Physical Therapy Specialties as a geriatric clinical specialist and is also a licensed member of the Oklahoma Bar Association. Professor Bender gives presentations on the topic of elder abuse to professional and community groups. Denise Gaffigan Bender, Department of Rehabilitation Sciences, The University of Oklahoma Health Sciences Center, Oklahoma City, OK 73190

Bonnie S. Fisher, Ph.D., is a Professor in the Division of Criminal Justice at the University of Cincinnati and a senior research fellow at the Criminal Justice Research Center. Her most recent work examines the abuse and violence against older women and the domestic violence community's response, issues surrounding the sexual and violent victimization of college women, and workplace violence. She coedited, along with Sandra Regan and Therese Zink, a special issue of *Violence Against Women* entitled "Overlooked Issues During the Golden Years: Domestic Violence and Intimate Partner Violence Against Older Women." She is the author of more than 80 articles and chapters on topics that include college student campus victimization, the measurement of sexual victimization, violence and sexual victimization of female college students, abuse and violence against older women, and domestic violence in the workplace. She is also the co-editor of the *Security Journal* and serves on the editorial board of several journals. Bonnie S. Fisher, P.O. Box 210389, University of Cincinnati, Cincinnati, OH 45221-0389; Bonnie.Fisher@uc.edu

Tina M. Fryling, Assistant Professor, Department of Criminal Justice, Mercyhurst College, 509 E. 38th Street, Erie, PA 16546

Nancie J. Mangels is doctorate fellow at the University of Missouri at Kansas City. She is a student in the *Department of Sociology, Criminal Justice and Criminology*. She has published two books and several articles in the areas of criminal justice and criminological related issues. She is currently working on a project involving sentencing disparities among African-American males.

Thomas W. Miller, Ph.D., ABPP is a tenured Professor and Head, School of Allied Health, University of Connecticut. He spent the last two decades as a Professor in the Department of Psychiatry, College of Medicine, University of Kentucky. He is a graduate of the State University of New York at Buffalo, is a Diplomate of the American Board of Professional Psychology in Clinical Psychology and is a Fellow of the American Psychological Association, the American Psychology Society and the Royal Society of Medicine. Dr. Miller has served as a trainer and consultant to the Governor's Task Force for interdisciplinary clinical treatment of abused persons. He has supervised the psychology service of the Domestic Violence Clinic, University of Kentucky, and has conducted research on interdisciplinary treatment of victims of abuse including the elderly. The American Psychological Association recognized him with a Special Achievement Award for his contributions to education, prevention and clinical services to children, adolescents, adults and the elderly, who are victims of abuse in our society. Dr. Miller was awarded the Master Teacher Award at the University of Kentucky; College of Medicine and is the recipient of the prestigious RHR International Award for Excellence in Consulting Psychology from the American Psychological Association.

Mary C. Newman, Ph.D., is a developmental neuropsychologist specializing in aging and age-related disorders. She has an appointment as an associate professor in the Department of Psychology, Missouri State University, and serves as the Coordinator for the Gerontology Program. Dr. Newman also has an appointment as Director of the Center for Multidisciplinary Health Education, Research and Services in the College of Health and Human Services. Mary C. Newman, Department of Psychology, Southwest Missouri State University, 901 S. National, Springfield, MO 65804

Dawn Oetjen, Ph.D., Assistant Professor, Director, Graduate HSA Studies, College of Health and Public Affairs, University of Central Florida, HPA II, Room 214, Orlando, FL 32816-2200

Reid M. Oetjen, MSHS, Doctoral Candidate, Department of Public Affairs, University of Central Florida, Orlando, FL 32816-2200

Saundra Regan, Ph.D., is a Research Associate in the Department of Family Medicine at the University of Cincinnati. She earned a Masters Degree in Gerontology at Miami University, Oxford, Ohio and a doctorate in Sociology at the University of Cincinnati, Cincinnati, Ohio. Saundra has 20 years of experience in geriatric research and teaching. Over the past few years she has concentrated on elder abuse and domestic violence of older women, physician home care visits of homebound elderly and increasing patient safety of older patients at family medicine clinics. Recently she has presented the domestic violence research work of her colleagues and herself at several national primary care, family violence and gerontological meetings and has co-authored several articles pertaining to domestic violence and older women. Saundra Regan, Ph.D., Department of Family Medicine, P.O. Box 0582, University of Cincinnati, Cincinnati, Ohio 45267-0582; regansl@fammed.uc.edu

Paulina X. Ruf, Ph.D., M.D.A., and M.A. is assistant professor of Sociology at the University of Tampa. She is a graduate of Western Michigan University, where she also completed a Graduate Certificate in Gerontology. Dr. Ruf studies different aspects of aging among ethnic/racial minorities, in particular their use and non-use of health and social services, family support and caregiving patterns, including grandparents raising grandchildren, and the impact of traditional caregiving roles on women's labor force participation throughout their life course. In addition, Dr. Ruf's current interests include the culture of honor and gender-based violence around the world

Helen M. Sorenson, MA, RRT, FAARC, is an Assistant Professor in the Department of Respiratory Care at The University of Texas Health Science Center at San Antonio. She has been a respiratory therapist for 27 years, with experience as a floor therapist, a department manager and for the past 20 years, as an educator. In 2000 Helen received an MA in Social Gerontology from the University of Nebraska-Omaha. In 2001 she was inducted as a Fellow in the American Association for Respiratory Care. Helen regularly gives presentations on geriatric respiratory care topics and has published numerous articles and book chapters related to geriatric patient assessment/ geriatric care. Helen M. Sorenson, Assistant Professor, Department of Respiratory Care, University of Texas Health Science Center at San Antonio, 7703 Floyd Curl Drive, MSC 6248, San Antonio, Texas 78229-3900; Phone: (210) 567-8857; Fax : (210) 567-8852

Dr. Therese Zink, MD, MPH. Board certified in family medicine with a Masters in Public Health, Dr. Zink is an assistant professor in the Department of Family and Community Medicine at the University of Minnesota. She has had foundation and government funding to examine family violence. The long term goals of her research are to help primary care providers identify and manage families living with domestic violence. From 1998–2004 she was an Associate Professor in the Department of Family Medicine at the University of Cincinnati where she collaborated with her co-authors on papers that examined the services available to older women living with domestic violence and the incidence and prevalence of different types of abuse against older women and their health effects. Therese Zink, M.D., MPH , Department of Family Medicine, P.O. Box 0582, University of Cincinnati, Cincinnati, Ohio 45267-0582; zinktm@fammed.uc.edu